AFRICAN ETHNOGRAPHIC STUDIES
OF THE 20TH CENTURY

Volume 14

TALES TOLD IN TOGOLAND

TALES TOLD IN TOGOLAND

A. W. CARDINALL

Routledge
Taylor & Francis Group

LONDON AND NEW YORK

First published in 1931 by Oxford University Press.

This edition first published in 2018
by Routledge
2 Park Square, Milton Park, Abingdon, Oxon OX14 4RN

and by Routledge
711 Third Avenue, New York, NY 10017

Routledge is an imprint of the Taylor & Francis Group, an informa business

© 1931 International African Institute

British Library Cataloguing in Publication Data
A catalogue record for this book is available from the British Library

ISBN: 978-0-8153-8713-8 (Set)
ISBN: 978-0-429-48813-9 (Set) (ebk)
ISBN: 978-1-138-49334-6 (Volume 14) (hbk)
ISBN: 978-1-138-49590-6 (Volume 14) (pbk)
ISBN: 978-1-351-02322-1 (Volume 14) (ebk)

Publisher's Note
The publisher has gone to great lengths to ensure the quality of this reprint but points out that some imperfections in the original copies may be apparent.

Disclaimer
The publisher has made every effort to trace copyright holders and would welcome correspondence from those they have been unable to trace.

TALES TOLD IN TOGOLAND

By

A. W. CARDINALL

F.R.G.S., F.R.A.I., &c.

District Commissioner Gold Coast

To which is added the

MYTHICAL & TRADITIONAL HISTORY OF DAGOMBA

By E. F. TAMAKLOE

Of the Gold Coast Civil Service

OXFORD UNIVERSITY PRESS
LONDON: HUMPHREY MILFORD
1931

By the same Author

NATIVES OF THE NORTHERN
TERRITORIES OF THE GOLD
COAST
A GOLD COAST LIBRARY
IN ASHANTI AND BEYOND

PRINTED IN GREAT BRITAIN

FOREWORD

IN the following pages I have collected tales told me by peasants and hunters in various parts of Togoland. The final chapter deals with the history of the Dagomba, a history collected by the sole efforts of Mr. E. F. Tamakloe. I have made no attempt at a comparative study of the folk-lore contained in this volume. Such a task is now too great to undertake, except after much study and reading, and in the quietude of some English home. Therefore I have merely recorded the tales and legends and myths as they have been related, contenting myself with the interesting task of their co-ordination.

A. W. C.

SEVENOAKS.
March 1931.

CONTENTS

Chapter One

WHICH IS INTRODUCTORY

NATURE OF THE COUNTRY—DISTRIBUTION OF TRIBES—HOW
THE ANIMALS OF THE BUSH PROTECT THEMSELVES FROM
MAN—VISITING GOD—INDIVIDUAL OWNERSHIP OF THE
MOON—MOON'S MARKINGS—MARKET OF SALAGA—THE
DOWNFALL OF SALAGA AND THE GROWTH OF KRACHI—
RAIN-DRIVING AT ODUMASE—A HYENA-WOMAN.

SHORTLY after the war the two Governments of
France and Great Britain divided the former German
colony of Togoland into two spheres more or less equal in
area. To the British Colony of the Gold Coast was allotted
the trusteeship of the western sphere which runs contiguous
to the former's eastern frontier. It is with the hinterland of
that portion of Togoland that these pages deal, but as the
tribal boundaries are not the same as the international,
reference is frequently made to tribes in the Gold Coast,
Ashanti, and Northern Territories.

Nearer to the coastline is a section known as the Southern
Section, administered as an integral part of the Gold Coast
Colony. It is peopled more or less entirely by tribes of Ewe
origin, but there are scattered all over the country remnants
of other tribes or relics of an earlier migration by the Ewe.
The nature of the country is such that it afforded an asylum
almost impregnable for fugitives and refugees from the
former bloodthirsty monarchs of Ashanti and Dahomey.
Range after range of hills and mountains, thickly wooded
and often precipitous, with abundant water and an easily
obtained food supply, offered a retreat for many a harassed
family or tribe. The people inhabiting this country have
been studied and written about several times, notably by the
German missionary Spieth, but those who live to the
north of this section remain even to this day practically

B

unknown to anthropologists. It is with these that this book is concerned.

Not one volume would suffice for a complete survey of their tribal customs and folk-lore. Scores of volumes would be required. The incompleteness of this present work is fully realized by me, but I venture to think that observations of native life and a record of folk-lore picked up at haphazard from the people themselves must always be of some little worth in these days of rapid development and fast shedding of old-time tradition. Moreover the science of anthropology is daily becoming more and more a collection of highly specialized subjects, and the worker in the field, if untrained, grows discouraged at his own ignorance. It is true that the science of anthropology was founded on the observations of untrained men, but it has almost outgrown those days, and it is only through the fear that the trained worker may not be forthcoming sufficiently soon that this little work has been undertaken.

It has often of late been pointed out how former surveys of native life in West Africa have been compiled by men whose work must have been prejudiced. Missionaries are said to have looked upon native customs as mere workings of a satanic power; others are generally officials whose inquiries have been regarded with suspicion and often accepted as a means of supporting spurious claims or explaining rights which were non-existent but were deemed desirable. That may have been the case; but those compilations have formed the basis of the science of anthropology.

In these pages I have taken especial care to have recorded only the views of the people, the peasantry, hunters, and villagers. Chiefs, and priests possibly, have other views. I know not. But it seems to me that in a survey, say, of England the religion of the peasant is likely to be of more value anthropologically than that of an archbishop; the beliefs of the cottager of more worth than those of the graduate.

The tribes of the Northern Section of the British sphere of Togoland are numerous. In the far north, bordering on the eleventh parallel of latitude, the Bimoba and Mamprussi are to be found. The former are a practically unknown tribe of wild people who still live in the bow-and-arrow stage of vendetta, secret societies, and occasional inter-family war; the latter are a highly-civilized nation—that is to say, for these parts—and resemble closely the Dagomba, who are frequently mentioned in the following chapters. Below the Mamprussi are the Chakosi, an interesting tribe of Twi[1] origin, still using that tongue to a very great extent but, unlike their Ashanti relatives, in a state of complete barbarism. South of the Chakosi are the Konkomba, a warlike nation of magnificent savages, who should be studied in detail as they have retained so much of their ancient customs and have remained so unsullied by outside influence. Their neighbours are the Dagomba, a tribe which boasts of a political and religious organization that cannot be characterized as other than civilized.

Closely connected with the Dagomba are the Nanumba, a small section only, surviving as a distinct unit. They are practically Dagomba, but seem to have intermarried with the Konkomba to a very great extent. South of these people is the district of Krachi, with which these pages mainly deal.

There, there is to be found a conglomerate of tribes— Nanumba, Gonja, Chumru, Krachi, Nawuri, Konkomba, Ajati, Adele, and Ntrubu. All told, in an area of some three thousand square miles, there is but a thin population, reckoned in the census of 1921 as approximately fifteen thousand, or five to the square mile.

The district itself is physically a replica of the Southern Section of the sphere with ranges of mountains running north and south along the eastern frontier and to a depth of

[1] The principal tribes of the Gold Coast comprise the Twi-speaking people: Fanti, Ashanti, Agni, Brong, and many others.

several miles. Elsewhere the country is traversed by many rivers. The Volta, or as it is locally called the Frao, forms the western border with the protectorate of Ashanti and its tributary the Daka or Kulukpene with the protectorate of the Northern Territories, to which the whole section is administratively attached; through the centre runs the wide but more or less sluggish Oti or Le, a river which is character-ized by its meanderings and pebble-covered cliffs; traversing the district from east to west are the rivers Asuokoko, a tributary of the Volta, remarkable for the redness of its water, whence its name is derived, and for its torrential waters, which render it completely unnavigable; the Tschai, a moun-tain stream flowing into the Oti, which dries up in parts during the dry season but always contains deep pools; the Bassa or Kwassa, so named from its raphia palm-covered banks, the home of elephants and a water to be avoided by man as being full of evil things; and finally the Mola, or Little BigRiver, whose renown is most unsavoury, and whose banks are completely deserted by man.

No better area could be imagined for fugitive tribes or outlawed families than this district of Krachi, and added to these physical features there is the far more powerful pro-tection of a multitude of godlings, whose reputation has stretched from Bambara to Lagos, from Assinie to Fada N'Gurma. It is in fact a veritable Land of Fetish, a paradise for the ethnologist if once he could gain the confidence of the people.

But in spite of this sinister aspect the District of Krachi is probably by far the best of all the bush stations in either the Gold Coast or its dependencies. Not only is it so from the anthropological point of view but for its natural beauty and its really fine fishing and hunting—mountain torrents, waterfalls, and boiling rapids, virgin forests and vast plains of treeless grass, distant panorama of river stretches that seem almost lakes, and a whole background of lofty hills all cragged and crested, almost alp-like. It is hard to imagine a better spot if only its healthiness equalled its beauty. Unfortunately Krachi must be reckoned among the most unhealthy places in the country. I do not mean that this applies to Europeans. They seem to keep fairly well; I refer to the native population. They themselves will tell of the ravages of sickness and disease; almost everywhere in the deserted bush one will find the ruins of former dwellings, villages of no mean size and of varying antiquity.

In great contrast is the northern area. Scenery there is negligible, almost wearyingly monotonous. Mere plains more or less covered with bushes and small trees—plains undulating and as uninteresting as the ground swell in a becalmed mid-ocean. But the land of the Dagomba and Konkomba is a land of people, well inhabited by man and his herds and flocks. In the dry season the whole is either burnt black by the annual fires as far as the eye can reach or remains a dreary drab of withered grass and sun-scorched trees, or an untidy stretch of bare soil, an arid area of badly ploughed and untidy land where the village fields have been recently harvested.

Similarly great is the contrast in the inhabitants.

In the south where the Ewe and allied people dwell one finds a system of culture not dissimilar to that which obtains among the Fanti and Ga tribes; in the centre among the tribes such as the Wora-Wora and Krachi the influence of the Ashanti has been so great that the two systems are almost unrecognizable the one from the other; among the Chumru and Adele one finds the civilization of the Dagomba mixed considerably with the Ashanti type, and farther north still there are the allied tribes of the Dagomba and Mamprussi where a state of civilization has been reached by far exceeding the cruder forms of the coastal and forest nations, whilst living close beside them are the almost savage tribes known as the Konkomba and Bimoba.

In spite, however, of these most evident differences it is remarkable how the lore of the people and the fairy tales are very similar and often identical. It is chiefly with these tales that this book deals, stories and beliefs held to-day by the peasantry, the hunters, and the women.

It is not surprising therefore to find many beliefs of the grossest superstition just as one would expect to find among the country folk of the remoter rural districts in Europe. But there is this real difference between African peasantry and European. It is that the superstitions are actually believed in and not half believed in. The stories of godlings and giants and fairies and werwolves are absolutely believed. They are not mere tales to while away the evening hours; they are real happenings. Those who relate these stories have often personally witnessed similar occurrences. There is absolutely nothing incredible, nothing out of the ordinary in them; they are occurrences of everyday life and to the native perfectly natural. Animals speak and so do trees. They have every human feeling and sense; they even have souls. It is sometimes the case that these animals and trees and rocks are the abode of some spirit who acts and thinks and speaks like Man, but more often than not it is the soul of the animal itself or that of the tree or rock which speaks.

Perhaps to make this quite clear the following incidents told me quite recently show how the native thinks and how to him such incidents actually occurred and are expected to occur.

I was walking along a path with a Dagomba hunter and in the course of our conversation he told me that he had never killed a bushbuck or, as it is otherwise called, a harnessed antelope. As this animal is extraordinarily common this seemed rather remarkable and I asked why, thinking and hoping that I should hear something about taboos and such-like matters. But he explained that the reason was that he never had been able to obtain the bullet necessary for killing

that particular type of meat. He further explained that each
bullet as a rule was destined for one particular sort of animal,
and that it would probably prevail only against that species.
Thus, if one were hunting buffalo one would take care to load
only with bullets which had the special magic power to slay
buffalo; similarly with all the other animals. He could not
tell me how the bullets obtained this magic property, but
said that when one went to the blacksmith to have bullets
made, or to some old hunter for the same purpose, then one
asked for the special brand of bullets. This, he explained, was
also the case with arrows, and accounted for the fact that
European guns were in a different category as the bullets
were made by the Europeans and were not of iron. He went
on to say that a proof of this was evident in the fact that
European hunters killed more meat and different species on
the same day.

His conversation continued on these lines for some time,
and he told me that in the village of Dutukpene, to which
we were then going, there lived a blacksmith who recently
had been approached by a stranger who had asked him for
some buffalo bullets. The blacksmith had agreed to prepare
them for him and told him to return in a few days' time
with the necessary money when they would be ready. The
stranger explained that he lived some way off and would
return on the third day. It chanced that this conversation
between the blacksmith and the stranger had been overheard
by an old hunter. This last waited on the third day for the
return of the stranger and watched him go to the blacksmith,
from whom he collected the bullets and then made off. The
hunter followed, and after they had gone some distance into
the bush the stranger, who was unaware of the hunter
following him, went behind a baobab. The hunter hid
himself and waited. Presently their emerged from behind
the tree a buffalo. The hunter had apparently expected this
for he had his gun already loaded and he fired. However,

his shot was of no use, and the hunter knew then that the man-buffalo had used the buffalo bullets as a magic against being shot. My companion then said that that is how often and often a bush-meat is missed, for it has by some means or other procured for itself immunity against bullets specially destined for its slaying.

That same day I came to Dutukpene, and in the Rest House there was, on one of the cross-pieces holding the roof of the verandah, a wasps' nest. It was hanging in a very inconvenient spot and one had to stoop to enter the house lest one should disturb the brutes. Now I was separately told by an Adele, an Issala, a Dagomba, a Moshi, a Lobi, and several Ajati that if one knocked down the cells or nest one could not be stung, and the wasps would go away without injuring any one. The same reason for this was given by all. The wasps must first sting their own house before being able to sting men.

A few days later an educated native, a man who was really well informed on European habits and thoughts, came to me and asked if I would mind him asking me a question concerning a matter that had given him a great deal of thought. I naturally agreed, and he particularly asked me not to laugh at his simplicity. Of course I told him I would not, and then he said that he had recently been down to Accra where for the first time he had seen aeroplanes. These had given him the problem which he wanted me to solve. Had the white men ever been in these aeroplanes to see God and visit Him in His house?

Those are his exact words. The man was and is a fervent Christian, but his idea of God is still exactly that of his unbaptized brothers. The Almighty lives close to Man and quite possibly accessible to some of us. I asked him what he thought God was like, and he replied that he did not know, but as he had heard from the white men that He was like us he presumed He was. This showed that he had himself no real reason to visualize a deity, that the deity existed, but that like all other things in this world, no matter what its shape might be, nevertheless it had all the attributes and senses and feelings of Man.

Thus it is that in the chapter dealing with the origin of things the stories related there are not to the native just fairy tales or imaginative yarns, but are absolutely real and quite comprehensible in the same way as one still finds many people even among the so-called well-educated ones at home who believe implicitly in the biblical stories of Genesis.

Of course, in the absence of religious teaching, each individual evolves theories for himself if he be given at all to ruminating over such abstract matters, which as one would expect is very rarely the case. But I know a youth at Danbae who is in a fair way to become a famous hunter. He is a strange fellow and is rather feared by the rest of the village as he is given so much to silence and aloofness and particularly because of his success in hunting. He was with me one day, and I asked him if he had ever reached the horizon. He said he had not and that men could never get there. I asked how that was and he said that Wulbari, which is the sky or the firmament or God, would never allow man to reach him, and for that reason he had set his children, which are the stars, to watch, and whenever a man got near him they were to warn him so that he could move farther on. He offered the suggestion, however, that it was possible that the white men were able to reach Wulbari for they had come from far away.

At the moment I did not ask how if Wulbari moved off at the approach of one man this was not noticed by the others left in the village. But native thought does not bother about trifles like that, for all whom I have ever asked about it are convinced that the moon seen, say in Ashanti, by a Dagomba is the Dagomba moon which seems to follow the individual Dagomba, and nearly all are astounded to hear that we in England see precisely the same moon as one sees in Krachi.

It was rather curious that some Krachi youths were interested in the shadowings on the moon's face and asked me for an explanation. This of course was too much for me to give them, and I asked in turn what they indicated according to their own ideas. One replied that there was an old woman seated on a stool there and a second suggested that he saw a man on a horse holding a spear, whilst the third considered that the marks showed a man drumming. I could not find out if these ideas were general or merely those of my informants, but the idea of the man on a horse and the spear is the usual one of the Moshi, which my informant may quite possibly have learned in the market of Kete.

This market is, or rather was, one of the most important in all this part of the country. It does not seem to have been of great antiquity but rather to have started in the 'eighties of the last century as a result of civil war in Salaga. This latter town was for centuries a mart for all the Western Sudan, owing chiefly to its geographical situation and to the fact that the chiefs were of Mandingo origin and consequently sympathizers with the emissaries of Islam who, in the other parts of this corner of the Sudan, received but a chilly welcome.

In parentheses it must be mentioned that all over the Northern Territories and Northern Togoland, excepting that small southern and eastern part of the Krachi District, the rulers are not of the same stock as the people and are evidently not only of a different nation but most probably of a different race.

Salaga was not the capital town but the chief commercial centre where the great slave and salt exchange was held— slaves and cattle from the north; kola and salt from the south. The abolition of slavery and overthrow of the Ashanti power affected Salaga directly, and when the market was visited by

Binger in 1886 it was already decaying. Then followed a civil war between the rival claimants to the overlordship of Gonja with interventions by the Dagomba, and finally the ruin was completed by the arrival of the rival European powers, Britain and Germany. The leading merchants sought peace elsewhere as trade was impossible in their own disturbed area. They fled to Kintampo in the west and to Krachi in the east. At this latter place there had always been a large settlement of foreigners gathered there in the interests of the salt trade, which is sent up from the coastal lagoons and reaches Krachi where, owing to the river being there blocked entirely for the passage of canoes by a series of cataracts and falls, an entrepôt is necessary. This salt is of vital importance to the peoples of the interior, and one of the natural trade routes is from Krachi to the Nanumba and Dagomba country or eastward through the mountain passes towards Borgu.

Krachi is therefore a natural emporium, and when the wealthy citizens of Salaga came there it grew in importance until it was almost as great as Salaga had been. To it came people from all over the Sudan, even Moors and Arabs from the desert itself. They lived in the special town for strangers, to which the name of Kete was given.

To-day Kete is no longer of so great an importance. Many are the reasons for its downfall—quicker transport by motors on the main North road which passes some sixty miles to the westward; abolition of slavery, which has led most of the cultivators of the food on which depended the township to return to their homes; and the temporary suspension by the Germans, although not eclipsed as they thought it would be, of the worship of the godling Dente.

With the gods I deal in another chapter, and Dente's story will be found related there. He had during the German occupation of this country been secretly worshipped in a small hut in the town of Kete, having removed himself from his rocky home by the riverside at Krachi. The Germans had destroyed the village of Krachi and had endeavoured to blow up the cave of Dente and cut down his sacred grove. They failed in the two last determinations, and since their day the village of Krachi has been rebuilt.

The cult of gods such as Dente is on a different footing entirely to the ordinary faith of the people. Just as in remoter villages of catholic Europe one finds a church with all its dogma and doctrine and learning and show and pomp, and close at hand one finds in the same place a truer worship by the local people of some saint or transmuted heathen god with all the superstitions and fears of peasantry. It is with these last as they are in this country that I particularly deal, such as the following.

When the other day I came into the village of Odumase I proceeded at once to my tent that had been erected just outside the village. The chief and his people were there, and after a few words of greeting I remarked that it was a pity a tornado was coming along as it seemed to me that the tent was not exactly firmly set up. They all looked at the sky and then rushed off to the town. The next I saw was the whole mob of them running in the direction from which the tornado was approaching and the men and boys shouting and abusing the rain. All sorts of epithets were used apparently, but the rain persisted in approaching. Then the people, getting more and more excited, shouted in unison: 'Rain, you lie, you lie; you are not coming here.' Thus they continued but in vain. The rain approached and a very heavy tornado seemed certain to break. However, it suddenly swerved off towards the mountain slopes and only the tail end touched the village. The tent did not collapse and all was well. I pointed out that they had not deterred the rain from falling, and the villagers replied that they had managed to keep the main part off, and that if they had perceived the storm earlier they would have stopped it altogether.

Many other such incidents are reported in the following pages.

It is not, however, necessarily the bush people who believe in these popular superstitions. One will find the educated in many cases do the same and are just as credulous and superstitious as so many still are in remoter districts of Europe. For instance, it would be very hard to find a native who did not believe or consider it quite possible that lycanthropy should be practised. Such beliefs seem to have been at one time universally held, and out here in the African bush one finds an implicit faith in it. I have not dwelt at any extent on this subject in the following pages because I have done so recently in another work, but the following incident is one of recent occurrence and was witnessed by a large number of people. It tends but to show how deeply laid is the belief in werwolves.

A certain clerk in Government employ at head-quarters had a bitch which had recently presented him with a litter of fine puppies. The family he allowed to sleep under his couch. One morning the clerk, who had passed a bad night through being disturbed by the bitch's growls and restlessness, searched about for the cause. He soon found a hyena hidden under a settle in the next room. Naturally he shouted out for a gun, and to his surprise the hyena asked him not to shoot as she was a woman and not a hyena at all. Several people had by this time run up to see what all the noise was about and witnessed a hyena-woman emerge from her hiding-place. She was a woman right down to her legs which were those of a hyena.

Every one was much alarmed at this unexpected sight and some constables were called in. The woman explained that she was from Kumbungu, that she had the power of turning at night time into a hyena, and that having heard that the clerk's bitch had given birth to a fine litter of fat puppies she had discarded her clothes and changed into a hyena and had then loped along to the clerk's house. Here, however, she had been kept off by the mother dog's growling and had been afraid to seize the puppies lest the clerk might be awakened. She had hidden herself hoping for a chance later, but the dawn had arrived before this had come so that she had decided to resume her natural form. This she was in process of doing when a fly had settled on her and thus had prevented the metamorphosis from being completed, for it is believed that if a fly sits on these werwolves they cannot change back into their human forms until the following night.

Now that scene was witnessed by some thirty people, many of whom were educated and supposedly Christian. They one and all believed implicitly that they had seen a being half-hyena and half-woman. The fact that a European who passed saw only a naked woman and nothing else detracted nothing from their faith. It merely showed that what the African sees is not the same as what the European can see. The woman was driven out of the town by the natives and returned to Kumbungu.

In the following pages I deal with several tribes, but chiefly the Krachi, Ashanti, and Dagomba. Not much do I write about the second, however, for they are only to be found here and there in the mandated area, but their influence, especially in the Krachi District, has been immense. So long ago as the early 'eighties European travellers in the Krachi area noticed the similarity in customs and, what is more important, remarked the use of Twi as the language instead of their own by the many tribes which dwell in that part. Indeed, to-day the languages of the Adele, Ajati, and Chumru are fast disappearing, and Twi or Ashanti is becoming the real language of the people. Therefore it will happen that in the following pages I shall often be using the word Nyame for God instead of the Krachi form Wulbari. And when relating Dagomba stories the form Wuni will be used. By doing this I have hoped that the source of the stories may be recognized at once without the need of continual distinctions.

Chapter Two

OF THE ORIGIN OF THINGS

THE SEPARATION OF GOD FROM MAN—GOD ESTABLISHES HIS
COURT—HIS CAPTAIN ASSURES HIMSELF OF HIS POSITION—
THE CREATION OF THE SUN, MOON, STARS, AND DARKNESS—
HOW DEATH CAME—GOD'S GIFT TO MEN OF THE KNOW-
LEDGE OF CULTIVATION.

IT is told by the Krachi that in the beginning of days
Wulbari and man lived close together and Wulbari lay
on top of Mother Earth (Asase Ya). Thus it came about that
as there was so little room to move about in, Man annoyed
the Divinity, who in disgust went away and rose up to the
present place where one can admire him but not reach him.
The form of the annoyance is variously stated. The Dagomba
and Krachi tell the same story, which also is related by the
Ashanti, to the effect that an old woman whilst making her
fu-fu (or mashed-up yam) outside her hut kept on knocking
Wulbari with her pestle. This hurt him, and as she persisted
he was forced to go higher out of her reach. But the Adele
agree with the Ewe and say that Wulbari was annoyed with
the smoke of the cooking fires which got into his eyes and
he had to go away. A second theory of the Ewe is that
Mawu, as they call Wulbari, being so close to men, made
a convenient sort of towel, and the people used to wipe their
dirty fingers on him. This naturally annoyed him, but it was
not so bad a grievance as the one which caused We, the
Kassena for Wulbari, to remove himself out of the reach of
man, for there it is said that an old woman anxious to make
a good soup used to cut off a bit of him at each meal time,
and We being pained at this treatment went higher.

Established in his new setting Wulbari formed a court in
which the animals were chief attendants. Everything seems
to have run smoothly for a time until one day Anansi, who

was the Captain of the Guard, asked Wulbari if he would give him one corn cob. Wulbari said: 'Certainly,' but wanted to know what Anansi wished to do with one corn cob only. And Anansi said: 'Master, I will bring you a hundred slaves in exchange for this one corn cob.'

And Wulbari laughed.

But Anansi meant what he had said, and he straightway took the road from the sky down to the earth, and there he asked the way from Krachi to Yendi. Men showed him the road and Anansi set out. That evening he came as far as Tariasu. There he asked the chief for a lodging, and a house was shown him. And when it was time to go to bed he took the corn cob and asked the chief where he could put it for safe keeping: 'It is the corn of Wulbari, and he has sent me on a message to Yendi, and this corn cob I must not lose.' So the people showed a good place in the roof and every one went to sleep. But Anansi arose in the night and gave the corn to the fowls, and when day broke he asked for the cob and lo! it was all eaten and destroyed. So Anansi made a great fuss and was not content till the people of Tariasu had given him a great basket of corn. Then he continued on his way and shortly sat down by the roadside as he was weary from carrying so great a load. Presently there passed along a man with a live fowl in his hand which he was bringing back from his field. Anansi greeted him and they soon became friends. Then Anansi said that he liked that fowl; in fact he liked it so much that he would give the whole of his load of corn in exchange if the man would agree. Such a proposal was not to be met with every day and the fellow agreed, and Anansi went on his way carrying the fowl with him.

That night he reached Kpandae and went and saluted the chief from whom he begged a night's lodging. This was readily granted and Anansi, being tired, soon retired. First, however, he showed his fowl to the people and said that it was the fowl of Wulbari and that he had to deliver it to Yendi. They were properly impressed with this information and showed Anansi a nice quiet fowl-house where it would be perfectly safe. Then all went to bed.

But Anansi did not sleep. As soon as he heard every one snoring he arose and took his fowl and went outside the village and there sacrificed the poor bird. Leaving the corpse in the bush and placing some of the blood and feathers on the chief's own doorpost he went back to sleep. At cock-crow he arose and began shouting and crying out that the fowl of Wulbari was gone, that he had lost his job as Captain of the Guard, and that the unfortunate village of Kpandae was most certainly in for a run of misfortune. The hullabaloo brought every one outside, and by this time it was daylight. Great indeed was the clamour when they learned what the fuss was about, and then suddenly Anansi pointed out the feathers and blood on the chief's doorpost. There was no use denying the fact; the feathers were undoubtedly those of the unfortunate fowl, and just then a small boy found the body. It was evident to all that their own chief had been guilty of a sacrilege too dreadful to think about. They therefore one and all came and begged Anansi to forgive them and to do something or other to divert the approaching calamity, which every one thought must be inevitable.

Anansi at last said that possibly Wulbari would forgive them if they gave him a sheep to take to Yendi. 'Sheep!' cried the people, 'we will give you any number of sheep so long as you stop this trouble.' Anansi was satisfied with ten sheep and went his way.

He seems to have had no further adventures but reached the outskirts of Yendi with his sheep. He was a little tired, however, and sat down outside the village and allowed his sheep to graze. Whilst occupied thus there came to him a company of people wailing and weeping. They bore with them a corpse, and when Anansi saluted them and asked

C

what they were doing they said that a young man had died and they were now carrying him back to his village for burial.

Anansi asked if the village was far, and they said it was far. Then he said that it was more than likely that the body would rot on the road, and they agreed. He then suggested that they should give him the corpse and in exchange he would hand over the ten sheep. This was a novel kind of business deal, but it sounded all right, and after a little while the company of young men agreed and went off with the sheep, leaving their dead brother with Anansi.

The latter waited till night fell and then walked into the town carrying with him the corpse. He came to the chief of Yendi's house and saluted that mighty monarch and then begged for a small place where he could rest. He added: 'I have with me as companion the son of Wulbari. He is the favourite son, and although you know me as the Captain of Wulbari's Host, yet I am only as a slave to this boy. He is asleep now, and as he is so tired I want to find a hut to let him sleep in.'

This was excellent news for the people of Yendi and a hut was soon ready for the favourite son of Wulbari. Then Anansi placed the corpse inside and covered it with a cloth so that it seemed verily a sleeping man. Anansi then came outside and was given food. He feasted himself well and asked for some for Wulbari's son. This he took into the hut, where being greedy he finished the meal and came out bearing with him the empty pots.

Now the people of Yendi asked if they might play and dance, for it was not often that a son of Wulbari came to visit them. Anansi said that they might, for he pointed out to them that the boy was an extraordinarily hard sleeper and practically nothing could wake him. That he himself each morning had had to flog the boy till he woke, shaking was no use nor was shouting. So they played and they danced.

As the dawn came Anansi got up and said it was time for him and Wulbari's son to be up and about their business. So he asked some of the chief's own children who had been dancing to go in and wake the son of Wulbari, and that if he did not get up they were to flog him, and then he would surely soon be aroused. The children did this, but Wulbari's son did not wake. 'Hit harder, hit harder!' he cried, and the children did so. But still Wulbari's son woke not. Then Anansi said that he would go inside and wake him himself. So he arose and went into the hut and called to Wulbari's son; he shook him and then made the startling discovery that the boy was dead. His cries drew every one to the door of the compound, and there they learnt the dreadful news that the sons of their chief had beaten Wulbari's favourite child to death.

Great was the consternation of the people. The chief came himself and saw and was convinced. He offered to have his children killed; he offered to kill himself; he offered everything imaginable. But Anansi refused and said that he could think of nothing that day as his grief was too great. Let the people bury the unfortunate boy and perhaps he, Anansi, would devise some plan by which Wulbari might be appeased.

So the people took the dead body and buried it.

That day all Yendi was silent, as all men feared.

But in the evening Anansi called the chief to him and said: 'I will return to my Father, Wulbari, and I will tell him how the young boy has died. But I will take all the blame on myself and I will hide you from his wrath. You must, however, give me a hundred young men to go back with me, so that they can bear witness as to the boy's death.'

Then the people were glad, and they chose a hundred of the best young men and made them ready for the long journey to the abode of Wulbari.

Next morning Anansi arose, and finding the young men

ready for the road, he went with them back to Krachi and from there he took them up to Wulbari.

The latter saw him coming with the crowd of youths and came out to greet him. And Anansi told him all that he had done and showed how from one single corn cob Wulbari had now got a hundred excellent young slaves. So pleased was Wulbari that he confirmed Anansi in his appointment as Chief of his Host and changed his name from Anyankon to Anansi, which it has remained to the present day.

Now Anansi got very conceited over this episode and used to boast a lot about his cleverness. One day he even went so far as to say that he possessed more sense than Wulbari himself. It happened that the latter overheard this, and he was naturally annoyed at such presumption. So next day he sent for his captain and told him that he must go and fetch him 'something'. No further information was forthcoming, and Anansi was left to find out for himself what Wulbari wanted.

All day Anansi thought and thought, and in the evening Wulbari laughed at him and said: 'You must bring me "something"; you boast everywhere that you are my equal; prove it.'

So next day Anansi arose and left the sky on his way to find 'something'. Presently he had an idea, and sitting down by the wayside he called all the birds together. From each he borrowed a fine feather and then dismissed them. Rapidly he wove them into a magnificent clothing and then returned to Wulbari's town. There he put on the wonderful feather robe and climbed up the tree over against Wulbari's house. Soon Wulbari came out and saw the glaringly coloured bird. It was a new bird to him, so he called all the people together and asked them what was the name of the wonderful bird. But none of them could tell, not even the elephant who knows all that there is in the far far bush. Some one suggested that Anansi might know, but Wulbari said that unfortunately he had sent him away on an errand. Every one wanted to know the errand and Wulbari laughed and said: 'Anansi has been boasting too much and I heard him say that he has as much sense as I have. So I told him to go and get me "something".' Every one wanted to know what this something was, and Wulbari explained that Anansi would never guess what he meant, for the something he wanted was nothing less than the sun, the moon, and darkness.

The meeting then broke up amid roars of laughter at Anansi's predicament and Wulbari's exceeding cuteness. But Anansi in his fine plumes had heard what was required of him, and as soon as the road was clear descended from his tree and made off to the bush.

There he discarded his feathers and went far far away. No man knows quite where he went to, but wherever he went he managed to find the sun and the moon and the darkness. Some say that the python gave them to him, others are not sure. But in any case find them he did, and putting them into his bag he hastened back to Wulbari.

He arrived at his master's house late one afternoon and was greeted by Wulbari, who after a while asked Anansi if he had brought back something.

'Yes', said Anansi, and went to his bag and drew out Darkness. Then all was black and no one could see; he then drew out the Moon and all could see a little again. Then lastly he drew out the Sun and some who were looking at Anansi saw the Sun and they became blind, and some only saw a little bit and were blinded in one eye, others were luckier and had their eyes shut at the moment, so they lost nothing of their eyesight. Thus it came about that blindness was brought into the world.

Now the Sun is male and the Moon is female. The two therefore married and had many children which are the stars. However, in due course the Moon became weary of the

Sun's attentions, she longed for variety, so she took to herself a lover. Unfortunately the Sun got to hear of her infidelity and there was a lot of trouble between the two. At last the Sun refused to allow the Moon to stay with him any more and drove her out of his house. He was not too hard on the errant woman, but divided with her all his fields and possessions. Some of the children went with their mother and some with their father.

In spite of this unmerited kindness the Moon was not content, and often even to-day she trespasses on the fields of her former husband. The latter's children get annoyed at this and seek to drive their mother away. There is then a battle between the star-children of the Sun and the star-children of the Moon. Then it is that we have the storms and thunder and lightning. But the Moon is a woman after all, and she soon calls her children back and sends her messenger, the Rainbow, to tell them to cease fighting. The messenger goes, and sometimes he is a long time and the Moon, his mistress, gets worried over his prolonged absence. The messenger, however, tries to be as quick as possible, and if he thinks he is late in returning he hangs out, or waves his many-coloured cloth, as a signal that he will soon be back. That is why we see the rainbow.

Sometimes the Moon herself is caught by the Sun in the act of stealing from his fields. Then he begins to flog her and even tries to eat her. We men see this at the time of eclipses, and if we did not shout and drum and threaten the Sun would finish the job and we should lose the Moon. But the noise we make frightens the Sun and he lets her go.

The Moon is of quite another use to men as well as the usual one of giving light, for the Krachis believe that she will give one a forecast of what will happen. For instance, should you see the new moon for the first time whilst standing you will know that you are soon to go on a journey, but if by chance you are sitting down, then you most certainly would not go on any journey, for then you would have ill fortune. Moreover, if the new moon appears first to us on her back then all men will have good luck that month, but if she is inclined to the north then the people in the north will suffer, as will those in the south if she points that way.

The Dagomba have a version very similar of the origin of the sun and moon. But they also tell how Wuni has a compound. It is apparently the sun. Outside there is a market-place. This one can see when there is a halo round the sun. In the compound Wuni keeps a ram. When the ram stamps with its feet then we hear thunder; lightning is the shaking of its tail; and the rain is the hair of the tail itself. As the ram rushes round and round the compound it makes a great wind. We see that in the tornados.

In the far north among the so-called Grunshi tribes the following stories are told:

There was a certain man who had a sweetheart who was already promised to another man. They therefore decided to run away. On their journey they were approaching a baobab tree when they were overtaken by a heavy shower of rain. They ran to the tree, and there found the house of a chichiriga[1] whose wife made them welcome. Her pots were all full of magic and medicine, and among these things was a man's leg. (I could get no explanation of this leg. I was just told that that was in the story.)

Soon the chichiriga came home, and as a result of his wife's magic he fell down dead. Then the man, his sweetheart, and the wife of the chichiriga ran off and presently came to a river. There there was, busily washing her things on the bank, a woman who said she was the wife of the river-spirit. So the man hid himself in the grass and when the river-spirit came along he killed him. Then taking the

[1] Chichiriga is a species of dwarf fairy. Later I devote several pages to them. Chichiriga is used when reference is made to northern tribes; Kulparga when to Dagomba; Mmoatia to Krachi and Ashanti tribes.

woman he ran off with the rest of his companions until they came to the far far bush where they decided to settle.

In course of time the women bore sons, and one day when they had reached manhood they quarrelled over a dead cow, as to who should have its tail. The father intervened but without success, so he said he would throw it up into the air and as the skin fell so should they know which part each should have. The skin was thrown up into the air, but it has never come down again, for the skin became the sky and the clouds, the horns the sun and moon, and the tail is the milky way.

Another version of the same sky myth tells how there were once three men who were almost dead from hunger. So they went to the chief's [1] compound and begged him for food. The first one said that if the chief would but give him some flour he might slay him; the second asked for beans and water and then offered his life; whilst the third asked the chief to be allowed to sleep with his daughter, and then the chief might kill him. To these requests the chief listened and gave the food to the first two, whom he slew as soon as ever they had partaken of the repast. The third received his request that night, and the chief told his dog to watch at the door of the hut and not to allow the man to escape.

Now the daughter overheard this, and early in the morning she awoke the man and calling to the dog gave it some food. The dog left his post for the food and the man and the girl escaped.

Soon after the chief awoke and finding the two had gone he sent ten men on horseback to bring them back. These galloped after the fugitives and came into sight of them near a river bank. They were bargaining with the ferryman as the horsemen approached, but the daughter of the canoe-owner took a fancy to the man and asked him for some fire. This

[1] It is very noticeable how in the north among the tribes speaking languages belonging to the Moshi and Grunshi groups 'chief' is used, whilst in the Twi group 'God' is substituted.

he gave her, and putting the ashes into the canoe paddled them across and left her father behind.

The three then continued their flight and soon came to a baobab where there lived a chichiriga. He was not at home, but his wife was there and asked them to come inside and have some refreshment. She showed them all her pots, which were different coloured—some red, some black, and the others white. These colours she explained were blood, hair, and brains.

After a while she told the man that she was tired of her husband and wanted to be rid of him. If he could give her some ashes she would be able to make some medicine which would effect this. The man then gave her some of the ashes brought from the river, and when the chichiriga came home the wife killed him and ran off with the man.

The latter with his three wives settled in the bush, and there they bore for him three sons. One of them was black, one red, and the third white.

In due time they grew up and reached manhood, and one day they quarrelled bitterly over a dead cow, for each wanted the tail. The father decided to throw the skin into the air so that when it fell down it would fall in such a way as to show which part would belong to whom.

He did so but the skin never fell down at all. In fact it remained up above, and the skin is the sky and the horns are the sun and moon, and the tail became the stars.

The women then quarrelled as to which of them had done most service for their husband. One cried out that she had saved him from the chief, the second that she had saved him from the horsemen, and the third that she had saved him from the chichiriga. He listened to them for a while, and then said that they were all alike and that each had saved him and that it was the same with his sons. They were all the same, and no matter whether a man was black or red or white they were men and there was no difference between them.

These stories can be compared to one from the Kassena country which relates how a man and a woman had but one child which one day was eaten by a snake. Their grief knew no bounds, but there chanced along four men who cheered the bereaved parents by stating that they might be of assistance as one of them knew how to track snakes, a second knew how to kill snakes, the third knew how to skin them, and the fourth knew how to restore the dead to life. Their help was accepted, and after a short hunt the snake was tracked and killed and skinned. The babe was found inside, and duly restored to life. Unfortunately these kind visitors began to quarrel as to the ownership of the skin. They grew very angry with each other, and the father of the restored baby had to intervene. He suggested he should throw it into the air and whomsoever it fell on that one should have it. This he did, but the skin has never come down again. We can see it still, for the sun is the head, the tail is the moon, and the stars are the spots on its skin.

But to return to the Krachi. Wulbari having established the Sun and the Moon and Stars, and thus having arranged for night and day took pity on men, his former comrades. He had heard that they were suffering from hunger, so decided to show them how to make farms and grow food for themselves. To this end he called the Captain of his Host and gave him seeds of every sort and showed Anansi how to sow them.

Anansi then called men to him and showed what he had learned. But Anansi was a careful man, and he only sowed half of the seeds. In a few days he called men again to see the result of their labours. They all repaired to the fields and found the crop had been completely destroyed by baboons. So he decided that he had selected a spot too far from the houses of men, and giving them instructions to plant near their homes and not too far away where baboons might come, he presented them with the remainder of the seeds and returned to Wulbari.

There is another version of this affair with the baboons. It is said that baboons are or were men. They received the seeds as well as men and were shown how to make their farms. The baboons were quite pleased at this and made great fields in the bush where baboons usually live. But it happened that there were a lot of mosquitos about which gave the monkeys a deal of trouble. They even got in their ears and buzzed and tickled there. This made work very difficult so the baboons got annoyed and said, 'Very well, we shall not work any longer'. So they sat down on their hoes, and they sat for such a long time that the hoes grew on the monkeys' nether quarters. That is why they have tails and their 'sit-upons' are bare like well-used iron, for the hoe blades became the latter and the handles the tails.

A third story runs on similar lines, but is not connected with Wulbari. There was a certain man named Kwa Cherebwa who had many slaves. They were so many that they got out of control and actually refused to work longer in his fields. Kwa was almost at the point of starvation when he sent for the recalcitrant ones, and calling the first he made him lie down on the ground and began to beat him with a stick. The other slaves seeing this ran away, and to protect their quarters put their hoes there to cover the place. Thus again the handles grew into tails and the blades into the shiny bareness characteristic of a baboon's hindmost parts.

Returning to Wulbari, the story continues that a certain bird, Animabri (blackbird), the Giant Ground Toucan, developed one day an evil liking for human flesh. He began to kill and devour all the men he encountered. Naturally the latter objected and began to cry out. The noise came to Wulbari, who asked what it was all about. On being told he called all his court together and told them that in future no one was to interfere with other people, but that each one of them was to mind his own business and not disturb his neighbour. He then asked each of his attendants to name each his people. The elephant told how he roamed in and controlled the far far bush, and all the other animals defined their respective realms. Then the goat came along and said that his people were the grass; and finally came the dog, who declared men were his subjects.

Wulbari gave the latter a medicine which would restore life to the dead whom the toucan had killed. And each made off to his kingdom. Now the dog did not have far to go, but on the way he found a bone and being hungry set down the medicine by the roadside and himself began to worry the providentially-sent toothpiece. Whilst so engaged the goat came along and noticed the medicine lying there unguarded. So he took it and scattered it all over his people. And the dog on finishing his meal could not find the magic drug. He returned to Wulbari, but the latter would do nothing. That is why to this day men die and do not return, but grass which dies every year comes back again.

A second version tells how in the olden times men grew weary of dying and therefore decided to send a messenger to Nyame to that effect and chose the sheep to convey their wishes. At the same time, as is the custom to this day among the people, to make sure that the messenger took his message correctly they agreed to send a second, and for that purpose elected the dog for the work. Now the dog knew that he was much swifter than the sheep so he did not leave together with the latter but waited some while behind. Meanwhile the sheep went along the road to Nyame's town, and on the way he came to a certain village where an old woman lived. This old dame had just been overhauling her stock of salt and had found some of it had been badly spoilt by water, and it was not possible for her to dry it again. She had therefore thrown the salt into the bush outside the village.

When the sheep came along he started to browse just there where the salt had been thrown, and finding the grass extremely palatable he stayed there a long time and his fellow messenger the dog coming along the road did not see the sheep in the bush. He therefore hastened on and reached Nyame's village first. There he told Nyame that he and the sheep had been sent on a message to him from men, and Nyame asked him what the message was, and the dog told him that men had said they wished to remain dead when they died and not to return again here. Nyame said that so it should be and the dog returned. On his way he met the sheep and told him what he had done. The sheep at once explained that a mistake had been made, and they both returned to Nyame. But Nyame refused to alter his first decision, and that is why men die and do not come back again.

But the Dagomba relate how in the olden time men did not die, and except for the chiefs they passed their whole time as slaves. They at last grew weary of this eternal bondage and decided to send a messenger to Wuni and to beg him to put an end to their servitude. They chose for this duty their friend the dog and he departed on his errand. As he ran along the road which led to the dwelling-place of Wuni he came to a village where there was an old woman cooking a pot of something over a fire. The dog thought it a good chance to get some food and sat down near by gazing at his hoped-for meal. The old woman tried to chase him away, but that merely made him more anxious to share some of the good things inside the pot. While he was thus waiting a young goat who had overheard the message of the men came along, and seeing the dog tarrying decided he would do a good thing if he himself took the message and delivered it to Wuni.

He therefore went on.

Now the dog had to wait a long time, and at last the pot was boiling. The old woman took it off and fetching a baby opened the lid of the pot, which after all was only full of water, with which she began to wash the infant. The dog was very annoyed and ran off down the road to Wuni. On his way he met the goat, who asked him where he was off to. The dog told him, and the goat replied that it was now quite unnecessary to proceed as he himself had given the message. The dog asked him what message, and when the goat told him that he had arrived at Wuni's compound and there told the god that men were tired of being slaves and now wanted to die, the dog was very upset and raced away to Wuni to correct the mistake. He came to the god, but the latter refused to listen to the new message, saying that he did not believe it and that he had already arranged for the death of men. Thus it is that death comes to all men nowadays and men remained slaves. It also accounts for men hating to see dogs watching them at their meals. Which last is a curious fact to be observed among all these tribes. If a dog sits down near men eating they will throw him some food, and then chase him away with sticks and stones. But to-day the young men are not quite so particular, and often they will allow their dogs to be near them at meal times.

A version of quite another type is told of the origin of death by the Krachi. It runs as follows:

Long, long ago there was a great famine in the world, and a certain young man whilst wandering in search of food strayed into a part of the bush where he had never been before. Presently he perceived a strange mass lying on the ground. He approached and saw that it was the body of a giant whose hair resembled that of white men in that it was silky rather than woolly. It was of an incredible length and stretched as far as from Krachi to Salaga. The young man was properly awed at the spectacle, and wished to withdraw, but the giant noticing him asked what he wanted.

The young man explained and begged the giant to give him some food. The latter agreed on condition that the youth would serve him for a while. This matter having been arranged the giant said that his name was Owuo or Death, and then gave the boy some meat.

Never before had the latter tasted such fine food, and he was well pleased with his bargain. He served his master for a long time and received plenty of meat, but one day he grew home-sick, and begged his master to give him a short holiday. The latter agreed if the youth would promise to bring another boy in his place. So the youth returned to his village and there persuaded his brother to go with him into the bush and gave him to Owuo.

In course of time the youth got hungry again and longed for the meat which Owuo had taught him to like so much. So one day he made up his mind to return to his master, and leaving the village made his way back to the giant's abode. The latter asked him what he wanted, and when the youth told him that he wanted to taste once more of the good meat the giant told him to enter the hut and take as much as he liked, but he would have to work for him again.

The youth agreed and entered the hut. He ate as much as he could and set to at the task his master set him. The work continued for a long time and the boy ate his fill every day. But to his surprise he never saw anything of his brother, and whenever he asked about him the giant told him that the lad was away on his business.

Once more the youth grew home-sick and asked for leave to return to his village. The giant agreed on condition that he would bring a girl for him, Owuo, to wed. So the youth went home and there persuaded his sister to go into the bush and marry the giant. The girl agreed, and took with her a slave companion, and they all repaired to the giant's abode. There the youth left the two girls and went back to the village.

It was not very long after that he again grew hungry and longed for a taste of the meat. So he made his way once more into the bush and found the giant. The latter did not seem overpleased to see the boy and grumbled at being bothered a fourth time. However, he told the boy to go into the inner chamber of his hut and take what he wanted. The youth did so and took up a bone which he began to devour. To his horror he recognized it at once as being the bone of his sister. He looked around at all the rest of the meat and saw that it was that of his sister and her slave girl.

Thoroughly frightened he escaped from the house and ran back to the village. There he told the elders what he had done and the awful thing he had seen. At once the alarm was sounded and all the people went out into the bush to see for themselves the dread thing they had heard about. When they drew near to the giant they grew afraid at the sight of so evil a monster. They went back to the village and consulted among themselves what best they should do. At last it was agreed to go to Salaga where the giant's hair finished and set a light to it. This was done, and when the hair was burning well they returned to the bush and watched the giant.

Presently the latter began to toss about and to sweat. It was quite evident that he was beginning to feel the heat. The nearer the flames advanced the more he tossed and grumbled. At last the fire reached his head and for the moment the giant was dead.

The villagers approached him cautiously, and the young man noticed 'medicine' which had been concealed in the roots of the giant's hair. He took it and called the others to come and see what he had found. No one could say what power this medicine might have, but an old man suggested that no harm would be done if they took some and sprinkled it on the bones and meat in the hut. This idea was carried out, and to the surprise of every one the girls and the boy returned to life at once.

The youth who had still some of the medicine left proposed to put it on the giant. But at this there was a great uproar as the people feared Owuo might come to life again. The boy therefore by way of compromise sprinkled it into the eye of the dead giant. At once the eye opened and the people all fled away in terror. But it is from that eye that death comes; for every time that Owuo shuts that eye a man dies, and unfortunately for us he is for ever blinking and winking.

However, neither the people of Krachi nor those of the other tribes in this Togoland hinterland believe that men are for ever dead. For a while the departed are wont to tarry near their former homes and often they may be seen as ghosts. Not all men, however, do this, but usually betake themselves at once to the city of the dead or to some remote spot.

A common belief is that the souls of the dead proceed on a long journey and return to life once more. Thus the Dagomba claim that the silincia (or souls) of men and animals depart after a while from their old homes and are born again in the same form as they had before, and this one can easily see for oneself by the striking likeness to ancestors which complete strangers often bear. The northern tribes believe their souls wander southwards to Salaga, which to them was the end of their geographical knowledge. The Krachi aver that they go to Gambaga, and in proof thereof the story is told of an Ashanti man whose family had removed to Elmina whilst he himself stayed in Coomassie. He had occasion to go to Gambaga and there to his surprise came across his family. All were there and seemingly prosperous. He stayed with them and then returned to Coomassie, where he learned that his family had all died in Elmina of some dire pestilence. That story is a modern one and is remarkable for its confirmation of a similar belief recorded over seventy years ago to the effect that the ghosts of the dead among the Fanti eventually depart to the north to the river Volta, where they build for themselves villages in which they sojourn till the time comes for them to return to their old haunts and be born again (Steinhauser, *Mag. der Evang. Miss.*, Basel, 1856,

No. 2, p. 135). That missionary records also that it was a common saying to a bereaved mother when one sought to console her for her loss 'He will come again'. He further states that men may return in the guise of animals.

Among the Mamprussi it is believed that the youths and girls who, having reached puberty, die before indulging in any sexual practices do not go to the world where dwell the other spirits of the dead who are awaiting their turn to be born again. On the other hand they are bound to hover at night-time near their old haunts, and one can often see them. They appear in front of one as one goes along the paths but are not recognizable, for they assume a mystic shape, limbless, a sort of white cloud somewhat higher than a man. They are to be heard weeping and moaning, and if the unfortunate person who meets them is afraid and runs away they will chase him or her back to the village, and often as a result the person will never speak again, but will die in a short while. If, however, one can conceal one's fear and not run away but just continue on one's road, there is nothing to fear and the ghosts will not harm you.

The Krachi see in the wind-devils and whirlwinds also the ghosts of the departed. These whirlwinds are called Pompontri, and whenever one approaches near the house the owner or any one of the inmates will offer it water and a little flour which is thrown on the ground. At the same time a prayer for help is uttered, as the ghosts are usually quite as likely to be malevolent as not.

There are also mysterious roads in the bush which seem to lead no whither. These are ghost roads. The most noticeable of such is one at Sandema in the country of the Builsa.[1] It runs right through the market-place, and though but little frequented by man yet has the appearance of being most constantly in use. It is said to go on and on to the

---

[1] A tribe of Dagomba extraction dwelling to the north-west of their parent stock among the Grunshi.

Moshi hill, where the City of the Dead is located, the dread city of Pilimpiku. Here no man will wander, but all take care to avoid its neighbourhood for the chimse, i.e. spirits of the departed, may seize you, and you would then never return to your home or friends.

However, ghosts are of quite a practical use, for if there is one thing they detest that is to see children robbing bees of their honey. So they will punish any such greedy urchin.

Among the Builsa and Nankanni there are maintained special houses called kuga where the ghosts can come and stay. Food is provided them, but in spite of this they are far from being welcome guests. Often and often will one hear at night-time the war-cry being raised. This is to scare away the ghosts of the dead who are troubling their living friends.

Animals have their ghosts as well as men, and the following is told by the Dagomba:

In the very long ago the Chief of Sunson considered that he was a very big man and wanted to show to all and sundry that he was greater than all others. He therefore called his people together and told them that he wished in future to ride a roan antelope and not a horse, so that whenever people saw him they would know that he was in truth a mighty chieftain.

The hunters went into the bush, and after a long time succeeded in catching a roan. This they brought back to their Chief, who was well pleased with them.

A few days later the Chief said he would try the roan and ordered his men to saddle it. After a lot of struggling they managed to do this and then the Chief mounted. No sooner was he in the saddle than the roan ran off and ran faster and faster till the runners could not keep up and the Chief was left alone. The roan went on and on into the bush and out of sight so that that Chief was never from that day to this seen again.

Thus it is that whenever a chief of Sunson is about to die

the people see in the night-time that ghost roan come to the town already saddled, and stand outside the chief's house, waiting for his rider.

It is only natural that Wulbari or Nyame should be accorded all the attributes of man, but it is curious how frequently it is related in the folk-tales that this all-powerful creator is foiled and humbugged. There is, moreover, a quaint story told how Nyame very nearly failed to become god at all. It is said that one day there were born two children, the first was named Ohene-o-Ohene, or The Chief-is-Chief, and the second, the younger of the two, was named Nyame-o-Ohene, or God-is-Chief. Now the father of the twins preferred the elder, and therefore one day, calling the two to him, he gave Ohene-o-Ohene a large calabash full of soup and meat. Ohene-o-Ohene ate all that he could and gave the residue to his younger twin. The latter could not find much food, but at the bottom he did find some medicine. That medicine has given him all his power, and that is why God commands men and has power over them.

The above is a curious legend of the Krachi which shows how the Supreme Deity is regarded as human by the people. One naturally presumes, therefore, that there must be stories of Nyame's marriage, and one is not disappointed.

We are told that his first wife was Akoko, the Barn-door Fowl. (One might see in this fact a reference to the dawn, cock-crow, and sky.) But Nyame does not seem to have appreciated the blessings of monogamy, for it is said that he took to himself four other wives. Of course Akoko retained her rights as the head-wife, and these other four obeyed her.

One day Nyame called the four new-comers and asked each what present she would give him in return for his having raised her social status. The first promised that she would always sweep his compound for him and keep the place neat and tidy; the second said she would always cook for him and never complain when there were many visitors;

the third agreed to spin cotton for him and to bring him all the water he might require; and the fourth said that she would bear him a child of gold.[1]

This last pleased Nyame, and every day he killed a sheep for this woman. But the child was long in coming, and just when Nyame's patience was giving out the woman conceived and Nyame detailed Akoko to tend and care for the woman.

So Akoko took the woman into her hut and when the time of delivery was at hand she told her that whatever else she did she was to be sure to shut her eyes when the child was born and not open them till she was told to. The woman obeyed, and Akoko hurried out and brought back a big pot.

Now it happened that the woman bore twins. The first one to be born was made entirely of silver, and Akoko at once took the babe and placed it in the pot. The second child was of gold, and again Akoko placed it in the pot.[2] Then she hurried outside and found two frogs. Returning with these she placed them on the couch and then told the mother to open her eyes and see her children. Meanwhile Akoko hastened out of the hut with the pot and ran with it as fast as she could to the far far bush where she found a dead odum tree. There she hid the pot with the two babies and then returned swiftly to Nyame's compound, passing by his hut on the way. She told her husband that the children had been born and asked him to go with her to see his offspring.

Nyame at once arose and went to the hut where the mother was lying. To his consternation and anger he found two frogs instead of the expected and promised gold-child. He gave orders that the frogs were to be killed at once and the woman sent into the farthermost corner of his kingdom.

Now it chanced that Nyame had a certain hunter whose hut was situated in the far bush. He happened to be out hunting on the day when the children were born and his

[1] These are the four duties of women.
[2] The second born of twins is considered the elder.

chase led him to the odum tree. There his eye was attracted by the glitter of the golden child and he cried out 'Why, what is this?' The children answered him: 'We are the children of Nyame.' But he could not believe that.

However, he took some of the dust that had fallen from their bodies and put it in his bag. Then he took up the children and carried them to his hovel. There he kept them secretly, nor did he tell any man of what he had found.

And every time he wanted money he would gather some of the children's dust. Thus he became a very rich man. Instead of a solitary hovel in the bush he built a huge compound and round him there gathered a great town.

Now not very far away there lived Anansi. One day he went out into the bush to gather some white ants for his fowls and came across the new town. He was astounded to see in the place where he expected a hovel so much wealth and so many people. His curiosity aroused, he entered the town to learn how the change had come about. By sheer accident he came across the former hunter playing with the children. At once Anansi knew the latter were the lost children of Nyame, and he hurried back home to send a message to their father. But the hunter had also seen Anansi, and he knew full well that that busybody would betray his secret. Therefore he called the children and told them that as they said they were the children of Nyame he proposed to take them to Nyame.

Next morning he prepared hammocks and fine clothes for the children and proceeded on the way to Nyame. On the road the children called their foster father and told him that he must collect some stones to play 'wari' [1] with as they could not themselves speak to their father but the stones would tell him all the story.

---

[1] 'Wari' is an African game somewhat on the lines of our game of draughts. It is played in many ways all over West Africa and is described in one form or other by almost all writers since the earliest times.

The man did so, and they arrived before Nyame. There the hunter set stools and asked Nyame if he would play him a game of 'wari'. Nyame agreed, but the silver child said 'No', that he himself wished to play, and that the stones would tell the story for which they had come.

Then the silver child and Nyame sat down to the game, and as the stones went round and round the board the golden child sang the story of their adventures from the time of their mother's promise till their birth; he sang of the baseness of Akoko and the kindness of the hunter who had fed them instead of killing them for their silver and gold.

Then Nyame knew them to be his children, and he sent straightway into the far far bush to call back the woman whom he had exiled. When she arrived she was all over dirt and her hair was uncut and ill-kempt. Nyame himself washed the woman, and when she was all clean and nice again he sent for Akoko.

Great was his wrath. He tied the evil fowl Akoko, his first wife, by its foot to a stick and cursed her. Then he threw her down from the sky and gave orders that every time the fowl wished to drink she would first have to raise her head to him and beg. Further, Nyame gave orders that every man would in future sacrifice fowls as the ordinary sacrifices to the gods. Are not these things done to this day?

As for the children: once every year they are washed, and dust from them falls upon the earth. Some falls on men, and those are the lucky ones who become wealthy.

That story tells one a lot about the native mind. The duties of women are laid down with care. They shall keep the house clean for their lords and masters; they shall cook for him and grumble not at the number of his guests; they shall spin cotton for his raiment and fetch him water from the streams; and they shall bear him children. The belief in gold falling from the sky is a common one, but there is also another theory of its origin, which is that all the gold is shown to us by the mists and clouds seen early in the morning hanging over the valleys, just as it is said that mystic fires indicate the burial place of aggrey beads.[1]

But the outstanding feature to my mind is the successful humbugging of a Supreme Deity. Nyame is a very human god.

To show further how the Supreme Deity can be overcome there is told the following tale—a story which not only accounts for how the present crops first reached man, but is full of other lore, and goes far to show how great is the belief in magic which these people hold.

It is a story common to all Twi speakers and runs as follows :

Many years ago there lived a certain old woman. She had eleven children. And she named them after the numbers 'One, two, three, &c., till eleven (Edubiaku)'. Now soon after the eleventh child was born a great famine came over the land, and the old woman and her husband could get no food. They did not know what to do. They and their children were starving.

When matters were very bad the old woman went into the bush to see what she could find. But alas ! she found nothing, and on her return her husband said : 'Shame has come upon me; I have many children and I cannot give them food. It were better to kill them.'

But Edubiaku overheard this and he called his brothers and he told them that great troubles were coming to them, and that he had learnt this through his magic and his dog Otwia (N.B. the old word for dog before the present one, Okraman). And his brothers told him that he lied, that he was only a baby, and they beat him.

But Edubiaku answered that he spoke truly, that whipping

---

[1] A bead of considerable value in the eyes of most West Africans, but intrinsically practically valueless. The value attached to them is derived from their personal contact with men or women of importance.

could not stop the trouble, and that they would see for themselves in three days' time.

And on the third day the old woman went with her husband to their farm. In the middle of the clearing stood
a large dead tree and at its roots grew a plantain. And the
woman asked the dead tree to help her, and said she would
call her children to the plantain at its foot, and when they were
all come the tree must kill them by falling on top of them.

The tree answered: 'It is a bad thing to kill eleven children. If I do this thing, what will you give me?'

And the woman answered: 'You are a big Tree, bigger
than all other Trees. Yet they have many young ones and
you have none. If you do this thing for me, I will take your
seed and plant many, so that your family may become a great
one.'

Now the Tree's name was Wingina—the silk cotton tree.
So Wingina answered: 'It is well. Send your children here.'

Then the old woman returned home and called all the
children together and told them to go to the plantain which
was at the foot of the Wingina tree; and she conjured them
not to separate, but all to go together as they would find
plenty of food.

So they started off to the Wingina tree, and Edubiaku took
his dog Otwia with him.

On the way he stopped his brothers and told them that
now the trouble he had foretold had come. Why were they
going to the clearing? What would happen there? He had
warned them and they had whipped him.

And the older brothers asked him how it was that he, still
a baby, should know these things. To which Edubiaku
replied that it was true what he said, that he knew all these
things, that the big tree had been told by their mother to kill
them, that God and the dog had given him this power.

But they went on, and when they arrived at the clearing
Edubiaku counted them: 'One, two, three, four, five, six,

seven, eight, nine, ten, eleven the magician (Konfo). Let all go and cut an akori (a pole with a hook at the end).' And they obeyed, and all got an akori and pulled down the big tree Wingina, so that it killed no one. Then they cut the plantains, and Edubiaku told them to put the plantains on the ground. And they did so. And Edubiaku called his dog, and the dog ran round the plantains three times and three times round the fallen Wingina.

While he ran round the big tree the dog found a dead parrot and he said: 'This is a parrot. Let all men make the parrot his friend, but let all men eat him also as the parrot will otherwise tell all men what you say.'

Then they all went back home with the plantains and their mother was amazed at their safe return. But she was angry.

Again she went to the clearing and there met Efre the pumpkin. She greeted him and asked him for his help. 'You are many,' she said, 'and I beg you to get a snake for each of your pumpkins. I will send my children to you to-morrow to gather your young ones, and the snakes will bite them and they will die.' And Efre made answer: 'I will help you, for man is my enemy and does not like to eat my presents to him except in the hungry time.' For you must know that in the olden days no Ashanti would eat pumpkins but that now men eat them always.

The woman was glad when she heard Efre's answer, and she called all the snakes and bade them hide among the pumpkins and to kill those who would come to get the fruit. And the snakes obeyed the woman.

She then returned home and calling all the children together told them to go to the clearing and to eat the pumpkins. Then they were all happy at the thought of food, and started off accompanied by Otwia the dog.

When they came to the clearing Edubiaku counted them 'One, two, three, four . . . eleven Konfo; Mate magyina (step aside). Let us all take sticks.' So they all took sticks.

Then he said: 'Let us knock the Efre down.' When they did so the snakes came out and were killed; so the children gathered the Efre and brought them home.

But their mother was very angry and did not know what to do to kill them. So she consulted her husband who advised her to go and see God (Nyame) about the matter, for surely he ought to know how to kill the children.

The next day both the old woman and her husband went to Nyame and told him how they had had many children (eleven children), that there was now hunger in the land and would God try to kill them, for they themselves could no longer give them any food. Nyame agreed, and told the woman and the man to send the children to him.

Then they returned home. When they got back to the house they called the children together and said: 'You must go to Nyame. He will give you plenty of food.'

Meanwhile God had assembled many men, whom he ordered to make an enormous hole in the middle of the road that the children would have to take. He hoped they would fall into it and so perish. And the men did as God told them and made an enormous hole.

As the children were all walking one after the other on the road to Nyame, Otwia the dog ran along in front. Presently he stopped, and Edubiaku at once counted his brothers and said 'Let every one pass along in the bush'. They obeyed, and so passed the hole safely and came to Nyame.

The God saw that of a truth Edubiaku was a great possessor of magic. So he bade the children go to a certain house and eat and sleep, and that on the next day he would see them.

On the next morning God sent for the children, and when they were come he asked which of them was Edubiaku. And Edubiaku declared himself. Then God told him to go alone without his dog into the bush and there to cut palm-nuts from a palm-tree as many visitors were expected and he wanted the oil. For God knew that it was not difficult to kill the other ten children; Edubiaku alone was different. Moreover, Abe the palm-tree which Edubiaku was to cut down was in reality a terrible spirit and no one dared go near him.

But Edubiaku was not afraid, and said he would go. First, however, he went to the blacksmith and bought two nkonya (bells). Then he left God's village and went to Abe the palm-tree. When he drew near the terrible spirit of the Abe came out and called in a loud voice: 'Who dares to come nigh me?' And Edubiaku replied: 'It is I.' Then the terrible spirit looked and saw a small baby boy and laughed and said: 'What! a small boy like you dares to come near me. What do you want?'

Edubiaku answered: 'I want you, Abe.' And Abe laughed and said he would kill him. But Edubiaku rang his bells and threw them away. Abe hearing the bells thought Edubiaku was with them and left the tree in pursuit. Thus Edubiaku had time to cut the palm-nuts down from the tree.

Meanwhile God, thinking Edubiaku would not return, killed the ten brothers and sacrificed a sheep. He placed the sheep's head on the fire to cook and gave the rest of the meat to the people who had killed the boys.

When Edubiaku returned, Nyame told him that his brothers had refused to stop any longer but had gone back home by what road no man knew. Edubiaku then asked for some water to wash in, and whilst so engaged his dog came running to him, and Edubiaku played with it, and the dog went and stole the sheep's head from the fire.

And all the people cried out: 'Edubiaku, Edubiaku, your dog has stolen the sheep's head.' So Edubiaku refused to finish his bath, but got up to follow the dog, who led him straightway to where his ten brothers lay slain.

When Edubiaku saw them lying thus he went into the

bush and gathered medicine which, on coming back, he sprinkled over his brothers, counting them: 'One, two, three, &c., rise up.' And they all rose up and with Edubiaku went to Nyame.

Then Nyame saw that of a truth Edubiaku was a great magician. So he said he was sorry, and he gave them all plenty of money and food. In the morning he told them to return to their father and mother, and he gave them seeds of all the things that grow in the farms to-day. So Edubiaku and his brothers and the dog went back home, where they made a clearing and sowed the seeds.

Thus farming came to Ashanti.

Another version of that story tells how Edubiaku arrived at the City of God with his brothers and three dogs. (In telling these stories it is interesting to note that an older language is used and words such as Otwia have now meanings only in an opprobrious sense.) The children were given a house to stay in, and Edubiaku took one of the dogs and buried it in the wall. The second dog he buried in the street and the third he kept as companion.

After two days God sent for the children, and having had Edubiaku pointed out to him, he ordered him to go to the City of the Dead (Owuokrom) and to bring back from there a gourd or calabash of gold, a musical instrument of gold, a golden message-stick and a gold-mounted fly-whisk.

Edubiaku agreed to go, but went first to prepare much food and magic medicine. When this was ready, he set out and soon came to a great river, which asked him for food. Edubiaku asked him why, and the river answered that if he the child was good to him, he the river would perhaps one day repay the kindness. This pleased Edubiaku, who took some of the food and gave it to the river.

Shortly afterwards Edubiaku comes across Wansane, the harnessed antelope, who also asks for food. The child gives the antelope some and proceeds on his road, meeting

Nkrani, the driver ant, who makes the same request, which is granted.

In a similar way Edubiaku has made friends with Ekura the mouse and Ahuria the tsetse fly, and at last he reaches the City of the Dead. The chief greets him and sends him to a house where he can rest. After a while palm-wine is brought to him in the golden calabash, which, when Edubiaku has sat down, is taken off by Ekura and hidden.

Edubiaku is about to sleep, but his 'magic' keeps him awake, and he overhears the Dead discussing how they will kill and eat him. This makes him restless, and he is asked what is likely to induce him to sleep. He suggests that if he plays music to himself it might be well. They bring him the golden musical instrument. After playing for a while he puts it down and Ekura at once hides it.

But still the boy does not sleep, and the chief sends his message-stick to inquire how it is that he cannot rest. Edubiaku suggests that if the stick were left with him he would be less uneasy and no longer afraid, and so might gain repose. When the messenger had gone Ekura came again and hid the message-stick.

A little later the Dead gathered in the street and made a great fire. Edubiaku arose and went to them, saying he was cold and could not sleep. So he sat down in the circle and presently Ahuria, the tsetse, came and bit the chief. At once a small boy ran off for the golden fly-whisk which he gave the chief. But the latter, once again bothered by the fly, hit at but missed it, and letting fall the whisk ran off in pursuit, followed by all the Dead. At once Edubiaku arose, seized the whisk, and made off down the road by which he had come.

Ekura the mouse met him outside the village and gave him the calabash, the musical instrument, and the message-stick.

Edubiaku thanked him and ran on. But the Dead had returned to the fire and found the boy and the golden articles were gone. They gave chase at once, but Nkrani the driver ant multiplied himself a million times. Now the Dead are very fond of driver ants as food; thus they were delayed. But they soon stopped eating and hurried after the boy.

Presently Wansane the harnessed antelope crossed their path. They could not resist the chase, and spent some time following the 'meat'.

Meanwhile Edubiaku had reached the river, which made itself very small indeed, so that the boy could cross quickly. No sooner had he done this than the Dead reached the other bank, but the river swelled and spread itself far and wide, so that the Dead could not cross, and thus Edubiaku managed to return to Nyame with his mission successfully accomplished.

The story now is similar to the first, but when Edubiaku wants his brothers he taps seven times on the wall, and the first dog comes out and tells him they are dead. He then goes to where he had buried the second dog, causes it to arise and to show him where the brothers are buried.

Over the grave Edubiaku makes 'magic' and the brothers are reunited. God admits he is defeated and allows them all to go home. On the way Edubiaku halts and makes lament that his father and mother and God and all men wished only to kill them. On his advice, then, all the brothers agree to change into something good, so that in future men will love them and not hate them.

Edubiaku makes medicine and calls out each of his brothers in turn and changes them into something good. One is changed into plantain; two into bananas; three, yams; four, cocoyams; five, cassada; six, tomatoes; seven, sweet-potatoes; eight, onions; nine, maize; and ten, okros. As for himself he became the small red chillie pepper, so that when men eat him they will cry as the peppers burn their mouths and tongues, and then they will remember Edubiaku with all his medicine.

Chapter Three

WHICH CHIEFLY CONCERNS THE SONS OF GOD

TANO AND BIA—HOW TANO TRICKED GOD—BRUKU—HIS
SACRED TOWN—THE BIRTH OF A GOD—DENTE'S BIRTH—
MYTHS CONCERNING HIM—THE SACRIFICE OF BARISU
KURI—AN ASHANTI LEAGUE OF NATIONS—THE DUEL
BETWEEN TANO AND DEATH—OF THE APPEARANCE OF
GODS—SACRED GROVE OF TA'HA—SATURNALIA—WORSHIP
OF TREES—SNAKE WORSHIP—SOULS OF ANIMALS—HOLY
RIVERS—GIANTS.

IN most books dealing with West Africa there is found
a long discussion as to whether the belief by the natives
in a Supreme Being, the Father of All, is one of native origin
or one that has been introduced to the native mind from
outside sources. I do not propose to enter here into this
controversy, for one could write a volume on the subject,
and one would, moreover, have to spend much time in
research among Portuguese archives for evidence of their
penetration into the hinterland, among the archives of the
various religious communities whose members shared with
Portugal these early explorations; one would have to search
the many Mohammedan manuscripts of Timbuctoo and other
Sudanese centres, and then sort out what was true and what
was mere flattery to their faith, for most of these records
are mere bolstering of their claims; and when all that was
done one would have to find out what influence Egypt and
Persia had in the centuries before the Christian era.

But all writers seem to agree that the worship of the
Supreme Deity is quite insignificant in its importance in so
far as the everyday life of the natives is concerned when compared with that of the minor deities, who are termed his 'sons'.

Now Nyame in Ashanti has many sons. Of these his
favourite was Bia, who was the eldest of the family. A second

son was named Tano. In due course the children grew to manhood, and as was and is the custom their father determined to award them some present to mark the occasion. The present would naturally be in accordance with the merits of the boys. Now Bia had always been a most obedient and helpful youth, whereas Tano had been the reverse. Nyame therefore decided he would give to Bia the most fertile and pleasing portion of the land, whilst to Tano he would allot but a wild and deserted area of little value and with few inhabitants. Therefore he chose for Bia the country of Ashanti where the people would worship him and give him sheep and eggs and other rich sacrifices, whilst for Tano he chose the dreary forest-land of the present Western Frontier.

When Nyame had made up his mind to this effect he called to him Akua Abirekyi, the Goat, who was his best and most trusted attendant, and having told her what was in his mind to do, charged the Goat with the message to call his two sons to him on the morrow and inform them that he wished to give them their portions.

Unfortunately, Akua Abirekyi was the intimate friend of Tano, and she was very upset to hear that the latter was about to be given so poor a share. Therefore she hurried to Tano and told him all, advising him to be very early in the morning and to reach Nyame's house betimes disguised as Bia, that thus he might deceive the Almighty. Tano agreed to this, and the goat went on her way to Bia. She delivered the message correctly, but added that there would be no need to hurry as Nyame would probably not be too early himself.

Next day Tano arrayed himself in all his finest clothes and for the first time in his life obeyed his father and reached the paternal roof betimes. There he completely deceived Nyame, who gave him his blessing and awarded him all that country through which the river Tano flows to-day, namely the rich parts of Western Ashanti and the gold-laden land of Sefwhi.

As soon as he had received this handsome present Tano hastened away.

Some time later Bia arrived at his father's door. Then Nyame knew what had been done, but he could or would not undo it. Therefore he gave to Bia that sad portion of the land which is of so little value, the thick forest and goldless land through which to-day the British and French boundary runs.

Meanwhile Tano had settled in his fair territory and there seems to have changed his evil habits, for he became rich and worked hard for his people so that they loved him and accorded him great respect and worship. They asked him what things he especially hated so that they might, by observing his desires, win his favour; and in memory of Akua Abirekyi's service to him he mentioned especially the goat. And that is why to this day the goat is not sacrificed to him.

Nyame had many other sons. Most of them seem to have been rivers and water-holes and lakes. Perhaps in this may be some dim remembrance of the time when the Ashanti dwelt not where they do to-day but in some hard unkindly land where water was difficult to get and thirst and famine frequent. For almost everywhere in this land one will find the tradition that the Ashanti came down from the north into the forest zone, from the arid wastes of the country bordering on the Sahara to the shady, fertile, and well-watered plains of Ashanti.

Now in the Krachi area the sons of Wulbari seem generally to be not rivers or watering-places but caverns and rocks. The actual rocks or caverns are not themselves worshipped but rather the spirits which are supposed to have taken up their abode therein. Possibly in this may be a fact reminiscent of the old-time Krachi tribes having dwelt in a country where hills and rocks were infrequent.

By far the most famous son of Wulbari lives in a rocky

nook in the mountains of Siari. He is Bruku, a god worshipped far and wide throughout West Africa. His cult is
preserved as secret as possible, and so far I have not penetrated to the actual dwelling-place. If one follows the
precipitous track from the town of Siari to the watering-place,
one will notice on the right hand a small path winding its
way up the almost perpendicular cliff through an alley of
overhanging verdure so dense that it is almost as it were
a tunnel. Strangers are warned not to progress, and as a rule
turn back. But I have been told by one who accompanied
some German officers that in a short while one comes to
a small clearing where a small pyramid of mud marks the
usual preliminary altar. The path continues further until
a cave is reached. Here is the very abode of Bruku; only the
chief priest and his assistant are allowed within these holy
precincts.

The usual function of this god is to render oracles and
such-like. Of course he is always willing to receive thank-
offerings as well as to accept gifts by way of reward from
those who come to him seeking help from him; but his chief
duty is undoubtedly that of oracle-giver, for which he has
gained a renown almost Delphic.

The town of Siari is a curious gathering of huts, beehive-
shaped, clinging precariously to the forest-clad sides of the
mountain sacred to Bruku. Five hundred feet below rush
the torrential waters of the Sabu, and five hundred feet
above rises the grass-covered summit. There are no streets
in Siari, merely alleyways between the huts, which are raised
on platforms of stones lest they should totter into the abyss;
and there are no cultivated clearings outside the town.
Those are some three miles away, at the foot of the valley, or
across the Sabu, not quite opposite to but visible from Siari.
It is a town of unknown age, but probably not very ancient,
if one can judge from the middens which are being formed
down the slopes of the mountains. But in many places in

the surrounding hills are to be found the remains of villages
which were constructed on stone terraces just as Siari is
to-day. Some are remembered as being inhabited, but most
are now forgotten and possibly belong to a fairly remote past.

The town is essentially an ecclesiastical one, and the main
industry is the exploitation of the god's oracle. The inhabitants are therefore all more or less intimately connected with
this work, and their houses are boarding-houses for the scores
of visitors who make their pilgrimage hither. Strangers are
not allowed to settle in the neighbourhood—a wise enough
rule, for apart from the sanctity of the precincts, there is no
room for many fresh houses—but must as soon as ever an
answer has been vouchsafed them from the god leave the
village and return down the valley, no matter at what hour
of the day or night the answer may be forthcoming.

Language difficulties seem to have been overcome, and
I was given to understand that in Siari are to be found
interpreters for all the principal tongues of West Africa.

The duties of the god seem chiefly to lie in assuring fertility of crops and women, and how efficacious he has proved
can be noticed in the fact that the name, Bruku, is so widespread and common, a name usually given to children born
after the parents have visited the shrine.

Bruku is also a famous detector of witchcraft, and some
time ago got into trouble with the Government for an
alleged practice of administering poison in order to find out
witches and wizards. But possibly his most important work
is the creation of 'sons', junior gods who act as his deputies
in remoter villages and who naturally provide good positions for the priesthood candidates. These are usually born
at Siari and carried away to the village which has asked and
paid for them. They do not differ from the 'sons' of the
Ashanti Tano, and their manner of birth is the same,
according to my informant.

Captain Rattray in his *Ashanti*, pp. 147 et seq., tells how this event occurs in Ashanti. 'A spirit may take possession of a man and he may appear to have gone mad, and this state may last sometimes even for a year. Then the priest of some powerful god may be consulted and he may discover, through his god, that it is some spirit which has come upon the man or woman. The one upon whom the spirit has come is now bidden to prepare a brass pan, and collect water, leaves, and medicine of specific kinds. The possessed one will dance, for sometimes two days, with short intervals for rest, to the accompaniment of drums and singing. Quite suddenly he will leap into the air and catch something in both his hands (or he may plunge into the river and emerge holding something he has brought up). He will in either case fold this thing to his breast, and water will be at once sprinkled upon it to cool it, when it will be thrust into the brass pan and quickly covered up. The following ingredients are now prepared: clay from one of the more sacred rivers, like the Tano, and the following medicinal plants and other objects: afema (*Justicia flavia*), Dama Bo (*Abras precatorius*); the bark of the odom, a creeper called hamakyem, leaves and bark of a tree called domine, another creeper called hama-kyerchene, any root that crosses a path, a projecting stump in a path over which passers-by would be likely to trip, also roots and stumps from under water, the leaves of a tree called aya—those are chosen which are seen to be quivering on the tree even though no wind is shaking them—the leaves, bark, and roots of a tree called Bonsam Dua (lit. the wizard's tree), a nugget of virgin gold (gold that has been in use or circulation must not be used), a bodom (so-called aggrey bead), and a long white bead called gyanie. The whole of these are pounded along with the original object already inside, while the following prayer or incantation is repeated.'

There is no need to give the words of the prayer, for prayers are much alike in humility and beauty be they offered to a spirit or a stone, but there is one significant paragraph which reveals the pure native standpoint as to the relationship between men and gods.

'And the laws that we are decreeing for you, you, this God of ours, are these—if in our time, or in our children's and our grandchildren's time, a king should arise from somewhere, and come to us, and say he is going to war, when he tells you, and you well know that should he go to the fight he will not gain the victory, you must tell us so; and should you know that he will go and conquer, then also state that truth. And yet again, if a man be ill in the night, or in the day-time, and we raise you aloft and place you upon the head, and we inquire of you saying, "Is so-and-so about to die?" let the cause of the misfortune which you tell him has come upon him be the real cause of the evil and not lies.'

From that it is evident how the native makes use of his god as oracles to foretell misfortune or success, to reveal the cause and therefore the remedy of illness and pestilence, to show how man may avert famine and catastrophe. The god speaks through his priests and priestesses, and the spiritual power in reality dominates, though sometimes flouted, the temporal power to such an extent that in this part of West Africa hierarchy rather than autocracy or democracy is sovereign.

A case that recently came to my notice in Krachi occurred at Makokwai and illustrates how the arrival of a god was learned. A certain man from Makokwai had gone down to a town called Mangoase in the Gold Coast Colony to earn some money in the cocoa-fields. He was accompanied by a young boy. One day while they were still at Mangoase the boy was seized with a fit of sorts, and as he did not recover the man took him back to their home village to ascertain what was the matter with the lad, and if possible to cure him. Arrived at Makokwai, the boy seemed to get worse rather than better, and it was eventually decided to send to consult the god Bruku. The latter informed the pilgrims that the boy was possessed by a god and instructed them how to proceed. The orders were obeyed and the boy recovered. Now it is rather disconcerting to the true believer when his gods quarrel. But it chanced that the god at Makokwai succeeded on several occasions in effecting some wonderful cures, and his name began to spread about the country. As his fame grew, he naturally attracted to him many who otherwise would have had recourse to the older-established shrines. Thus it came about that the success and growing cult at Makokwai began to affect the revenue of the priests of the shrine of Dente, who will shortly be described. Now Dente is one of the sons of Bruku and therefore was the elder brother of the new-comer at Makokwai. His priests therefore learned from him that the latter was an upstart and no real god at all. His cult therefore must be abandoned. Now it happens that to-day the political power at Krachi, which is suzerain over Makokwai, is the same as the priestly. Orders were therefore sent to discontinue the new cult and a propitiatory offering was sent to Bruku to obtain his consent to the command. Naturally there was considerable discontent among the younger members of the priesthood at Makokwai as they therein saw the complete disappearance of an easy revenue. But heresy among these people must, as with us, be uprooted, and no man better than the native priests realizes so well that the inevitable end of allowing any disturbing element in his own religion to survive will bring about the ruin of his church. The elders, even of Makokwai, were therefore in accord, and in spite of the miraculous disappearance of the youth who was first possessed and who after many days absent in the bush was found once more under a tree close to the village, in spite of his story of a marvellous voyage to the house of his god, the cult was condemned and, it is to be hoped, heresy stamped out.

Dente, who seems to have been so jealous of his younger

brother, is said to be the eldest son of Bruku and his favourite.
It is possible that his shrine obtained its first step to really
extensive worship through the Ashanti. This warlike tribe
invaded the Krachi country some two hundred years or so
ago, and in accordance with their usual practice did not
destroy the local shrines, but rather sought to obtain the
assistance of their in-dwelling god in their enterprises. Thus
Dente drew Ashanti worshippers to him. There is a tradition that Dente was in reality brought to Krachi by the
Ashanti and established in the cavern where he now resides;
that he loathed the spilling of blood, and that if once a nation
accepted Dente as its god that nation disarmed itself and was
considered to be under the protection of Ashanti. In short,
there centred round the shrine of Dente an African League
of Nations, and Krachi sees in Geneva a mere replica of
itself.

But local tradition is not thus. It is said that Bruku, who
is a god of such standing and of so extensive a cult that even
the extremely well-informed missionary Müller mistook him
for the Supreme Deity of the Akposso, a neighbouring
transalpine tribe, was able to produce sons without the
need of any wife. Thus one day he laboured in travail and
from his womb there issued his first-born, Dente. One can
see to this day the actual birth-place, for there at Siari, down
the precipitous path that leads to the watering-place, is
the great cleft in the cliffs whence Dente issued forth.
Moreover, you can be shown how he, urged by some divine
impulse, pushed his way through the mountains, leaving
behind him a deep track, where now torrential Ssabu flows;
how, as he came near their verge, he was met with the vast
wall of Kedjebi's hill. But, godlike, he cared not for
mountains or their ilk. He desired a passage through to the
smiling plains of the Oti and to the distant banks of the
Volta. So with one mighty push he forced the hills aside
and there to-day in the precipitous flank of Kedjebi we

have witness of his power. Thence he strode to his pre-destined home in the cavernous grotto amidst the dark, dank groves near-by the banks of the Frao and close to the thunderous roar of Krachi's mile-long cataract.

But there is another story told, which I give from the account recorded by the missionary Rottmann. His source of information is, maybe, tainted for political reasons. It is less poetical but possibly more African.

This is how his story runs:

In the olden time there lived a god in a grotto close to the village of Date, which is not far from the town of Akropong in Akwapim, an important division of the Gold Coast Colony. His name was Konkom. He was a terrible monster to behold, for he had but one eye and one arm. Moreover, his nose was eaten away by leprosy and was all covered with ulcers. So loathsome was he that he never showed himself to man, but contented himself with putting forth his single arm to gather in the sheep and goats and other good things which his devotees brought to him. But the latter were curious to see what manner of thing it was that they worshipped. So they decided that somehow or other they would learn the nature of their god.

One day therefore some of the villagers, bolder than their brothers, approached the grotto quietly, and when the god put forth his arm to receive the offering they leapt out and seized it. They pulled and pulled until at last the god was forced to come out in spite of all his cries and protests.

But as soon as they had succeeded in their task and the god stood before them they were seized with fear. His awful appearance, his ghastly form, and no doubt the fear their sacrilege must have inspired, were more than they could bear. Incontinently they fled. In vain the god recalled them. In vain he promised forgiveness for their curiosity. They would not return. Then the god grew angry and he swore a mighty oath that one day they would regret their sacrilege and be sorry for their fear.

Then he withdrew into the recesses of his grim grotto. In time his worshippers gained courage and came back to the shrine, bringing ample offerings to appease their offended god. All seemed well. The offerings were accepted; they gathered that forgiveness was accorded them; they even imagined in their conceit that a blessing was vouchsafed them.

Konkom, it is said, told them that if they obeyed him they would reap a harvest so rich and wonderful that man had never seen the like. Gladly they promised and asked him what to do. The answer was unexpected, but its instructions were carried out.

They were to cut all the fruit that still remained upon the trees, uproot the fields, and burn all that had already been garnered.

This done, the god withdrew once more into his cavern, and from that day to this he has never been seen again at Date. Famine followed his departure, as might have been expected, and the people cried to their god aloud, but in vain, for he treated them as they had treated him, and would not turn back.

Meanwhile Konkom wandered far away to the north, until at long last he came to where Krachi is to-day. The people of the place asked him whence he came, and he replied 'Date'; but as his nose was so disfigured his pronunciation was not clear and the men of Krachi thought he said 'Dente'. Hence the modern name of this important god.

The story continues that Konkom was well received by the people, who showed him the grotto, his present abode, as soon as they learned that he was a god. Moreover, the town began to grow in population and in wealth after he had settled there. His fame and that of his adopted town spread far and wide, and at last the people of Date learnt where their god had gone.

Konkom seems to have been rather a nasty god, for he played two more tricks on his former worshippers, who, after all, were only guilty of a little sacrilegious curiosity. It is said that he directed a man to appear before the people of Date and tell them that he was an emissary from Konkom and that he had been directed by his master to show where there lay buried a great treasure. It was under the great village tree. The people, only too anxious to get their god back and not perhaps indifferent to the prospect of easily gained wealth, cut down their ancestral tree and dug and dug beneath its roots. In vain; there was nothing there, and when the emissary went with them to the old shrine, lo and behold, no man could find the way thither, and to this day the whereabouts of the grotto of Konkom in Date is known to no man.

Even then Konkom was not satisfied. He sent to Date a spirit which entered into a woman of the place. She frothed at the mouth, she entered into deep trances, she stiffened her limbs so that they were like boards, she talked tongues of unknown nations. The priests soon diagnosed that it was Konkom himself who had possessed her. Somehow they calmed her and learned that indeed it was their old friend Konkom who had returned. They ascertained further that Konkom wished the people to observe the following rules. Goats were to be abhorred. They were neither to be allowed in the town, nor could their flesh be eaten, nor yet could their dung be touched. Konkom, moreover, would expect cattle to be sacrificed to him at the larger festivals instead of sheep, just as he would prefer gin to be offered him instead of palm-wine. His worshippers were to refrain from wearing native cloths of indigo dye, nor were they to promenade the streets at night with lanterns lest they should intrude on the secrets of the 'sons' of Konkom who might send them disguised as the whirlwind or travelling with the thunder-clouds.

To all this the people agreed, but the possessed girl

proclaimed that if they were to reap the benefits to be expected from the return of their god they were to make an extra special sacrifice. In short, nothing less than a human offering would satisfy him.

For long the elders debated this. Dared they risk committing such a crime when an ever-watchful Government was so close at hand? But at last it was decided to obey the behest of Konkom.

A young boy was bought in the market at Anum and preparations made secretly to perform the sacrifice. A night was chosen, and after warning all the uninitiated to keep to their houses lest they should meet with Konkom's sons, who were expected to visit the place, they dug a deep hole at the entrance of the town. Into this they thrust the boy, leaving his head above the earth. In spite of his tears and entreaties they covered his head with clay and on the following day summoned all the villagers to come and build over the cone a pyramid of mud. This done, the priests thought all was well, and that Konkom of a truth would return. But alas for their desires! Konkom did not return. He had played them another trick and had even managed to inform the Government, who sent officers and soldiers to investigate. The corpse of the unfortunate youth was found and the priests arrested, and those guilty paid their debt on the scaffold.

The story does not give the date of the first disappearance of Konkom, but the latter part is obviously of recent occurrence. Dente has, however, been at Krachi for well over two hundred years, and when one considers that the Akwapim people were at one time interested in claiming rights over the Krachi the story is quite likely to have been mostly invented to support that claim. In any case the Krachi themselves refuse to admit that they have ever heard of such a romance, and relate instead the far more poetical myth of Dente's birth in the womb of Bruku in the beautiful gorge of the Sabu.

It may be of interest to record here that whenever the Krachi people make sacrifice or pray to Dente they first call on Bruku after the usual greetings to Wulbari the Supreme. This is usual among most tribes, for in all prayers that have been recorded the openings refer or are addressed to all the senior gods in order of their rank until the deity is reached who is especially being invoked.

In addition to their duties as oracles the gods have considerable control over the fertility of women and cattle and crops. Barren couples resort to their shrines and hope by gifts and prayer to learn what steps should be taken to obtain children. Here as in so many similar cases the lesser gods have occasion often to remember the senior ones, and after revealing the nature of the sacrifice they wish for themselves advise a greater one for their greater 'fathers'. Thus if Dente makes known to the supplicant that he wishes for a sheep, he will more than probably add that a sheep or two to Bruku would not be amiss.

When a woman wishes to have a child she consults the local deity, which in this area is invariably a 'son' of Dente. It usually happens that the village priest informs her that she must make the sacrifice known as Barisu-kuri, which means 'on top of God-husband'. This name refers to a belief the natives hold of a former life spent in the land of Wulbari before being born on this earth. Sometimes the supplicant is a would-be father. Then the sacrifice is called Barisu-chii (on top of God-woman).

A date is fixed by the priest after the usual consultation at the shrine, and early on the appointed morning the woman issues forth from the village till she comes to the first cross-roads. She carries with her a new cooking-pot, a new spoon made from a calabash, three pieces of shea-butter tree-trunk or large branch, some sticks from the same tree, pito (millet beer) in a second pot, a new calabash, and a white fowl. If the worshipper is a man, he takes the same articles.

The supplicant is accompanied by an old man from the village. It does not matter who he may be; it is merely necessary that he be old. This man charges a fixed fee, 300 cowries if the supplicant is a man, 400 if a woman. Here once more one finds the numbers four and three; four where a female is concerned, three where a man. In previous books I have mentioned this curious association of numbers, and so far have learned no explanation. No one seems to know how the figures are arrived at, nor does there seem to be any well-known story accounting for the fact.

Arrived at the cross-roads, the old man asks the supplicant to kneel down facing the sunset. (The sacrifice, however, is taking place in the early morning.) He then pours some of the pito on the ground and calls the name of the god to whom the supplicant has been instructed to sacrifice. The supplicant then locks her fingers and holds the locked hands over her head, palms upward, with the fowl, properly trussed but still alive, between the hands and head.

The old man then rings his bell which he has brought from the village and calls on the woman's spiritual husband, thus if her husband is named Kobina, he would call 'Kobina Barisu-Kuri'. This he does four times. But if the supplicant were a man, he would call the spiritual wife. For instance, if the real wife were named Ajua, he would call 'Ajua Barisu-chii' and repeat the call but thrice. These spiritual husbands and wives refer to the belief that simultaneously with our existence in this world we have a secondary existence in the world of spirits.

The old man having called on the spirit of the husband or wife, then tells him what is required of him, that the woman before him desires a child and has been instructed to bring him the sacrifice. Three times the old man repeats this if the supplicant is a man and four times if a woman.

All the time he continues ringing his bell and begs and begs the spirit to grant the request, and continues thus until the fowl on top of the woman's head is dead. As soon as he is sure that the unfortunate fowl has died, he tells the woman to throw it down. If the fowl falls on its back it is a good sign, but if it falls on its breast it is an evil omen, and in that event the sacrifice is in vain and one would have to return and ask from the god what further sacrifice he required.

But if all is well and the fowl falls favourably, the supplicant makes a fire with the sticks she has brought with her, sets the three small logs in such a manner that they will support the new pot over the fire, fills the pot with clean water, cleans the fowl, and cooks it in the pot.

She can add whatever spices she may like to make the broth more savoury. Yams and salt and pepper are the usual ingredients, but these have in reality nothing to do with the sacrifice proper and are left entirely to the choice of the cook-supplicant. As soon as the brew is ready, the old man pours some more of the pito on the ground and once again calls on the spirit-husband, saying that his food is ready. Then the pot is removed from the fire by the supplicant, and while the fire is still burning she places on the three small logs the head, the feet, the feathers, and the entrails, as well as some of the yams if they were used in the cooking. The rest of the food is then eaten by the supplicant, but not the smallest bit given to the old man.

When all is finished the old man usually asks for some of the pito, which one can give him or not as one may please. The fire is then extinguished with the rest of the water and then the old man claims his fee of cowries. These given, the woman marks her forehead and temples and all her joints with white clay and returns to the village. If the supplicant is a man, he does exactly the same and marks himself in the same way with the clay.

The old man retains the pot and spoon, &c. These he must carry back to the village himself, as the supplicant must on no account touch them again. They may not remain in the village, however. The old man must either get rid of them to a stranger who is going far away, or he must take them himself into some distant place. He does not accompany the supplicant back, but remains behind in order to pick up the three small logs which are only a little burnt. These he must throw away into the bush, and these little logs are quite a striking sight whenever one enters a Krachi village during the dry season when the grass is either burnt or laid low so that they become visible once more.

As for the supplicant, she must not look back on her way to the village, nor may she that day do any manual work. It is a day to rejoice, and only dancing and laughter are to be allowed.

Dente, however, enjoys a far-spread fame. After the Krachi had made the mistake of allying themselves with the Chumru, Gonja, and Brong tribes against the Ashanti power, which hopelessly defeated the allies near Kulpi, the Krachi had to acknowledge the overlordship of Coomassie. Now Dente had always disliked bloodshed, hence wars and murders were hateful to him. Human sacrifices had to be made without the spilling of blood and took the form either of burial alive under the pyramids of clay which are to be seen at the entrance to every village which worships him, or of breaking the sacrifice's neck. This was done by laying the victim on the ground and placing a log across the neck. Two assistants stood on either side of the log whilst a third lifted the victim's feet up until the neck broke—not precisely a speedy method of slaying.

The Ashanti saw in this peculiarity a possible advantage to themselves, and as was their usual practice they paid proper and meet respect to the god. Dente chose to accept their offerings favourably, and when the Krachi tribe placed themselves under Coomassie their god automatically entered the ranks of the Ashanti theocracy. His dislike for bloodshed thus made a natural no-man's-land on the north-eastern frontier where war and fighting was forbidden not by human law but by divine. Thus Dente's fame spread afar and many of the smaller nations placed themselves under his protection, an action tantamount to accepting the overlordship of Coomassie. Nations such as Buem, Wora-wora, Tapa, Adele, Ajati, Akposso, and others thus came peacefully more or less under the yoke of Ashanti.

To this day service is given to Dente, but the creation by the priesthood or miraculous birth of 'sons' to Dente has lessened his power at Krachi itself, for each village holds at least one of his offspring. To Bruku, however, all look alike. He, dwelling in the mountainous region of Ajati, is on a pedestal one grade higher than Dente and next to that of the Supreme Deity himself.

Of the other sons of Bruku there are many. Mostly they dwell near their father among the mountain ranges, abiding in rocks and caves. One has found a home in a mountain torrent, but most of them seem to have preferred a stone or stony place.

It seems to me that in this fact may be found some clue as to the origin of the people. For if the worship of rivers by the Ashanti be taken as a positive proof of their coming from a riverless land, it might be urged that the people who are awed by and therefore eventually come to worship rocks and caves originate from some land where rocks and mountains are almost unknown and from their very rarity were there considered the holy places of their gods.

The natives endow these gods with all the usual human attributes as well as superhuman powers. They mostly incline to picture them as disgusting and loathsome in appearance, but their resemblance to man is undoubted. Sometimes men see them, but that is not a common occurrence. Rarer still is it that those favoured with a view of their god would relate the story. But in Perregaux's *Chez les Achanti* the following tale is told.

F

A certain hunter in the long long ago went into the forest a-hunting. Many a goodly meat he saw, but it was of no use; he could not kill. At last after many days of this non-success he espied an antelope in front of him. He fired and hit; but the animal bounded off. A long chase ensued until the antelope entered a cavern. The hunter was close behind and followed on its heels. To the man's terror he saw the animal change suddenly into a god, the very god Tano himself.

But the god told him not to be afraid but to take him up, and promised to protect the man in future. Then the hunter picked up the god and set out for his abode. On the road the travellers met Death, who cried out: 'Hallo, Tano, where are you off to?' 'I am off to dwell with man,' the god replied. 'That I shall not permit,' said Death.

The god was furious at this daring, and when Death began to sing a song of defiance he retaliated in kind. The two of them sang and sang the one against the other without cease for the space of one whole month. But Death was unable to force Tano back along the road he had come, nor was Tano able to proceed to the towns of Man. At length the two contestants made a compromise. It was to the effect that whenever a man fell ill the first comer of the two would have his way with the sick man. Thus if Tano reached the bedside first the man would recover, but if Death arrived the first then the man would die. Thus Tano came amongst men and unfortunately Death as well.

These gods are usually conceived as giants. In this they resemble the dread monsters who so often take up their abode in the monstrous trees, especially the odum and the baobabs. Possibly some African Rackham saw in the grotesque shapes, their tortured branches, their gnarled trunks, their gaunt buttresses the semblances of some distorted human form. Possibly the frequent accidents these trees have caused made them objects of fear, respect, and worship. Be the explanation what it may, the fact is that the natives in

Krachi and Dagomba alike believe that many of the larger trees are inhabited by some spirits who are evilly minded towards men. This belief, however, is not to be confused with the practice among all the northern tribes of regarding the clusters of trees as the fane of the local Earth-god.

Perhaps one of the most famed of these latter is the sacred grove not far from the Chief Commissioner's house at Tamale. It is not only visited by the local people but by Dagomba from all over the country. The name of the grove is Ta'ha, and its priest is entitled Buglana. The latter lives in a near-by village of the same name as the grove. Baobab trees thrive in these sacred precincts and are full of swarms of bees who may live here unmolested by man. I am told that the old combs hanging from the branches, exuding from the many holes which are so common in that species of tree, are a wonderful sight.

An annual sacrifice is made to the deity. It takes place some time after the dry season has set in, and grass-burning is supposed not to be allowed until the sacrifice has taken place. The grass is never burned inside the grove, and in order to prevent this happening the people have to clear a wide fire-guard around it. On the fixed day the priest enters the grove. There he drums and sings and if the bees do not come out and sting him he knows that the god is willing to accept the offering. Fowls are sacrificed and sheep and cattle, but fowls that may wander into the grove on their own are deemed sacred and must not be killed.

After the sacrifice has been made the people return to the village of Ta'ha and dance and drink millet beer throughout the day. All restrictions are raised and free indulgence in one's passions are tolerated, provided always that such does not take place in the bush. On the following day the people again set out to the grove and set fire to the grass. It seems that a similar dance ushering in a period of saturnalia is practised in Adele.

Here the dancers are women and they pretend for the occasion that they are men, and in the dance mimic and satirize all the usual actions of their manfolk from hunting and stalking game to the lewdest actions conceivable. I managed twice to witness this dance in rehearsal, but have not yet succeeded in visiting the particular village where the dance takes place at the time of the exhibition proper. The village is called Odumase, and when I asked the village headman how it was that his village had an Ashanti name, he told me that the name was so difficult to pronounce that the people had agreed to give it the more easily uttered Ashanti one. It may be, of course, that the name is a sacred one, not to be uttered or mentioned by the common herd, but the chief made no bones about giving it me. I failed to be able to reproduce it in any recognizable form at all.

Trees which are known to be the home of these evil spirits are avoided as a rule. But sometimes offerings are made, especially if the giant-inhabited tree happens to be near the home or fields of men. This is natural, for the spirits could do much damage. It is, however, the rule that any tree which kills a man by dropping a branch on him or falling on top of him is utterly destroyed. The natives cut it up into the smallest pieces, which they then burn *in situ*. Great care is taken that no one should carry off pieces for their cooking fires. The same is done to any tree which may have served to kill a man. Thus at Krachi the tree on which the Germans had hanged the priests of Dente was given to the people shortly after our occupation of the place and was by them cut into the smallest of pieces and then burned. Again recently at Krachi a certain man hanged himself on one of the mango trees in the avenue leading from the station to the river. After some time the Chief of Krachi asked me for permission to cut down this tree. Leave was given, and I saw a man busily engaged in felling it, and after he had dropped the tree, cutting it into the smallest pieces, which he carefully collected and burned. But first he offered a sacrifice of a fowl to the spirit of the tree, not to the spirit of the man who had perished there.

Trees too are sometimes the manifestation of some former member of the family. Not far from the town of Danbae stands such a one. Danbae is a town of comparatively very recent growth. It stands on the banks of the Oti, half-way between Kpetsu and Dutukpene. The Germans seeking a way around what was for some years regarded by the British and Germans as neutral ground found that they could not construct and maintain a road between the two places unless they could get people to settle along it somewhere. They persuaded the people of some villages, slave-born families, to settle at Danbae, and thus the place began to be opened up. Now not far from this new village there are middens of some former inhabitants. From the middle of one of these there sprang a tree, a silk cotton. The people of Danbae learned through their god's utterance that the soul of some former important man had entered this tree. Therefore the people of Danbae take him offerings of food and drink and provide him also with firewood and fragments of cloth.

Trees are in most cases treated with respect. Before a man dare fell one for a canoe he must and invariably does sacrifice to its spirit and apologizes for the harm he is about to do it. Other trees are considered necessary for the shade of some spirit, son of Bruku or Dente, who will have told the people what sort of tree they are to plant to shelter their offspring. It is curious, however, that among Krachi and Dagomba the planting of a mango tree is considered to be an evil thing to do, and woe betide the rash fellow who does so. He will surely die that selfsame year when first his tree bears him fruit.

The spirit of these trees is, as I have said above, usually imagined to be a man of gigantic stature and loathsome appearance. But often he will disguise himself and show himself to man in the guise of a snake. This is natural enough when one remembers that these trees so often have convenient holes at their base where snakes can live in comparative quiet, or hollow trunks or branches offer a friendly domicile.

That the spirits should take a snake-like form is natural too, for the worship of pythons is widespread. Possibly this cult has penetrated inland from the coast of Dahomey where snake-worship is very popular; possibly it is the natural expression of fear and therefore reverence savage man would have for beasts so dangerous and so uncanny.

The following is a story of such worship in Dagomba sent to me in a note by Mr. Tamakloe. The locality of the python-spirit is at Tampiong, on the British side of Dagomba. His name is Wunwon and he is a large python which has his home in a rocky hollow amid a cluster of thick trees set in a swamp whence flows a goodly stream. The spirit's especial function is to provide rain when the latter is badly required.

In time of drought the priest of Wunwon, who holds his office by hereditary right, will advise the villagers that it is time to visit the god and to offer him the usual sacrifice. This consists of three balls of millet flour made into a thick paste with water. No fire may have touched the dumplings. Nor may any other grain save that of millet be used. Then the priest and his followers and any one who may like to go, proceed to the thicket with the fowls and possibly goats as well. Arrived at the grove, the priest and the people form a procession and march three times round it shouting out a song. The python is supposed to be deaf, hence noise more than ordinary is made in this singing. Sometimes, no matter what the clamour may be like, the python does not hear. Then the gathered people take sticks and twigs and set to work to flog the thicket. This action will most certainly draw the python out. It will make its way to a cleaned space where the dumplings have been placed and there in full view of the people will devour them. Then rain will surely fall even before the villagers can get back home.

Sometimes the python refuses to eat the balls of paste. Then the priest hurriedly prays to it and asks what is the reason of its daintiness. Is it that he, the priest, will die that year, or perhaps some of the python's children are seedy and will pass into the world below, where the dead of all sorts gather?

It is said that the python will at last approach the offering, and if it touches the paste with its lips one will know that that year the priest will die; if, however, it licks them with its tongue, then it is a sign that one at least of its offspring will perish. When the paste-balls are devoured the priest sacrifices the fowls or goat and the meat is roasted *in situ* and there devoured by the gathering. The python gets none of the meat at all.

In many of the stories I relate in these pages pythons are represented as the spirits of the marshes or rivers or swamps, and most of the natives hold them not only in awe but also in some sort of reverence. Thus at Krachi there are several pythons, one of which is said to be the spirit of a swampy place called Brubruku. I saw a leopard there one morning, and when I mentioned that fact one of my hearers said that it was the spirit of Brubruku, who sometimes assumed that guise; but another said that that was not so, rather that it was the wife of the python.

This difference of opinion shows that they did not actually know what guise the spirit would take, and that any animal or beast that came from the swamp would probably be, temporarily at least, his form. This being the case it is to be expected that the people do no harm to them, but they do not mind strangers running the risk of meddling with a spirit. Thus one day some Krachi men were engaged on building a house not far from my bungalow. One of them had taken with him a fowl and some chickens to his work,

a common practice, as not only can the owner protect them
from cats and snakes and hawks, but he often finds a nest of a
species of termite which is particularly good food for them.
This time, however, the owner had bad luck. A python came
out of the grass and carried off the hen and one of her chicks.
They sent for me and asked me to kill it as they knew the
python would be quite close and they themselves did not
know how to drive it away.

I complied with their request and shot the brute. The men
would not at first approach the corpse at all and declared
that in reality it was their own brother. But they gradually
went up to look at it and then some spat deliberately on the
ground and others took a pinch of earth and threw it at the
corpse, but none would touch it. A Moshi showed no fear
at all and asked to be allowed to eat it, a suggestion which
seemed almost nauseating to the Krachis who heard it.
The Moshi dragged the body to my bungalow, for it was
only a small python, not more than twelve feet long, and
a Dagomba woman seeing it at once took a pinch of dust
and threw it on the dead snake. She told me that it was her
brother.

But in addition to the possibility that monsters such as
pythons, crocodiles, leopards, and their kind may be used
as disguises by the spirits of groves and rivers and swamps,
these animals have their own private spirits as well.

These have to be appeased by the hunters, and often
a funeral custom will be held for important animals. This
also takes place with trees and the soul of the fallen tree thus
laid to rest. The idea that trees have souls is met with amongst
all the tribes, and as has been mentioned the Krachi ask leave
from the tree before they cut it down and they offer it some
small sacrifice. The Konkomba when preparing their poison
from the strophanthus plant will first tell the plant itself what
they want to do, whether it be merely to kill small animals
such as hares and duikers, or larger and more dangerous

beasts such as the buffalo or the magic-endued red-flanked duiker, or for the more important work of man-slaying.

It would seem that in the generality of cases an animal which has been entered by some spirit still retains his own private one. However, special animals are deemed to be none other than the spirit itself.

Thus in the Moshi country where stands the sacred hill of Pilimpiku, in whose side is built the City of the Dead, and from whose flanks the sound of drumming issues forth, foreboding some dire calamity to the Moshi race, such as the death of their Na or King, there runs a wondrous stream. It twists and turns about like no other stream known to man. It is a stream of greatest sanctity.

At a certain season in the year the time comes when the tindana or priest of the earth-gods considers the stream should be fished. He assembles the villagers and they all proceed to the banks where the sacrificial stone is set. There a fowl is offered to the spirit of the river and the usual observation made as to the manner of its dying, i.e. if on its back the sacrifice has been accepted, if on its breast the sacrifice has been refused. It is particularly important on this occasion to make quite certain that the sacrifice has been accepted, because that is a sure sign that the crocodiles, who are numerous in the stream, have been ordered to their holes by the river-god, their master.

Then the people begin their fishing. This has to be done by emptying the water in calabashes on to the banks, baling the river! When the water is all but gone a certain fish is seen. Its name is Perle. It is the river-god himself. The fish has a beard and on its back is a double line of cowries (presumably cowrie-like markings, for it is unlikely that even gods should show to all and sundry their bank balance). As soon as the fish is seen the tindana is called. The fish is carefully picked up and carried to another pool. Not once may it touch the ground, for should it do so then the fishers will surely die if they get even the smallest cut or scratch during the fishing.

Just such another sacred stream I know in the country of the Builsa close to the Sisilli River. There the river-god lives just undergound and makes the earth so soft and treacherous that people are sometimes swallowed up in it. Some such quicksand did, not long ago, take the wife and child of one of the sergeants of the Northern Territories Constabulary. It was considered at the time that the river-god coveted the woman and thus took her to his home.

Fishing itself has probably as many restrictions and taboos as hunting. I know not. But there is a certain custom observed at Krachi. If one succeeds in catching a Nile perch, one presents to the chief the head. This is apparently one's duty. Should the chief accept the present, he then automatically becomes responsible for the donor's debts. I gave him a head once which he accepted. Some days later I reminded him of his indebtedness, but he explained that the fact of my being a European made it different.

Among most of the tribes in the Mandated area the rivers and ponds each have their respective gods or indwelling spirits. These partake more of the nature of local earth-gods and are not considered as direct offspring of the Supreme Deity, although they are ordinarily termed his sons. This appellation of son must be understood in the same way as it is applied to human beings. The sons of man are all his nephews and grand-nephews, grandchildren as well as his own progeny. The term is also applied to servants, clients, and their offspring.

In addition to the belief that such spirits as river-gods and tree-spirits are generally seen by men in the guise of giants, there is also the belief in the existence of giants *qua* giants. This may be the result of a conquered race of small stature having given ground to an invasion of a race of taller men, when the dwarf mother-parent might relate to her children stories of dreadful men of brobdingnagian stature, or possibly it may be the result of an alien influence, as the following story would suggest.

Many years ago a certain man of the Dagomba tribe who lived at Yendi decided to become a Mohammedan. Soon after he was seized with such religious zeal that he decided to make the long trip across the wild lands to Mecca. Now on that road there is an immense stretch of uninhabited bush, which lasts for five long days' marching. Water there is none and the way lies across many rocks and other hard places.

When our Mohammedan came to that place he took his two donkeys and placed on their backs skins full of water and himself took yet another skin, and then, after praying, set forth across this evil place. When he had reached half-way he was surprised to see come out from behind a rock an immense man. So high was he that when he stood upright it was impossible to see his face, and when he talked the noise was like the noise of thunder. The giant was naked and covered with red hair. The unfortunate Dagomba was terror-stricken and could not move; but the giant did not seem anxious to hurt him, merely asking him for some water. It must be remembered that all these giants can speak every language in the world.

The Mohammedan gave the water he was carrying and the giant swallowed it at one gulp. He then asked for more and took all the water that the donkeys were carrying. He seemed satisfied, but the unfortunate human began to cry, saying that now of a truth he was as good as dead, for he was still too far off the next dwelling-place of men to reach there without water. The giant told him not to be afraid, that he would carry him there. This he did, picking up him and his two donkeys and in one step transporting them to the next town.

But the essential point of the story is that the people

actually believe that such a story is true and do not hesitate for one moment to accept it for a fact. There is nothing in it to them which seems impossible; in fact it is quite a likely sort of adventure one might expect when travelling afar and in foreign parts, just as the existence of fairies and pixies is beyond doubt.

Chapter Four

WHICH DEALS WITH PIXIE-FOLK AND THEIR WAYS

BELIEF IN DWARFS—THE TREE AT TAMALE—PALBE HUNTER'S EXPERIENCE—MISCHIEF DONE BY FAIRIES—CAUSE OF TWINS—DAGOMBA AND KRACHI—METHODS OF DEALING WITH TWINS—IMPORTANCE OF ORDER OF BIRTH—SICKNESS DUE TO DWARFS—THEIR FONDNESS FOR STRONG DRINK.

THROUGHOUT Togoland, as in Ashanti and the Northern Territories, there is a confirmed belief in the existence of mischief-loving dwarfs. The Ashanti call them mmotia and in the north they are known as kulparga or chichiriga, the words differing dialectically in each tribal division. These dwarfs are of either sex and are extremely numerous. Men say that often and often they are to be seen, but few will admit that they have themselves seen them, lest people should laugh. Those who most frequent the wild and solitary places are not so averse to admitting this privilege, and hunters will often relate at evening time adventures they have met with in their encounters with these pixie-folk.

It is difficult to explain the belief, but it seems to me that in the tradition of the existence of these dwarfs there is surely a remembrance of some dwarf race or tribe of smaller stature which held the land before the present peoples came here, traces of which may be found in the small-made and delicately-featured families of the Coast. One is often struck by the difference some of these show to the majority of their fellows in the village. This is a question which might be explored by anthropologists who are enthusiastic over measurements.

In any case most folk-lorists accept that as an explanation for the almost universal belief in a race of dwarf fairies.

Here we find them nearly always associated with large and thickly-leaved trees, with rocky places and dark pools, precisely those spots where one would expect a conquered race to hide in their endeavour to escape annihilation.

There is told a story in this connexion concerning the large tree which stands at the entrance to the drive leading up to the bungalow known as Number Two on the ridge at Tamale. The tree itself was in earlier days the abode of some spirit, and sacrifices were made to it. To-day this is still done, but owing to its position on the European Ridge naturally not as frequently as in the past.

Some time ago this bungalow was temporarily occupied by a European who lived alone in the house save for his boy, a Dagomba and a native of the neighbourhood.

One evening the former was invited out to dinner, and left the boy in charge of the house.

The boy tells how after his master had gone he himself went upstairs and having locked the back door lay down to sleep away the time till his master returned.

He knew that everything was safe, as nothing of value was downstairs and no one could get upstairs without passing him. At about nine o'clock he was disturbed by the noise of people talking. He went round to where the voices came from, but could see no one, and after listening a while he heard the chattering coming from the other side of the house. Thither he went, but again could see no man. This continued for some time and the boy was kept on the run. He challenged the people, but could get no reply, and though he could make out quite clearly the voices, he was unable to understand the language which was being spoken. Then began a bombardment of the house with small stones— a form of annoyance characteristic of these pixie phenomena among all tribes.

The boy was in sore fear by the time he saw his master returning down the road with a hurricane lamp in his hand.

Now it so happened that when the latter drew near the tree he saw three very small children on the road, and when they were passing he asked them what they were doing. He got no answer and the children ran into the grass. He asked his servant who they were, but the boy was too afraid to say that they were fairies and merely replied that he had seen no children.

Of course it must be remembered that even if the European did speak to the children they could not have understood him, as he would either have spoken English or Hausa, neither of which local natives understand.

Another story of Kulparga living in trees is told by a certain man who used to live at Palbe on the Great North Road. This man was a famous hunter and the number of the heads of animals outside his compound was beyond reckoning. He was always in the bush hunting. But one day he returned after killing a roan and from that time he never went hunting again; and this is the story he would tell to any young man whom he might have noticed as likely to become a good hunter.

'As you know, I have killed many animals. Do you not see the heads of all I have killed at my door? But I do not go into the bush now to hunt, for I have seen a fearsome thing. All men who hunt learn strange things, but this is more fearful that any other I have seen or heard.

'I had killed a large roan. When I shot it, it ran away and I followed the blood trail. This led me to a great baobab tree and there it finished and I could see no more marks. I looked and looked everywhere, but I could see nothing. I grew tired and I sat down by the tree to rest, and as I was sitting there I saw an old man coming along.

'He was carrying on his head a part of a white ants' nest for his fowls. When he came up he asked me what I was doing, and I told him how I had shot the large roan and how the trail had finished at the large baobab. He told me that was what one might have expected, and that if I followed him he would show me things.

'He told me to leave my gun behind against the tree and then took me into the tree through a long dark hole. We came out into a wonderful village which I knew at once to be the village of the Fairies. It was a very rich place and the houses were much larger than ours and cleaner, and the people had rich clothes. But as we drew near we heard the noise of much weeping, and we learned that the eldest son of the chief was dying.

'We went to the house of the chief and there saw the young man. He was a very fine man to look at, but he had been wounded in the chest and his life was certainly near its end. I asked how the accident had occurred and I was told that there was a certain hunter in my own village who was always killing the young men of this fairy township and that they were very afraid of him. They told me that they did not understand why he was always doing this as they had never done him any ill thing. I knew then that they spoke of me.

'At last the young man died and my friend the old man told me to come away. We went back the road we had come and passed through the baobab tree. Then the old man left me. And as I came out there at the foot of the tree lay my roan shot through the chest.

'From that day to this I have never hunted. And you will hear that many other hunters have seen the same thing which I have just told you.'

This dwelling in the tree is not so common in the far north where the Kulparga choose usually rocks. I have elsewhere told how among the Kassena a woman might be so incautious as to sit on one of these rocks and so produce a Kulparga child. But fortunately there is in Dagomba country a safeguard against the evil and mischievous machinations of these dwarfs. For if you happen to pass near a large tree and you find your hair beginning to stand on end or goose-flesh creeping down your spine, you can save yourself by knocking two pieces of iron together. 'Iron—cold iron—is master of them all!'

It is perhaps of interest to record here that a traditional race of giants were the first iron-makers among the Dagomba, and in the fact that it was the giant people who introduced the iron which would appear to be so prejudicial to the smaller race, who have become the fairies, we may have an overlapping of two distinct lores.

The Kulparga are described by all the tribes as being naked hairy folk. They have long noses and have their feet turned the wrong way. They talk in twitterings like birds, which reminds one of the Theban priestesses who were carried away by the Phoenicians.

They are always throwing stones at one when one is in the bush and the stones can hurt one quite a lot. This characteristic is believed in everywhere, but what the explanation can be I do not know; perhaps it is the souvenir of a race which used slings in warfare, an unfair method of fighting that is not now countenanced by even the wilder tribes. It may of course be a symbolical way of stating that they are for ever on the look out to make mischief.

It is interesting to note that when one sees in the bush those portions of land which are completely bare of grass, one is told that it is there that the Kulparga come of nights and dance, and further that if one were to fall asleep in such a spot then one would return home crazed and maybe blind.

Nightmares and evil dreams of every sort, including all sexual dreams, are attributed to these dwarfs who play the fool with one's wandering soul in this manner. It seems that they are particularly interested in sexual matters and cause endless troubles in that way.

G

Here is a typical story of their work:

There was living in a certain village a very rich girl. She refused to marry any man, and at last fell in love with a boy so poor that there was only one old cover-cloth for him and his mother and a father to share. The girl arranged to meet the boy out in the fields and told him that she intended to marry him. He was very much afraid at this, and although he liked the girl, he pointed out that there would surely be trouble with her parents.

However, she insisted and promised that she would obtain the consent of her parents. In due time she managed this and married the poor boy. After a while she asked her mother to give her some money so that she and her husband could fare forth and see if they could succeed in getting wealth by trading. The mother gave her daughter some bags of cowries and some extra money for their food, and the two went away to a country where they heard that there was plenty of dried fish to buy.

They reached the place and spent all the money on some fish and then wandered back to a large town where they sold the fish at a profit and again returned to the fishing-place. They did this several times and each time succeeded in obtaining a profit.

At last the boy told his wife on their return to the town that he would leave her a while and go to fresh markets in the remoter villages and there get rid of the fish. He did not want her to accompany him as she must be tired after all their travels and he would go alone.

At first the girl would not agree to this, but in the end she consented. However, she first told her husband that he must take an oath on her guardian spirit to the effect that he would take no other woman to be his wife or concubine so long as he lived. He demurred and pointed out that seeing that he was a penniless person and all that he had was hers, he was not in a position of a free man to go and take other women.

But she insisted, and he agreed if she in turn would take the same oath.

So they went to the sacred grove (tingani) and both putting their hands on the sacrificing stone swore that they would be faithful to each other all their lives.

Now it so chanced that in the tree above the place there was hidden a Kulparga. He heard all that they had said and agreed to, and he determined to take the woman for himself.

The two returned to the town and to the house where they were wont to reside, which was the first one as one approached the place from the fishing-grounds. The boy told his landlord that he was going off for a few days to sell his fish and that his wife would remain with him in his care and the man agreed to look after the woman.

Next morning the boy went off with the fish and his wife busied herself with the usual household duties of the women-folk. On the following morning as she was thus occupied she saw enter the house a young man richly garbed and accompanied by two slaves bearing chests of money. The slaves put these down and their master asked the woman if the landlord was at home. She replied that he was and before going to tell him of the visitor she went and got him some fresh water to drink and gave it to him in a respectful manner in a new calabash and brought for him a stool.

She then went and fetched the houseowner. The stranger asked if he could stay there and was told he could. Then he inquired as to who the woman was, and hearing she was the wife of a poor boy who had gone away the day before, he called one of his slaves and had one of the chests opened and took from it a bag of money, which he gave to the woman and thanked her for her kindness in giving him the water and the stool.

Now the stranger was really the Kulparga who had disguised himself. But no one knew that.

The girl was so pleased at getting so large a reward for

nothing that she went forth to the market and bought there a small fowl which she cooked and placed in the young man's portion of soup. In short, she did everything to please him and make him happy.

That night the stranger came from his room and went to the girl. But she refused him, and told him that she had taken an oath on her guardian spirit and would die if she were faithless to her husband. The stranger then withdrew.

The next morning the girl said nothing to her landlord of what had passed in the night, and when the man had withdrawn the stranger called her and thanked her for her silence and gave her two bags of money.

These the girl took to her room and sitting there she began to think that if the stranger gave her so much money for nothing, how much more would he give her if she yielded to him, and that the spirit would not know, and even if he did he could not really kill her.

That night the stranger again came to her and she yielded to him. In the morning he arose and told her that she was foolish to remain with the poor boy and that she had better come away with him that very day. She agreed to this, and they got up and went and told the houseowner.

The latter was very angry. He abused the stranger, who merely mocked at him, and the two guilty people went off. Scarcely had they gone than the poor boy returned and went at once to his wife's room. Not finding her there, he asked the landlord where she was and the man told him all that had happened. Then the boy arose and said that he would follow after the couple and that he would kill the man.

Asking the direction of their escape, he hurried away and very soon came up with them. Then he called to the stranger and began to fight with him. But the stranger easily conquered and threw the young man to the ground. He then asked the woman what he should do with her husband and she at once replied: 'Kill him.'

Then the Kulparga allowed the boy to get up and told him everything and said that he would let him go. But the woman died that day from her guardian spirit and the money which the Kulparga had given her disappeared too, for it was only Kulparga money after all.

Now that story tells us never to trust a woman, for we never know what they will do next nor what value there is in a woman's promises.

But the pixie-folk are always like that, for is it not told how a certain man had nine wives, but no children at all? This grieved him and one day while he was bewailing his lot in the bush a Kulparga spoke to him and asked what was the matter. The man told him and the Kulparga answered that that could soon be remedied and climbed back into his tree. Presently he came out with some medicine which he gave the man and told him that now he would have nine children in the first year.

The man thanked him and asked what were the charges for the medicine. The Kulparga answered that they were nothing. At the end of the year the man would have to bring some food for his dogs, of which he had nine. The man asked what food the dogs wanted, and the Kulparga said: 'Bring either one of your children or your own mother. My dogs like man's meat.'

Now what was that man to do? It is just the kind of mischief a Kulparga would make, placing a man in a fool dilemma.

Another belief held by all the tribes of the north without exception is that twins are due to the machinations of these Kulparga or chichiriga.[1] Triplets are, on the other hand, naturally born, and as a proof of this the Dagomba tell how some years ago there was a certain woman who lived at Kpabia. On four separate occasions did she give birth to triplets. All the children were normally developed babies

---

[1] Pl. Kulparsi or chichirsi.

and grew to manhood; there was nothing the matter with
them, nor did any trouble come to their parents.

But twins are in quite a different category. For the first
few years of their lives they still retain the characteristics of
the Kulparga from whom they were born, and only after
reaching puberty do they assume their proper human character and lose to a certain extent the magic powers with which
their fairy father had endowed them.

That twins are born from Kulparsi is proved by the
following stories:

There lived at Kumbungu quite recently a certain man
who had two wives. He was unfortunate and had not got
any children. One day the two women went to the market
in a village near-by. On their return, they each bought a few
cowries' worth of ground-nuts to eat along the road. They
came to a tree and sat down in its shade. Now there happened to be concealed in that tree two Kulparsi who had
agreed to be born as men. Seeing the two women there, they
saw their chance, but first wanted to test the women to see
which one of them would be likely to prove the more gene-
rous in the matter of food. Presently the women took out
their ground-nuts and began to eat them. Now the Kulparsi
had chosen one of the women already and watched her for
the reason above stated. As she broke the nut, they knocked
her hand and the nut fell to the ground. She picked it up
and ate it. Three times did they do this and each time she
picked the nut up again. Then the Kulparsi decided she was
too mean and they tested the other woman in the same way.
This one, however, did not trouble to pick up the nuts but
left them on the ground. Then the Kulparsi decided she had
better be their mother, so they entered her and were carried
back to Kumbungu where they were born.

In course of time they grew up and were able to talk and
play about. One day they were playing with their younger
mother, i.e. the one who had not left the ground-nuts on

the ground and told her that they had first chosen her to be their mother. She asked how that was and then they told her all about the tree and the ground-nuts. The woman remembered all and went and told the townspeople.

That is pretty strong proof of the Kulparsi origin of twins, but if it is not sufficient, there is told the following. A certain man had twins presented to him one day. They were very forward children and soon able to walk and talk. One day they came to their father and asked him to give them a goat to ride and play with. Now it is the custom never to refuse any request of twins; but in this case the request was incapable of being granted, for the man had nothing in the way of wealth and was so poor that he even could not purchase a cloth for himself. However, the twins insisted, and their father went to consult the sorcerer, who could give him no comfort, but merely told him that the twins must have what they asked for. This made matters no better and on his return he told them he could not grant their request. Next morning the unfortunate man woke up blind.

The boys grew up and one day were playing about in front of the compound. Their father was sitting on the ground outside, taking the air. In their play the children kept knocking the old man and falling over his legs. At last he complained and told them that it was quite enough for him to bear the jeers of the town children without his own sons abusing and making a mockery of him. Then the elder of the two spoke and said, 'Father, is it true that the boys of the town abuse you because you are blind?' And he told them it was. Then the elder told him that it was he who had made him blind because he had refused the goat, but that he was sorry that the children of the village had made a mockery of his father and promised that next morning the old man would wake up cured. And sure enough on the next day the old man could see as well as ever.

The birth of twins is a serious event in the life of all communities. There are several ceremonies to be observed. Shortly after the birth the father goes round to all the houses, both of his friends and of strangers, and shows them to the people. The latter are expected and in the past never failed to give presents. It did not matter much what the presents were, provided they were two in number of exactly the same character; for if one gives to one twin, one must give also an identical present to the second.

They receive special names varying according to the tribes. Thus in Dagomba twins are known, if they are both boys, as Da'wuni and Da'na; if both girls, Pag'wuni and Pag'na; if a boy and a girl, Da'wuni and Pag'na. The meaning of these names is Da, man; Wuni, God; Na, King; and Pag', woman. And the old custom was that the ownership of the twins was vested not in the father but in God or the King, the eldest being for Wuni and the younger for the Na. To-day this has slightly altered and the Na has claims only in the event of both being girls, the father keeping his rights in them in the other two cases.

To determine the elder of the two is easy. He or she is the second born one, unless a boy and a girl are born, when the boy is always the elder. The reason for this is that the elder exercises in the womb the rights he will enjoy on earth of obedience from his younger brother or sister, and therefore he sends the younger one into the world first in order to see if all is well. The elder who remains in the womb is informed as to the state of the world by his younger brother, who, if he finds this earth a good place, begins to cry at once, but if he thinks it a bad place he won't cry at all and then his brother will be born dead, whereas if he cries out quickly the elder will be born without any trouble. Should the younger take some time to make up his mind as to the pleasantness or otherwise of the world, he will not cry out for some time and then only with reluctance will the elder be born.

Children who die when still babies are buried in the middens or sometimes at the bathing-places outside the compound, where the women wash. But it is not so with twins. Should they die, they are taken down to the watering-place and buried alongside where the ground is always damp and cool.

The ordinary burial is accorded them, however, if they die after they have grown up or reached puberty, for then they are looked upon as ordinary men except that they enjoy more freedom than most. For instance, it is on record that twins have in the Mamprussi country refused to allow themselves to be circumcised. This is unusual as they may be laughed at by the other young men. The twin girls also enjoy a certain amount of liberty. Though they belong to the Na, yet they can choose their own lovers and cannot be punished for so doing.

In the procession mentioned before there is no drumming. The father or mother as the case may be carry the babies in their arms, the elder on the right side and the younger on the left, and in front marches a man playing with a calabash which has been hollowed out but which still retains its pips, so that thrown from hand to hand and shaken the pips rattle together and actually produce quite a rhythmical noise. An old calabash is also carried by one of the grandparents, and into this the people place the cowries or money which they wish to give the twins. This money is then taken by the parents, who buy with it a pair of goats, if there is enough or they are able to make the amount up to the necessary sum. The colour of the goats to be bought (they must be the same) is determined after consultation with the sorcerer. These goats are the property of the children and in due course may make quite an inheritance. However, during the babyhood of the twins the goats enjoy a certain amount of magical protection. For they can never be taken by hyenas, and if lost will turn up again in a few days. It is said, too, that during the night-time the twins will take their goats and go riding on them round the countryside.

The Chumru and Nawuri would not tolerate twins at all. They were taken at once into the bush and left exposed on ant-heaps.

We learn, too, that among the Krachi twins were never popular. But as the god Dente forbade the spilling of blood they were disposed of by the easier method of throwing them into the Frao, or as we call it, the Volta River, first placing them in a calabash.

As elsewhere, the birth of deformed children or those inclined to yell too much was pretty clear evidence to the Krachi parents that a mmotia had been playing tricks and that the mis-shapen brat was not a human one at all. There was only one remedy for this and the child was taken, once the parents were quite sure on the point of its evil origin, to the remote bush and there either knocked on the head or just left there. The spot where this took place could never be visited by either parent again. The actual deed was, however, performed not by the indignant parent, but by a special man who was to be found in every village. The Konkomba do the same, whilst the Dagomba parents would poison them.

The order in which children are born is carefully observed, and various results arise according to whether a girl precedes a boy or the reverse.

In the Krachi district the order of birth is of importance in the interpretation of omens. For instance, sneezing, which among many of the northern tribes is an indication that the sneezer is about to tell the truth (I have never noticed any sneezes in my Court), among the Krachi will tell you if you are about to be lucky or not. If you are a male and the child born to your mother immediately after you is a female and some one sneezes on your left-hand side, then you know you will have good luck; but if the sneeze comes from your right-hand side, then you will have bad luck.

However, if you are a girl and the next child of your mother is a boy, then a left-hand sneeze will bring you bad luck and a right-hand one good fortune.

In the event of a boy being born after you and you yourself are a male, then the right-hand sneeze is the lucky one and the left the bad one. But the reverse is for the girl who is succeeded by another female child, for then the right-hand sneeze is a sure sign of bad luck and the left will be the fore-teller of good luck.

Stubbing the foot is similar. A male born before a female stubs his right foot. He will of a surety have ill luck that day; but if he had a brother born immediately after him, then he would have good luck. With women the exact reverse, as in sneezing, is foretold.

But to return to the pixie-folk.

Mushrooms are looked upon by many in the same way as they are at home. They are the shelters, umbrellas, for the little people, but this does not prevent them being eaten. There are three kinds of edible mushrooms known to all. Possibly there are many other varieties known only to the few. Of these three sorts one species is almost exactly like our own; a second is found chiefly in the thick forest, growing out of rotten tree-trunks, especially the silk cotton, and the third is actually cultivated.

On the middens one often sees in the Krachi District an untidy heap of sticks or rather twigs and bits of bush lianes. Under them is a rotting mass of cassada and yam skin. Women collect the skin and then after choosing a well-manured part of the midden cover the mass of skin with the sticks and twigs and each day water the heap. In the course of time a bluish kind of toadstool appears and this is allowed to remain until the whole heap is covered with the fungus, which is then collected and made into soup.

Our mmotia, however, who seem to lead me into as many by-paths in my script as they lead men astray in Togoland, are ever out for mischief. They will even bring sickness, and it is told that all illness originated from their machination.

People relate how in the olden days a certain hunter while out hunting grew tired and sat down to rest under a large baobab. Presently he was astonished to see coming out of the tree a large number of Kulparsi, who took no notice of him but began to dance and drum and sing. Their words were only 'Talatta' often repeated. The hunter, inveigled by the drumming, arose and joined the dancers and sang with them 'Talatta, Talatta'. When the dance was finished the Chief of the Kulparsi called the hunter to him and praised his dancing. He then by way of reward gave him thousands of cowries. After which all the Kulparsi withdrew into the tree.

The hunter, overjoyed, went home with his wealth. There he met another hunter, who asked him why he was so happy. When he heard the story he begged to be told the place so that he too might go and get wealth. The first hunter told him and directed him on his way.

Next day the second hunter went to the tree and soon there issued forth the band of Kulparsi who began to dance as before and sing 'Talatta, Talatta'. The hunter joined in the dance but added words of his own. Now Talatta means Friday and the hunter continued Saturday, &c., and so spoilt the song of the Kulparsi.

When the dance was finished the chief of the little men sent for the hunter and, thanking him for his dancing, said that he did not want men to come and teach him the days of the week and that he would reward him, not with cowries, but with a bag which he was to open on his return to his village.

The hunter hastened back, and calling all the people together to see what the Chief of the Kulparsi had given him, he opened his bag and there came out fever and all the ills that visit man. And that is how sickness came into the world.

It is not surprising then that sacrifices are made to mmotia and Kulparsi by all tribes. These consist almost invariably of sweet food, such as bananas, sugar-cane, ground-nuts, &c. Meat is never offered, as they are supposed to be present when women make the food and take whatever they want for themselves without any one noticing the loss. The offerings are placed under the big trees which the mmotia are supposed to frequent, or in those clean parts of the bush near old ant-hills where the mmotia are wont to come and dance and play.

Madness is frequently attributed to the machinations of the Kulparsi. Especially is madness noticed among hunters, who frequently become crazed as I myself can testify, for many times have I known hunters go temporarily out of their wits and act as real madmen. Further, it is believed that if one sleeps out at night and does not take the precaution to get under cover when the night-breeze springs up then madness is certain to follow. This breeze is the property of the mmotia, who make it by their too rapid dancing.

In the Krachi District there came to my notice the case of a certain hunter who lived in a small village called Kojo-krum. He was a friend of mine and we had on several occasions been out hunting together. One day he came to Krachi to buy some powder and that evening he went quite mad. He began by walking about the market-place in a strange manner, talking and muttering to himself. The madness increased until he was singing and shouting. Then he discarded his clothes and openly expressed his determination to end his days, but with an éclat worthy of the slayer of elephants. He proposed that I should be his victim and came up to my bungalow shouting out his intentions. Fortunately there was some one around who explained his design and I could deal with him in time. Next morning he was quite dazed and stupid. I sent him back with his friends to be looked after, as they assured me that he would recover all right if they could get him home. He did, and some four weeks later on passing through Kojokrum he came to me and tried to explain what had happened, for he apparently likes me.

He had killed two elephants near a certain tree but on different occasions. This tree he naturally looked upon as a lucky one for him and often he would go and sit under it hoping more good luck would come his way there. One day he had fallen asleep and had been dancing with the mmotia. On awaking he had come to Krachi for the powder and then it was that the mmotia had allowed the medicine they must have caused him to take or touch to do its work and he had gone out of his wits. On his return home his friends had taken him to consult the local soothsayer, who had told him that he could never be quite free from the madness till he had killed a red buffalo. This he had succeeded in doing and now he was quite sane.

Again at a small village called Tintum there was a youth who went one day out fishing. He grew tired and went to sleep under a large tree. He did not return to the village for a week and the people searched everywhere for him. They reported his disappearance to me and almost immediately afterwards there came in a messenger to say the lad had been found under the tree. The matter was quite inexplicable to them as they had passed the tree many times and no one had seen him there. However, the youth was demented and could tell nothing of his adventures. He was taken to the shrine of the god Bruku and after a month or so was restored to his senses. He then told how when he had fallen asleep the mmotia had come out of the tree and had begun to dance. He had joined in and when the dance was over they had asked him to go home with them. He agreed, and they called a crocodile from the Oti. The youth was told to mount the animal and follow. This he did and was led under the water where he found a fine large town full of mmotia. Everything was as it is in the outer world; but the light was different, for it was neither daylight nor darkness. Everything too was much smaller and the people did nothing but dance and eat sweet things. He stayed there for some while and then asked to be shown the way home. The mmotia agreed and the crocodile was called and took him back to the tree where he was found later.

Apart from their predilection for sweet things, the pixie-folk are very fond indeed of intoxicants. I have not heard if they care for the product of Europe, but they certainly do like palm-wine and millet-beer. One has to take all sorts of precautions to prevent them getting at the drink. It must be remembered, however, that they do not consume it in such a manner that the loss could be perceived, any more than they do with the meat already mentioned; but when they do manage to get at the drink one will soon know, for the whole brew is spoilt and rendered unfit for human consumption.

To prevent such an untoward occurrence, the Dagomba women will place five or six chilli-peppers in the pot after the final boiling, or if there are no peppers available three or four glowing lumps of charcoal will suffice. A further precaution is to lean a knife against the brim of the pot while the beer is brewing.

The Krachi have to take similar precautions. It is usual to make a circle of ashes round the pot which will receive the brew and again a knife should, as an extra protection, be leant against it. In the pot where the wine is actually being received from the tree one should, if wise, place a small lump of charcoal, not glowing, but cold and it must be quite black. It is natural that the mmotia should be on the *qui vive* when you are returning from the bush with the wine, and therefore one has to put a red pepper in each pot. This one has to do, moreover, each time one moves the pot from village to village.

These precautions are necessary even when one has not yet begun to brew the beer. For if you buy or otherwise have to transport fermenting millet, you should put a small pyramid of wood-ash on top to prevent these mischievous mites from getting at the stuff.

Chapter Five

HUNTERS AND SOME OF THEIR LORE

STORY OF THE INTRODUCTION OF FIRE-ARMS—MAGIC STICKS—
THE SLAYING OF A GIANT—STORY OF THE TAIL OF THE
QUEEN-ELEPHANT—HOW ANIMALS SEEK REVENGE—THE
HUNTER OF TAWIA—HUNTING TABOOS—OMENS—SNAKES
AND PIGS—TOADS—LIZARDS—LIZARDS AND LIGHTNING—
RAIN AND HUNTERS—SOAP-MAKING—TYING SLAIN GAME—
DEAD ELEPHANTS—BAMBUA THE RED-FLANKED DUIKER.

IT cannot be so very long ago that all these various tribes
depended on the chase chiefly for their sustenance. All
over the country one meets with the tradition of the foundation of the villages by some hunter, who finding the site
good for 'meat', settled there and raised a family which
eventually became a large village. Moreover, we know that
some four hundred years ago the country on the coast itself
was full of animals which to-day have been almost extermi-
nated. But it must not for a moment be thought that hunting
in this part of Africa at all resembled or resembles the inten-
sive form found on the eastern side of the continent among
such tribes as the Masai.

Firstly there does not seem to have been so large a variety
of animals, and secondly there is no doubt that just prior to
the arrival of Europeans on the coast the natives indulged
chiefly in snails and grubs, as to a great extent they do to this
day. Guns were of course unknown, and bows and arrows
were the chief weapons together with spears. There is
a delightful picture in De Bry of the coast natives hunting
in this way, and the story of the first coming of guns is thus
told by the Krachi.

There was once born in a Krachi village a wonderful boy,
for no sooner had he arrived than he was able to walk and
talk just as if he were a grown man. Naturally he was

H

possessed of great magical powers and was looked up to with great respect by his fellow tribesmen. One day, Kwaku Ndyente, for such was his name, went on a long journey. It is said that he even reached the sea. On his return he brought with him a stick of the most wonderful power. It sufficed merely to point it at a man and that man fell dead.

Now the Ashanti at that time were troubling Krachi, enslaving them and making them pay tribute. Kwaku Ndyente made up his mind to put an end to this state of things, so calling the people together he told them he was going to sally forth against their oppressors with his magic stick. They tried to prevent him, but he said that there was nothing to fear, as all he had to do on reaching an Ashanti town was to point the stick at the people and say: 'If you sit down there will be trouble for you; if you stand up there will likewise be trouble,' and then the Ashanti would all fall down dead.

Kwaku set out on his campaign and sure enough whenever he met with the Ashanti he pointed his stick and repeated the provocative words and the Ashanti all fell down dead. In time he came to the place where the King of Ashanti himself was and Kwaku Ndyente slew him in the same manner. Then Kwaku was satisfied and the Ashanti made peace and he returned home where some time later he died.

Quite possibly this is a remembrance of the defeat of the great Osei Tutu by the Ewe of Dahomey, to whom the Krachi are, as all other Guan people, closely related. In any case it seems a clear legend of the introduction of fire-arms, although the pointing of a magic stick at something, thereby killing it, is not necessarily a reference to fire-arms, for the people of Krachi used to relate how until about 1914 there lived close to the town of British Krachi a sacred crocodile. It was wont to bask in the sun close to the landing-place of the canoes which bring salt from Addah and was apparently quite harmless to men. The saurian was remarkable for carrying its bank about with him, for the people tell me that its back was covered with cowries. There was no doubt about its sanctity and a special house was erected for it to shelter in and small sacrifices were frequently offered to it. Moreover, each year there was one great sacrifice. A young bull was purchased by subscription, and on the appointed day all the people accompanied their priests and the bull to the place where the crocodile used to lie and there tied the bull to a stake. After many incantations and prayers the priests raised their magic sticks and pointed to the unfortunate bull. Three times they pointed and at the third time the bull is said to have fallen dead. Every one then moved off and left the carcass. No man whatever could partake of the meat; the whole was left to the holy monster.

Hunters, whether armed with arrows or guns, are everywhere looked upon as men imbued with much magical power or medicines. It is, of course, usual in towns such as Kumasi to mock at them as 'bush men', but at the back of every one's mind there is a certain regard akin to fear of them, for these men, as all know, see wonderful things and hear wonderful tales. Many hunters are supposed to understand the tongues of the birds and the languages of animals; they frequently meet giants and dwarfs; they visit underground cities; they can make themselves invisible or change themselves into various forms at will.

Some few miles north of Krachi lies the village of Wururuto. There lived a certain man, the son of a most mighty hunter. The latter one day went out on his business of the chase in the far bush across the Frao or Volta River. For long he saw no meat and was almost determined to return, but thought he would first ascend a small hill to see what was the other side. This he did, and to his surprise he met an enormous thing, man-shaped, but of a hugeness such as the mind could not conceive. He determined to kill it as he knew there must be much medicine in so vast a monster.

Quietly he drew near and when quite close he fired his gun. That he had hit the giant he knew, for the latter felt the stricken spot but otherwise took no notice. Again the hunter fired, but with no result, except that the giant turned to see what gnat was troubling him. The hunter was afraid, but again loaded his gun. The noise aroused the giant, who perceiving the man, tried to catch him, but the hunter was too quick and changed himself immediately into a tree, where he made medicine rapidly, and spitting on the bullet, once more loaded the gun. He fired, and the giant, after glancing at his wound, fell dead.

The hunter made haste back to his village and called the people to come and help him bring in the meat. Then after making a sacrifice and preparing more medicine he returned with the people and they brought back the meat. He himself only kept the hair.

The proof of this story is that you can even to-day buy some of that hair from his son. I managed to obtain a little of it.

Now it seems to me that here one has an example of an etymological legend in its very beginning. If my surmise is correct, the hunter slew a lion, which is never called by its real name of lion, but is referred to either as Lord of the Bush (sirem'sei) or Great Animal (aboa kese). This great animal became merely 'giant', and as giants are firmly believed in and lions are uncommon in these parts, the confusion in terms has quite naturally ensued.

The value the hunter attached to the hair of his victim is to be compared with the story of Owuo (*vide supra*, p. 32), where the source of Owuo's power lay in his hair, or with the following tale, in which medicine is kept in the hair. It is a Krachi story and runs:

A certain old woman had two children, both sons. They

were devoted to their mother and one day to show their affection told her what they intended to do for her when the time came for her to die. The eldest promised he would obtain two slaves to send to attend her in the next world, and the younger said he would not be content to bury her unless he buried with her the tail of the Queen of the Elephants.

Now, soon after, the old lady passed away and the elder fulfilled his promise, sacrificing two good slaves to follow his mother and look after her. But the younger found he could not keep his word and wandered all over the country-side crying bitterly, saying: 'My eyes are red for my promise.'

One day he came across an old woman who asked him what it was all about. The boy told her and she took pity on him for his piety and gave him a medicine, named Depo, and instructed him to go into the far far bush where he would find a great senya tree, whom he was to greet, and the rest he would learn in good time.

The boy thanked the old dame and went off. After a long while he came to the senya tree and saluted him. The tree asked what he could do for him, and the boy made answer that he wanted the tail of the Queen of the Elephants. Then the senya split into two and told the boy to get inside and remain very quiet and that in a short while the elephants would come to sleep near-by. Moreover, the tree said that the eleventh would be the Queen. The boy did this and in a very short while the elephants came. As each one approached the tree he gave a great sniff and asked the tree if man was around as he thought he could smell him. But the tree denied the presence of any man and the elephants were quieted.

Presently the eleventh came and the boy knew at once that it was the Queen. She was of an enormous size. She asked the same question of the tree and when reassured entered the circle of her followers. The tree then whispered to the boy that he must wait till he told him the elephants were all asleep, for even when they were quite quiet, only making the sound krikri, they were still awake and would kill him if they saw him.

A long time went by, but at last the tree told the boy that all were asleep, and Kwaku, for such was his name, came out. Quickly he went to the eleventh and cut off its tail. To his surprise he found inside a lot of gold and a large brass pan. (This detail is not referred to again and my story-teller said he did not know what the gold and pan had to do with the story.) Then he hurried off home.

No sooner had he gone than the first elephant woke up and complained that he had had a dream in which his tail had been cut off. Then each in turn awoke and said they had all had the same dream. Last of all the Queen herself awoke and repeated the dream, which seemed so true to her that to prove it wrong she tried to shake her tail. Thus she found out her loss. Great was the anger of the elephants. They knew that a man must have done this and that the tree had helped him. So they tore down the senya and broke it up into the smallest of fragments and then gave chase to the marauder.

His tracks were quite clear to them and they soon began rapidly to overhaul him, but Kwaku begged the tail to help him and he whirled it about so that the tail made a large pond of water [1] to which the elephants soon came. They were overjoyed at the chance of a good bathe, so waited and played about. (I think that the gold and pan might possibly have served to perform other acts of delaying the pursuit.)

The Queen came up and abused them and said she would go on alone and that they could await her there. On their agreeing, she continued the chase, but when she came near the village she turned herself [2] into a young girl and thus disguised entered the settlement.

[1] Tails and water are often found to be closely allied with each other, especially in rain-making.

[2] This is one of the commonest beliefs, as it is also vice versa. It is not even looked upon as a magical happening.

Meanwhile Kwaku had given the tail to his people and the chief was so pleased with him that he gave him the name of Kwaku Obaduia, which means Kwaku the Cutter of Tails.

Now the elephant-girl had arrived at the village meeting-place under the great shade tree and there she sat, admired by all the young men of the place, for she was very beautiful indeed. The youths soon learned that she was quite alone and opined she ought to be married. Apparently they suggested this, for the elephant-girl said she would marry any one of them who was able to get her calabash for her, for she had brought with her a long calabash which she had thrown into the tree-top. All tried, but in vain.

Kwaku's sister was present and said that if her brother had been awake he would certainly have got the calabash down for her. The elephant-girl was interested and persuaded Kwaku's sister to awake the boy. Kwaku came out and immediately shot down the calabash with his arrow. Then the elephant-girl married him.

One day she said to her husband that she would like to go with him to his farm, for she had never seen it. He agreed to take her, and they went off together. The farm happened to be close to a palm-wine camp and Kwaku went to get some. On his return he offered his wife some, but she refused, so Kwaku drank it all himself. This made him very sleepy; so, lying down, he went to sleep. At once the elephant-girl searched through his hair, for she knew the medicine must be there. She soon found it and threw it into the fire.

Then Kwaku awoke and found his wife turned back again into an elephant. The stump of her tail was bleeding and she demanded the return of her tail forthwith. Kwaku did not know what to do, but pleaded to be allowed to call his medicine three times. She agreed and Kwaku called 'Depo, oh! Depo, oh! O my medicine! Where are you?'

At the third call Depo replied: 'What do you want? Had

you really liked me and wanted me you would never have allowed the elephant to have found me.'

But Kwaku explained that it was only because of Nsa, the palm-wine. So Depo said he would help and told him to jump a little into the air. Kwaku jumped and at once was changed into a chicken-hawk. Thus he escaped, and we know this is true, for do we not see at every grass-burning Asansa the Hawk hovering over the flames looking, looking for Depo his lost medicine?

Hair is, of course, commonly regarded with reverence. Among the Dagomba, for instance, the widows of a man have to shave every bit off as soon as their man is dead as well as to cut their finger-nails to the quick. For it is said that the man must have played with their hair and their nails must often have scratched him. In the same way they may not go outside uncovered or unaccompanied, for the dead man will probably be near at hand, and if he recognizes them he might call them by name, so that they too would have to depart and follow him.

But one could digress far on the subject of hair. To return therefore to hunters. In the story just told of Kwaku Obaduia the chief point is the desire for revenge on the part of the injured beast. This is only to be expected, and all hunters have to observe the strictest of ceremonies after killing dangerous or magic-possessing animals. Funeral customs are given to many; sacrifices of all sorts have to be performed lest they should come back either to haunt one at night or, what is worse, damage one in daylight. Here is another tale which is heard among both Dagomba and Krachi illustrative of the belief that animals, injured by men, seek their revenge.

A certain hunter killed one day a female buffalo, but did not perceive a heifer whose mother the buffalo had been. The young cow determined to be revenged on her mother's assassin and followed the hunter home to his village. When near the place she changed her shape into that of a beautiful maiden and entered the market-place in this guise. Every young man fell in love with her, but she refused to marry any one except the hunter, who took her home as his wife.

One day the latter asked him how he managed to be so clever a hunter, for he would bring home each evening plenty of meat. The infatuated husband then began to relate all his magical powers. He told how he could change into a tree, into a stone, into water, and so on. He had nearly completed the catalogue of his powers, when his mother overheard the conversation and told him to be quiet, that no man in his senses ever told everything to his wife. The hunter at once stopped talking in the middle of the word 'needle'. He only managed to say: 'Then I become a nee.'

Next morning he went forth to the bush and had not got far on the road when he met a buffalo. This was his heifer-wife turned once more into her own shape. Without warning, she charged the man. He turned into a tree; she began to uproot him. He turned into a stone; she began to stamp him to pieces. He turned into water; she began to lap him up. He turned into a needle and hid in her tail. The buffalo could find him nowhere, so tired at long last with searching for him, she made off into the bush and her husband fell from her tail and when she was out of sight changed into his man-shape and returned home, grateful indeed for his mother's warning.

It must not be thought that these tales are just simply fairy yarns. They are not. They are to a very large extent believed in, and I once actually overheard my orderly explain to a hunter that I had the power of rendering myself invisible. This was after they had witnessed my standing well out in the open grass whilst a female kob with her young came up to within ten yards of where I was watching them.

Hunters, moreover, see marvellous things in the bush. But it is forbidden to them to relate these until they are too

old to fare forth any longer on the chase. Thus it was that
the old hunter of Tawia on the Tamale-Yendi road used to
relate the following adventure. He was a famous killer of
elephants and buffalo, claiming seventy head of the former
and two hundred and forty of the latter. He never killed
any other meat, scorning such as roan and hartebeeste. His
name was Salifu, and when too old to hunt he would join
in the 'obofo' or hunter's dance and tell of the strange
happenings that had come to him in the bush.

Thus one day he and two others had decided to go forth
to get meat for their village, for a festival was at hand and
they thought it a good thing to supply their brothers with
fresh meat. The three had argued as to the most likely spot
to find their quarry, and as they failed to agree on the point,
decided to go each his own way.

Salifu made for a place where he had seen many tracks of
buffalo, but search as he would, he could find nothing.
Weary, he sat down under the shade of a large tree and shook
out a little tobacco-dust on to his thumb-nail to snuff. Just
as he did this he noticed an old, old man approaching, so old
that he could not stand upright nor walk properly. The old
man greeted Salifu and begged him for some tobacco, saying
that he had sent his wife many times to the market to procure
him some, but she had not succeeded.

Now Salifu was rather frightened, as he knew there was
no village near and that the old man could not possibly have
walked far. However, he gave him some tobacco and the
old man sat down and began to converse with him. He
asked what Salifu was doing in the bush and Salifu explained
that he had come to get some buffalo as he had seen many
tracks hereabouts. The old man replied that it was useless
for him to look for the buffalo as he had locked them all up,
for the buffalo were his cows and he had overheard the
conversation of the three hunters in the village, so had taken
the precaution to hide all his animals. However, as Salifu

had been so kind, he would allow him to have one. He added that as soon as he had gone away there would come along three very fine large buffalo; Salifu was to let the two foremost pass untouched and could take the third.

Then the old man got up, and Salifu, tearing off a piece of his cloth, wrapped up a lot of tobacco in it and gave it to the old man, who, thanking him, went away. Scarcely had he gone than the buffalo, as foretold, came along. The hunter carefully allowed the first two to pass and then when the third was quite close slew it and returned to the village. He met the other two hunters, who had had no success at all.

Salifu's killing was confined, as stated above, to buffalo and elephant. This is by no means an uncommon practice among the older hunters, to keep to the killing of one animal in particular. One can easily understand this, as it is only natural for a man to become familiar with the habits of one type rather than those of many.

In this connexion there is told by the Krachi the following tale of how hunting first started and why hunters follow this practice. For it was not always that men hunted. In the olden times there were only three real hunters. These were the lion, the leopard, and the wild dog. But one day a man did kill a duiker and while he was still gazing at the dead meat, the three hunters came along and the man was afraid. He hid himself in a big tree and watched what the animals would do.

The lion said he had killed the duiker, but the leopard claimed it as his. The wild dog also put in his claim and there was a great dispute. While they were all wrangling the leopard perceived the man and asked him why he was all trembling. The man replied: 'I am afraid. It was I who killed the meat.'

The leopard told him not to fear, and the man, gathering courage, asked the leopard if he might be allowed a portion of the kill. The leopard agreed and the man chose a hind quarter. This the leopard at once gave him and the man, seeing that the leopard was still in a good humour, asked if he might have too the skin and the head. The leopard gave him these and still the man remained. So the leopard asked him what was the matter and the man replied that he was afraid. The leopard told him not to fear but to speak out all that was in his mind. The man then said: 'You, Master Leopard, are a great hunter. I beg of you to give me some of the medicine which you use for hunting.' The leopard was not at all angry and agreed to give the man a little of his magic. Then the man went away home.

Now this medicine was truly a magic one. For it gave the owner power to understand the talk of all the animals and trees and bushes. And the man used to take this medicine with him and would go into the bush to hunt and he would hear the conversation of all the animals and birds and trees and so would learn where the animals he wished to kill were feeding. Thus one day he saw two buffaloes and one of them was a cow. And he heard her say to the bull: 'Husband, I hear a man coming and he will kill us.' But the bull replied that he did not fear, and that the grass there was excellent so that he would not go. The man came up and he killed both the cow and the bull.

On another day he was returning home and his way led him to cross a river. Whilst he was doing this he put his foot on the back of a fish. The latter called out to his brothers: 'See here is this man and he is not content with killing all the animals but he must now begin to kill us.' Hearing this the man succeeded in catching a lot of fine fish.

But one day when he returned home tired and was resting inside his room, an old one-eyed woman was outside husking the rice. There were two fowls also there and one of them had found the fallen rice. His comrade, seeing him busily eating, came up to share the feast; but the former, seeing this and being greedy, said: 'Brother, look over there, there is plenty of rice.' And he pointed to the spot where the husks were falling. The man saw this and understood all that the fowls had said. This made him laugh aloud.

When the old woman heard the man laughing she grew very angry and wanted to know what he was laughing at. For she thought he was making mockery of her appearance. The man told her what he had seen and heard, but the old woman refused to believe him and grew angrier and angrier. At last she summoned him to appear before Nyame to explain his behaviour and to pay for his mockery of her.

Now Nyame heard the case carefully and asked the man what he had to say. The man explained what he had seen and what he had heard, and Nyame then asked him how he had come by so wonderful a medicine. The man then said that he was not allowed to say how he had got it, for if he revealed the secret he would then die at once. But Nyame insisted, and the man had at last to tell that he had received the medicine from the leopard. At once he fell down dead.

Then Nyame was sorry, but he took the dead man and cut him up into small pieces. So small indeed were they that they were like sand. These he threw all over the world, so that to this day when a hunter takes his medicine he gathers up some of the pieces, and according to the nature of the piece he picks up so will he succeed in hunting. Thus if he picks up a bit of the buffalo, he will kill chiefly buffalo; if of duiker, he will kill duiker; if of bushbuck, he will kill bushbuck. And that is how men learned to hunt and why it is that some hunters are always lucky with certain animals more than with others.

Hunting being so full of magic it is to be expected that there are a vast number of taboos to be observed and other rules to be obeyed. Thus no man may have sexual intercourse with a woman for seven days before he goes hunting. If a woman should be tolerated at all in the hunting camp, she and the hunters are under the most stringent rules bound to observe continence. At the same time she must leave the camp at once on the first signs of menstruation, for the animals of the bush and various spirits therein hate the sight and smell of human blood, and if such be spilt at all on the ground they will in their anger injure and kill the hunters. Thus during the seven days preceding the departure for the camp no man may have brought to him water by a menstruating girl. Should he drink such water, not only will he be killed in the bush but the girl too will perish.

The observance of continence is carried even further, and it is ordained that no man shall touch the wives of those away on the chase. Death to the hunter will follow. Fortunately a breach of this regulation is at once known to the animals in the bush, and they have sufficient sporting sense to warn the hunter of the infringement, when, if he be wise, he immediately returns.

For should one, while out hunting, perceive two birds or two animals, or even two insects, having intercourse one knows that one's wife is faithless. Should you perceive this whilst on the way to the hunting-place a neat distinction is drawn. Trouble has not yet come, but one should return lest it might arrive.

Sexual matters apart there are several ways of learning beforehand what sort of luck one will have out hunting. For instance, to meet a tortoise on the road is a pretty sure sign that you will see no meat at all. If you touch it and continue on the chase you will have even worse luck and might possibly be killed or mistake your brother for an animal. The best thing to do is to pick it up and take it back to camp.

The chameleon is also a forerunner of ill-luck if you touch it. This lizard is considered by the Dagomba to be closely related to fire. They hold too a curious belief that after one is bitten by it one must take it and wrap it in leaves and bite it in return. Otherwise leprosy will come to you.

Again bees can tell what luck one will have. For if they swarm past you on the left-hand side while you are on the way to hunt you will have bad luck; if, however, they pass on the right you will have good luck. This belief does not apply alone to hunters nor does it matter which side they pass when you are sitting down or at one's ordinary work.

There is too a certain bird, often pointed out to me but which I never can recognize. If you hear it on the right hand you will have bad luck; if you are out hunting you will know that unless you kill a 'meat' you will surely meet on your return home a corpse. On the other hand, if you hear it on the left you will have good luck, and no matter if you kill nothing still you will find plenty of meat when you get back home.

Another bird very similar in appearance is known as the ni-baga. It is a witch. It is not a bird at all, and the best thing to do is to go straight home. But my information is of little worth since I can identify neither bird.

Hunters, leading as they do a life of danger, are as might be expected learned in all sorts of medicines and science of the bush. Perhaps snakes are their most formidable foe. They are often deadly in their bites; they are difficult to see at most times and almost invisible to a stalker eager on his prey. Some of them are vindictive; some are witches in disguise; some can fly; others jump hundreds of yards; others leap backwards. The lore concerning snakes would fill a goodly chapter.

There is the horned Cerastes, which leaps enormous distances according to local belief. It is ordinarily quite a quiet snake but it hates any one passing round its back or tail. There is a snake which resembles the black Mamba. It spits at you, especially at the eyes. If you are hit you will become blind, but if you are very quick and manage to wash your eyes in your own urine before the poison takes effect you will be all right and your eyesight will not be harmed.

Again there are two-headed snakes and even three-headed ones. These must be avoided at all costs. The two-headed one may be a species of slow-worm; I have no explanation for the three-headed one. Possibly fear or rapid swaying of the snake's head may account for this belief which all hunters hold.

The latter have as a rule antidotes, or rather charms, against this danger from snakes. There must undoubtedly be some real antidotes known which, assisted by the psychological effect of faith, do often procure cures. If, however, one is without one of these safeguards the following is the behaviour of a stricken man in Dagomba. It is governed by strict laws observed by all, and as far as I have yet learnt similar customs obtain among the Krachi.

The law is that he who holds the medicine must give it to him who is bitten. Payment can be arranged later. This forced saving of another's life is curious, as the general rule throughout these parts is not to interfere with the decrees of the Almighty. However, with snakes it is apparently different. It is necessary to find out what snake has bitten one and if possible to kill it. Its belly should then be opened, and if the inside is all broken up and bloody one will know that it was not a snake at all but a witch disguised as a snake, and the services of the owner of the antidote are not required.

A case of this came to my notice in Krachi. A Dagomba who was working for me got bitten by a very bad cobra. He killed the snake and at once made for Kete, the nearest village. There he knew a certain man who had the antidote for this particular species of snake. But before sending for him he cut the snake open and found that all the inside was smashed up and black. He knew it was a witch, and therefore being well protected from their machinations took no further trouble in the matter. He did not succumb, but told me the story himself about a week later when I had killed just such another snake.

Now although one must hasten to the antidote-owner, one may not, if a townsman, proceed direct to the fellow's house. First, one must call out, even at night-time, to let every one know what has happened. For this is to warn people, lest peradventure one should meet a man or woman still unwashed after sexual intercourse. Snakes hate that, and should the bitten man have the misfortune to meet such an unclean one he, not the unclean, will die. The Krachi in particular believe that if a man bitten by a snake meets another man who has had sexual intercourse with a woman with whom he also has cohabited, then the snake poison will prove fatal.

Fortunately the law is different for a stranger. He may enter the town without any evil falling on him, no matter how many unclean people he may meet.

Again one does not as a rule refer to snakes. One must always seek some paraphrase. Of such, the commonest used, if one meets a snake on the path, is: 'Take care; there is a rope.' And if one's friend has been stricken one calls out, not 'So-and-so has been bitten by a snake,' but rather 'Quick; my friend has hurt his foot on the road. He has crushed a rope.' It is not necessary to add the last sentence as every one would understand the first.

Another curious belief held by these people is that a man never dies in the bush of a snake-bite. He always manages to reach home first.

Europeans who come out to West Africa are prone to aver that there are few snakes in this country. That is because they are either town-dwellers or unobservant. Snakes are exceedingly common in all parts, but naturally difficult to see. Deaths from snake-bite must average about the same as in India but they are not recorded, and, as they usually take place in the bush far away from European doctors, are unremarked. Seventy different species were identified by the Germans in South Togo. The northern

I

parts, probably a more likely country for snakes, were not so thoroughly examined by them.

Offhand I could describe at least a score of types myself, including the long whip-like green snake, non-poisonous, which the natives say loves the milk of women and is often found suckling them. However, I cannot identify the snake which crows like a cockerel, nor the one with the red plumes on its head, nor yet the snake which devours its young. These are special snakes reserved for native belief.

There is in the native mind some close connexion between snakes, scorpions, and pigs. Wild pigs and domestic pigs are everywhere regarded as having especial power against the bites and stings of these pests. As has been stated, there are certain men in every tribe who own medicine or anti-dotes against their poisons, and this is how they procured that power.

Many, many years ago there was a certain hunter who had made for himself in the bush a small field of ground-nuts. When the nuts were nearly ready he noticed that a family of wart-hog were in the habit of marauding his field. He there-fore set a watch and one evening he saw nine of the pigs approaching. He hid himself and succeeded in killing one with his arrows. The same thing occurred next day, and soon he had slain eight of them. The following night when the ninth and last one drew near the hunter was astonished to hear himself addressed by name by the pig. He asked him what he wanted, and the pig replied that surely the hunter was by now satisfied; he had slain eight of his brothers and now only himself was left; he would give the hunter medi-cine against all snakes if the hunter would let him go free. The hunter was sorry for the pig and agreed, and from that day to this there are certain men who have inherited this power. At the same time the hunter gave the pig a magical medicine which would ward off arrows and spears, and that is why it is so hard to kill wart-hogs and other bush pigs.

There is also a very close connexion between snakes and toads. It is alleged that all toads are poisonous and that they are addicted to swallowing snakes whole, beginning with the tail and leaving the head of their victim in their mouth so that the snake thus swallowed can add his bite to that of the toad.

It is perhaps because of that belief that the following story is told:

In the olden days snakes and toads were quite friendly. However, one day they disputed as to which of them was the more powerful and more dangerous to man. The toad suggested a trial, and the two proceeded to a path and there awaited the coming of a man, it being agreed that the snake could have the first bite.

Presently a man came along and the two hid in the grass. Just as he passed the snake struck out and bit him on the heel and then made off quickly into the bush, lest the man should kill him. But the toad remained by the roadside. The man looked down to see what had struck him and seeing the toad exclaimed, 'Good. That is nothing, merely a toad.' So he went his way.

The snake then returned and the two sat down to await a second passer-by. Presently he came along, and the toad sprang up and hit him on the ankle, and then made off. But the snake remained. The man feeling the blow, looked down and saw the snake. Thoroughly frightened, he began to cry aloud and bewail his lot, for his last hour had come. And soon he fell dead.

The snake perceived then that the toad had more poison than he, and from that day to this snakes hate toads, for they are jealous of them, and whenever they see one they haste to devour it so that the poison of the toad may in that manner become theirs.

Lizards are to a certain extent, but not universally, thought to be near relatives of snakes, and some people, especially the

Dagomba (though I have met Krachi who believe the same) hold that lizards eventually turn into snakes or vice versa. Proof of this is visible they say in the two-legged snake frequently met with in the grass country. One can see in it the actual process of metamorphosis.

It is not surprising therefore to find quite a lot of lore concerning lizards. The iguana, which is fairly common, is said to whip you with its tail, and small boys are warned not to molest them. A smaller species of iguana seems anxious to die. I have not yet learned the story why this should be so, but the Krachi tell me that it will wait quietly for a man to kill it and make no attempt either to escape or resist.

There are two varieties of small lizards which frequent houses. They are pretty little reptiles, very shiny brown on the back and almost silver-bellied. One has a remarkably long tail and two pale yellow stripes along its flanks. These two are reputed to bring luck to the household. That is a Krachi belief.

A third lizard, perhaps the commonest in the country, is of a most dreadful appearance. The males are of a slate colour with orange or lemon heads and tails. The females are of a brownish hue with markings on which I presume are founded the patterns of the so-called Fair Island jumpers. These are exceptionally pugnacious, and battles between males are serious affairs. They flog each other mercilessly with their tails, and one can hear the blows for a considerable distance. Throughout the battle they keep raising their heads up and down, balancing themselves on their forelegs in a manner reminiscent of physical jerks; they blow out their cheek pouches, and in their rage actually change their colour to a paler tinge. Once one begins to win he follows his adversary and frequently does not leave him till he is dead. He begins to bite him as soon as he is too tired to swing his powerful tail, and continues to bite him till he succumbs.

This variety of lizard is closely connected with fire, and

in the remote north of the Protectorate the annual burning of the grass is ushered in by the cruel ceremony of tying a brand to its tail and loosing it in the bush. The direction it takes will be the direction for the first burning. Its dung also is one of the usual ingredients in the making of tinder from kapok, a custom prevalent among the northern tribes of Togo as well as in the Protectorate.

Then there is a lizard believed to be deadly poisonous. It is quite harmless till one touches it, when it will turn and chase you from the bush. Its poison is alleged to be in its tail. Not long ago there was a plague of these at Tamale, and the local inhabitants would not go out at night without a lantern. The Europeans in that station, however, were sceptical and laughed at the mention of the lizard. I recently heard that an M.O. had found one and had sent it home for identification. The result I have not heard.

Only once did I myself come near one of these. That was at Krachi, but a local native drove it off with sticks before I came up to the place. He explained that it was a very bad thing indeed and that he knew I would disregard any warning and get myself hurt. He did not know me.

Another lizard very common among rocks and old trees has a vermilion belly. Its scales are closely knit, thereby giving it a shiny appearance. This fellow is said to be in close connexion with lightning. Sparks will issue from its belly, and it is highly desirable to keep away from close acquaintance with it; moreover it too can sting with its tail.

The connexion between lizards and lightning I do not understand. But there is another lizard which is common in most houses. It is chiefly remarkable for its stone-like colour and its very beady black eyes. It is said by all to bite one and to cause considerable pain. But it is particularly noteworthy for its total disregard for Saa, the god of lightning and thunder and rain. Whenever storms approach this lizard is said to defy the god, for at that time one most usually hears its voice, a kind of croak. Saa is always, and naturally so, annoyed at this and seeks to kill it. Thus it is that houses are struck by lightning and cracks come in the walls. My own bungalow is somewhat cracked, and the explanation is obvious to all who enter, for there are scores of this lizard inside, clinging with their feelers to the ceiling. That too is remarkable, for lizards as a rule have claws.

If lizards are closely connected with the god Saa so too are hunters. Rain-making and rain-stopping are usually one of their provinces, though this is not necessarily so, for I have frequently met in the Krachi area this power in the possession of quite young boys.

I had occasion to cross a wide area marked on the map as uninhabited. A tent was therefore essential. The rains had already commenced and when wet the tent weighed very heavily. Now the carriers were all from one village, a Nawuri one, and they took with them a youth of about sixteen summers as a guard against rain falling. For they were aware of the weight of the canvas when wet which they would have to carry. We were nine days on the march and no rain fell during that time though it threatened constantly.

The youth would sally out of camp whenever it looked as if a storm would break, and taking certain herbs and grasses would go and secrete himself a good distance away. There he proceeded to 'tie' the rain. An essential part of his duties was to refrain from washing himself. Water had not to touch him at all. On the evening of the ninth day, after a very long march, we approached human habitation. We did not know, of course, what place we were coming to, but as there were plenty of cultivated patches we presumed it was a settled village. I had also told the carriers that that evening I expected to reach a town. As we came down to a stream the boy insisted on washing against the wishes of all the other men. He excused himself on the ground that we would sleep in a village. However, that village was a long way off and rain began to fall long before we reached it. Every single man was convinced it was the boy's fault and abused him 'properly'.

Elsewhere the people who had to carry that tent were wont to beg the chief of each stopping-place to try and stop the rain whenever this threatened. I noticed the following practices:

At Kpandae an unwashed boy took leaves and grass and a cow-tail and went into the bush in the direction from which the rain was coming, and began to abuse it. At Dambabin a man sat down in front of his house-door and set in front of him a large number of cow-tails and bush-meat tails, especially hartebeeste. These he raised from time to time and beat on the ground, all the time abusing the approaching storm. At Adumadun a man went running through the bush towards the rain and abused and threatened it. At Bassa three men were engaged on this work. They had with them cow-tails. Two buried them in the earth in a little hole which they scooped out, murmuring abuse, and the third covered his with ashes. At Bantama a man went into the bush, and when he had found a certain creeper he tied it into a knot calling on the rain to remain tied until the white man had gone with his tent.

In the Dagomba country there used to reside an old man at Tamale. He had a magic stick, which prevented rain falling wherever it was carried, though rain might fall close alongside.

Mention has been made of the dislike snakes have for sexual uncleanness as well as the prohibition to hunters to indulge therein when hunting or about to engage in the chase. This prohibition is carried still further among the Konkomba, who are bound to refrain from such intercourse throughout the period of the poisoning of their arrows and the trials of that poison's effectiveness.

But although a digression from the subject of hunting, it

may be permissible to record here a further curious time when sex matters are more or less taboo. I have not found this custom except in the Krachi district. It is the period of soap-making.

Among the tribes to the north, such as the Moshi, Nan-kanni, and the so-called Grunshi, soap cannot be made if a menstruating girl approaches the place or one who is un-washed from her blood. But among the Krachi and their allied tribe the Chumru no one at all is supposed to come anywhere near the soap-making place.

Soap is manufactured by the old women outside the village. Certain grass or guinea-corn stalks are burnt, together with the wood of a tree which resembles somewhat our elder, till only a white ash remains. The ash is then collected and placed on top of some grass in a pot pierced like a sieve. Then water is poured on and allowed to filter for one night. The filtered water is next day boiled and boiled; shea-butter is added according to the recipe of each individual maker. The whole is then allowed to cool, and it is especially during this period of cooling, while the soap is visibly forming, that the approach of unclean people will ruin the brew. One is forcibly reminded of the belief at home that ham cannot be cured if menstruating girls have a hand in the process.

Another curious custom prevalent, especially among the tribes who still use arrows rather than guns, is to give names to their weapons. The names are usually meant to assist magically in stopping the animal hunted. A Konkomba told me how one sits in a tree along the path of 'meat', and after firing at an animal one sings a song to the arrow fired telling it what to do. Thus a favourite name is 'Rotting Meat' or 'Smell of Death'. This will cause the meat of the animal to spoil so that it dies or causes the aroma of death to surround the beast so that it perishes.

They name, too, their quivers, and particularly the ring

worn on the middle finger of the right hand to guard against the cutting of the bow-string. That finger being the aiming one it is easy to understand that the ring influences the shot.

Apart from thus arresting the flight of a wounded beast, there are many other ways to make sure one will eventually pick up the meat. Each hunter probably has his own medicine for this purpose. I have met the following methods. One hunter had a medicine to rub in the form of a cross on the soles of his feet. As soon as he trod in the footprints of the animal he was hunting that animal's head would turn backwards till the hunter drew near enough to have his shot. Another man had a medicine which he carried in one of those hollowed-out seeds of the fan-palm used commonly as snuff-boxes. He would sprinkle this on the tracks of his quarry with the excellent result that the latter rested till the hunter came up. This was, he told me, particularly efficacious with elephants.

A third to whom I had related how I had lost meat to vultures through failing sufficiently to cover it informed me that it was really quite unnecessary to bother about that. I had just killed a water-buck and he plucked a little grass, not a handful, spat on it, and muttering some words threw the grass upon the dead meat and spat on that. This he told me was quite enough to ward off any vulture or other scavenging animal.

But in spite of these medicines and scores of similar ones it is necessary always to be on guard. For it is quite well known that the unwary hunter who treads on elephant dung will soon after fall a victim to elephantiasis. Otherwise elephant excrement is of considerable value as a medicine in certain illnesses and can find a ready market in the south. Excrement of other animals is likewise of use, as has been noticed in connexion with tinder-making, when lizard and cock dung is necessary. Moreover, it is said that if bird dung fall on one good luck will follow, just as the old story of the sea-gulls of London Bridge and tall hats. But if a vulture's dung were to fall on one, then one must expect bad luck to ensue.

It would take many years to learn all that there is to be known about hunters' lore. Each animal is surrounded with many beliefs and superstitions. The hartebeeste is said never to injure you with his horns; rather does he savage you with his teeth like a dog. And woe to the man thus bitten! The Dagomba believe that Isiga, the crowned duiker, has lamps instead of eyes, and probably gets his oil from the shea-butter fruit of which he is so fond. Elephants suffer terribly from toothache, and when the pain becomes insupportable they will thrust the offending tusk into an ant-heap and break it off.

This last fact is proved by the frequency with which tusks are found near white ants' nests. Apparently the cleanness of the ground in the vicinity and therefore the ease with which one can perceive the fallen tusk are overlooked. However, one must take care to have nothing to do with a dead elephant. That will surely bring one bad luck, especially if one takes his tusks away.

In any case the discoverer of a dead elephant is in the same category as its slayer. He must make the funeral custom for it. This ends usually in the hunters' dance which, so far as I have learned, is common to every tribe from the sea to the desert.

That dance must also be given at the obsequies of the red-flanked duiker, a little and beautiful animal which though excessively common throughout all the country bordering on the great forest is regarded with the utmost awe by all hunters. His size and extraordinary vitality possibly account for this. He is regarded with such respect that most people look upon him as the most important and powerful animal in the whole bush with the sole exception of the tortoise. Hunters refrain from killing this duiker, presumably because

he is rather small. Only youngsters kill it. That is the
Krachi practice. But among the Dagomba Bambua, as he
is called, is not killed as he is thought to be a friend
to hunters, for in him are all the animals of the bush. His
duiker mark on the spine is the elephant in colour, as are
his legs; all the other animals are found in his other colour-
ings, and his tail is tufted like that of the lion. Therefore he
is held in respect. Moreover, he is full of wisdom, as this
story tells:

There was a certain hunter who lived in the far, far bush.
One day he killed a roan and it was a very large one. The
meat was much too heavy for him to carry, so he decided to
return and collect some people to help him.

On his way back he met a very old crocodile which was
blind and which was looking for some water-place where he
could rest. But owing to his blindness the crocodile had
become lost.

When the hunter came up the crocodile said to him:
'Hunterman, Hunterman, help me. I am old and I am lost.
I cannot see, and all I want is for you to show me where there
is water so that I may end my days in peace.'

And the hunter said that the water was not far away, and
if the crocodile liked he would show him the way there.
The crocodile thanked him and asked if he would carry him
to the place as he was old and tired. The man agreed, and
picking the crocodile up he slung him across his shoulder
and made for the water-place.

Arrived there the crocodile asked the man to carry him
into the water. The man did so, and still the crocodile asked
to be carried farther, until at last only the head of the man
remained above water. Then the crocodile seized the man's
shoulder and said that he was going to eat him. The man
begged, but the crocodile refused to listen and said that he
would certainly eat the man.

Just at that moment Bambua, the red-flanked duiker,

chanced to pass that way and hearing the dispute inquired what it was all about. He was told, and then he asked if they would agree for him to hear the case and make a decision. Both assented and came out of the water.

Now Bambua pretended that he could not quite understand, so he told the man to pick up the crocodile and to carry him back to the spot where he had first picked him up. The man did this, and immediately the crocodile was on the ground the duiker told the man to leave him there and to go on to the village to fetch the people for the meat. Thus it is to this day all hunters are friendly to Bambua the Red-flanked Duiker.

Chapter Six

CUNNING VERSUS STRENGTH

THE BEGINNING OF CUNNING—MAGIC OF ANTIAKOTI—
DAGOMBA VERSION OF HOW LIES TRIUMPH OVER TRUTH—
RETRIBUTION SOMETIMES COMES THROUGH BOASTING—
ANANSI OR BRER RABBIT TALES—ORIGIN OF ANANSI.

THE native is a profound believer in wisdom or guile. He thoroughly agrees with the philosopher that 'wisdom is high above the strength of men and the swiftness of horses'. To him the wily Odysseus appeals far more than the hero of the battlefield or the chase. Perhaps this may be due to a gradual process of mental evolution as outlined by Professor Routh in his *God, Man, and Epic Poetry*, or perhaps it is the outcome of centuries of servitude, the natural way of thinking for the hewer of wood and the carrier of water. Many, many are the tales told in which the hero is served by guile and conquers his superior in muscle and power.

I have told the story of Edubiaku, the wonder-child who overcame even the might of Nyame and by whose magic or guile there came to Man the blessing of crops and harvests. Similar tales seem to be told by all the tribes with which this book deals.

The Krachi relate the adventures of one called Krakra Nyansa, a name which signifies 'small, small sense', or in other words guile. It runs as follows, and tells us of the origin and importance of wiliness :

In the very olden days a certain woman had a boy-child. No sooner was he born than he ran out of the house and came to his father who was working in his field. 'Greetings, father mine,' he cried. The man turned to see who had spoken and, seeing the infant, he naturally asked him who he was. The latter replied that he was his own child. This so astounded the man that he decided to return home at once. Taking up

his belongings he set forth together with the babe. Now it
chanced that on the way they had to pass across a river, and
when they were in the water the man put his foot upon a
fish. At once the child called out: 'Give me the fish. For
it was I who first saw it.'

The man was afraid and gave the fish to the child who
took it home and cooked and ate it, all except the head.
This he dried and hung up in the hut.

Some time later the chief of the village lost his favourite
bull. There was a great to-do about this, and the chief
swore a great oath that he would kill terribly the man who
had stolen it. News of the theft reached Krakra Nyansa.
At once he went to the chief's compound and told the great
man that he knew where the head of the bull was to be found
and that the thief could not be far away. The chief at once
sent men with the child, who led them to his father's house
and there showed them the dried fish's head which he had
changed by magic into the head of the bull.

The unfortunate father was taken and put to death. But
the chief and villagers were annoyed at having in their midst
a boy who could thus betray his own father and they drove
him from the place.

As he fled he came to a river near a very large town.
There on the bank he saw a number of women, the wives of
the chief who ruled in those parts. Now they were all busily
engaged in washing and had brought with them their pots
to fill with water for their household. One of these pots was
of gold, a pot which was very highly valued by the chief.
Krakra Nyansa saw this pot and picked it up. The women
shouted to him to put it down at once, but the child refused,
and taking it to the river dropped it into so deep a pool that
it could not be recovered.

The women were very angry indeed, and began to chase
the child, who ran and ran till he quite escaped them. He
had now come to some farms where there were a lot of men

gathered who had been out hunting. He greeted them and began to play about. No one seems to have taken much notice of what he was doing until they saw that he had collected all their guns and set them against a dead tree. They called to him to know what he was doing, and he answered that he was doing nothing. But quickly he took some fire and set light to the dry wood and some of the powder which he had spilt from the powder flasks that had been left with the guns.

The men could not put out the fire, and all their guns were destroyed, but they gave chase to the mischievous child and swore they would finish him off entirely if once they could catch him. However, he made good his escape again, and in due time came to a group of women sitting by the road-side. These had just returned from the market where they had bought rice. The pots full of the grain were on the path and Krakra Nyansa sat down and began to amuse himself with scattering the rice all over the place. The women did not at first notice this, but when they did he had almost finished his work of waste. The women were very angry indeed and ran to catch the boy.

Krakra Nyansa ran and ran, but the women followed hard on his heels and entered the village close behind him. The chief happened to be sitting under the village shade tree and called out to know what was the matter. He was told, and then he decided to hear the palaver and called Krakra Nyansa to him. Meanwhile all the parties who had been injured by Krakra Nyansa had arrived and had seated themselves round the chief and the boy. They told their stories, and the chief asked Krakra Nyansa what he had to say. He replied that he had nothing to say, that they were all fools, and that he alone had any sense.

This rather tactless remark decided the chief to have the boy killed. He therefore gave orders to that effect and Krakra Nyansa tried to run off. But every one shouted out:

'Catch him, catch him,' and the women took their calabashes and pots and the men their clothes to throw over the boy, who leapt from pot to pot till at last he came to the very last one which was in front of the chief himself. The boy could leap no farther, so just as he was about to be taken he jumped straight into the eye of the chief, and that is why we all have that little black thing in our eyes, which is the fount of all our knowledge.

The story is not a very edifying one but it illustrates the importance guile holds amongst these people, for it enabled a very mischievous and far from praiseworthy urchin to escape a just retribution. The Ajati tell this story:

One day a child was born who was able to walk and talk at once. He ran out of the house to the farm of his father who was heaping up his yams. The man seeing the child exclaimed: 'Who are you?' and the child answered: 'I am your own son born to-day and my name is Antiakoti. (N.B. People have as a rule several names, one at least they select for themselves.) You are my father and are a farmer but I shall be chief of the village one day.'

Now it chanced that those words were overheard and reported to the chief, who began to fear such a wonderful child. But for some time he did nothing, until, his fear increasing, he summoned all the elders and consulted with them as to how he could best get rid of a child obviously possessed of much magic and who had openly threatened him.

They advised their chief to go to the Village of Ghosts (N.B. Twi and Moshi alike believe in the existence of ghost villages or towns of the departed), and there to consult with the departed, and promised to accompany him. Antiakoti overheard this and watched the old men. When he saw them all go off he changed himself into a bird of most beautiful plumage,[1] and taking with him some sand, an egg, and a white ant he flew away to the Village of Ghosts. The

[1] Cf. p. 20.

chief and his elders had already arrived and had persuaded the ghosts to kill the boy, when he flew among them. They all admired the bird and wondered what it was when it said: 'I am Antiakoti. I have heard all your plans and you are all bad people and not fit to be chiefs.' This made the chief and the elders and the ghosts very angry, so they called their dogs to catch the boy, who had changed back into his proper shape. But he ran away, and as he ran he threw down the sand, which grew and grew until all the country was sand, and the dogs could no longer run. Thus Antiakoti had some time to get a good start, but the dogs soon crossed the sand and then Antiakoti broke the egg which became a big river. He then crossed and waited for his pursuers. They were some time, and seeing the river was too large for them to cross they cut down a tree and began to make a canoe (dug-out). Then Antiakoti released the white ant, which multiplied itself enormously, and all the ants swarmed on the canoe and ate a large hole in it so that it would not float.

Then the chief forgave Antiakoti, but only for a while, for he called the elders together to decide how to kill the boy. They advised him to dig a big hole in his compound, to cover it with sticks, and to place on it a chair. The chief could then invite Antiakoti to his house, and when he sat on the chair he would fall into the hole, and if the women would prepare enough boiling water they could pour that upon the boy and so he would perish. But Antiakoti heard all this and he made friends with some rats who bored a hole from the chief's house to Antiakoti's.

When the day came the boy went to the chief, sat on the chair, and, while all the people laughed when they poured the boiling water into the hole, he escaped by the tunnel and sat down. Then indeed were the people very angry, and Antiakoti's father decided to send the boy away.

Next morning Antiakoti started on a long journey to see

K

a relation. At midday he came to a stream where a woman was washing her clothes. She had thirteen children with her, but too small to help her, and she had given them some palm-nuts to cook and a dead mouse to each one. Antiakoti saw this and told the children he would make very good oil for them if they would give him the nuts. They agreed, and he set to work, and as the children were looking at him he threw them into the boiling water and so killed them all. Then he took the corpses and placed on each of them a dead mouse.

But the woman came up from the river, and seeing her dead children began to lament when, noticing Antiakoti and knowing that he was the murderer, she got very angry and raced after him. At once Antiakoti changed himself into a civet cat, and ran in front of the woman. Presently he came to a silk cotton tree and climbed it. The woman sat down under it and made some food for herself. Antiakoti then amused himself by dropping chewed-up leaves into her soup. Looking up she saw the cat and at once went off to the village to tell a hunter. Antiakoti followed her, changed once more into his own shape.

The woman, however, had slipped into the bush, and when she saw the boy pass followed him quickly and quietly. Arrived in the village Antiakoti saw some people playing at 'wari',[1] and wishing to hide himself and at the same time to cause trouble changed himself into one of the 'wari' marbles. But the woman had seen this, so she stopped the game and said: 'I have lost one of my "wari" marbles. There is one too many here. If you count them you will see I speak the truth and you can give me mine.' Then it was found that the woman had spoken the truth, and they gave her the 'wari' marble, which she wrapped up in her waist cloth.

The woman went away from the 'wari' players out of the village in order to kill Antiakoti, but he changed himself

[1] *Vide supra*, p. 38.

into guinea-corn and fell out grain by grain from the woman's cloth on to the path. Unfortunately for him she saw it, and before he had completely fallen out she changed herself into a hen and ate up all the grains. Antiakoti had no more magic left and thus he died.[1]

The Dagomba even go so far as to praise lies and cunning for they tell how long ago there were two friends and one day they had a dispute. The one said that it was best always to tell the truth, but the other laughed at him and said that by telling the truth one would gain nothing and that only by lies could one grow wealthy.

They decided then to go for a journey and see which of them was right. The one who wished to tell the truth was given the first chance, and the two of them told nothing but the truth for a week. At the end of that time they had won nothing and had already lost their money.

It was then the turn of the deceit-loving man.

On the very first day of his week the travellers came to a large village. Every one was weeping there and they asked a passer-by what was the matter.

'Do you not know our chief is dead?' he replied.

Then the deceitful man said that that was nothing, and if they would pay him he would soon bring back their chief for them. The elders met and agreed to give him whatever he wanted if he did this, for they loved the dead man, who had been a good and just chief.

The deceitful one asked to see the body and he was told that it had already been buried for some days. So they led him to the grave and showed him the place. He ordered them to clear the earth away from the top and to expose the covering stone. They did this. He then told them to bring a bed mat. They brought it.

[1] In many respects this story of the Ajati resembles the legends of the Gow and Sorko, hunters and fishers, of the Songhai race. Cf. Dupuis-Yakouba, *Les Gow*, Paris, 1911, and Desplagnes, *Le Plateau Central-Nigérien*, Paris, 1907.

He then told them to go away while he made magic and said he would call them back when he was ready.

When every one was gone he went into the bush to a certain tree and caught a number of those black and white birds which make a noise like this. (Here the teller imitates the birds.) He then went a little farther and caught a dove.

He returned to the grave and covered himself and the birds with the mat and then sent for the people of the village. When all were come he told them that he would make the chief talk. He then shook the calabash in which he had put the black and white birds and they twittered. He then asked if the people recognized the voice. They answered at once that it was the voice of their old chief. He then shook the other calabash and the dove protested. He asked the people if they recognized the voice, and they answered that it was the voice of the chief before the last one. He then said:

'By my magic I have made the chiefs alive, and if you want them you must have them all.'

But the people called out at once 'No' and begged him not to release the chiefs, saying that it were better to try a new chief and leave the dead to rest than to call back many who had troubled them.

So the deceitful man agreed and he came out and helped the people to cover the stone again.

The elders thanked him and gave him a donkey and a cow and thirty thousand cowries.

On the following day the deceitful man and his friend went away and they first sent back the cow to their own village.

Soon they came to another village and there they lodged at the first compound they came to. It was owned by a rich man who treated them well. In the evening the deceitful man told his host that the donkey was a very valuable one, that every night it used to drop cowries instead of dung! He therefore begged to be allowed to sleep in the outer stable and not in the room the host had given him. The latter agreed to this, and at the first cock crow he came out to see the wonderful thing. There on the ground by the donkey were the cowries. And it was so on the second night.

Then the rich man was envious and wanted the donkey. He asked his guest if he would sell it, and after much disputing he agreed to give a cow and a donkey and forty thousand cowries.

The two friends decided to return home and took the donkey first to the chief of the village and gave it him, then with the cow and the cowries they set forth on the way back.

Now the following morning the rich man arose very early to see his good fortune. But he found nothing. The same happened the next day and he became very angry. He decided to follow the thieves and set out after them.

But the deceitful man knew this, and he told his wife that when she saw the stranger coming she was to bring water when he called for it and then to abuse him and curse him, and he would then show her something.

Having arranged this he took the rich man's cow and killed it and took the blood and put it into the cow's stomach. This he carried into his wife's hut and then went and sat down outside the house.

Presently he saw the rich man coming. He soon arrived, and after greeting his former guest asked him why he had so deceived him. The deceitful one began to make explanations. This angered the rich man, who began to shout and abuse him. Then the deceitful one said: 'Wait, let us first take some water and then we can talk of this matter.'

He then called to his wife: 'Woman, bring the stranger some water.' The woman did so, and having saluted the two men she turned on her husband and began to abuse him cursing his father and his mother. The deceitful one told her to go away and the woman ran to her room. Her husband followed her and quickly wrapping the woman in the cow's stomach and her own cloth he cut the stomach and the blood ran out into the compound.

The rich man was very upset: 'What,' he cried, 'do you kill your wife for nothing like this?' 'Oh, that is nothing,' said the deceitful one, 'it is a good lesson for her. In a short while I will bring her back to life. It is good for bad women to know what death is.'

Saying this he took a black pot and went into the bush and collected the bark of several trees. He then returned to the rich man and said: 'Do you see this? This is my magic medicine, and with it I shall bring the woman back to life.'

Saying this he went into the hut and told the woman to get up and go outside. She came out all covered with blood and her husband told her to go and wash herself.

The rich man marvelled at this and said that if the deceitful one would show him the medicine he would forget about the cowrie-laying donkey. To this the deceitful man agreed, and he took the rich man into the bush and showed him several trees and told him to take particular note of them and to mix them in the way he would show.

They returned to the compound and then the rich man departed for his home.

Arrived there he said nothing of his new knowledge but waited. One day there was a big rain and he thought that it would be a good thing to send his people out to make the farm. So he called every one and told them to go out. He then told his wife to make some flour, and when she had done this he told her to go to the field. She grew angry and asked him if she were a slave. Then he seized a knife and cut her throat.

All the people ran up to see what was the matter, and when they saw the dead woman they asked what she had done. The rich man told them, and added that after all it was nothing, and that he would easily restore the woman, after she had learned what death was.

They told him to be quick, and he took the barks of the trees and washed the woman. But nothing happened. He tried again, and then seeing that the woman was really dead he began to be afraid and ran away. But the young men ran after him and caught him in the bush and beat him to death.

Thus there was no one to know where the deceitful man was and he grew wealthy in his own village.

From this we learn that by cunning and deceit a man can grow rich and that truth is a foolish thing.

However, not always is guile triumphant, for the Dagomba also relate the following story of how retribution overtook two men of guile.

There was a certain young man and he fell in love with the daughter of the chief. The girl also loved the young man, and one day he asked her if she would agree to marry him. She replied that she would like to marry him but he must go and see her parents. But he was a poor man and it was no use going to see the mother of the girl empty-handed. But he had nothing.

He managed to collect two thousand cowries and took these to the girl. She thanked him but told him that he must try to get some rich present for the mother and the father.

This he could not do and the girl loved him no more, and the poor young man used to see her at the market-place giving pito [1] freely to the strangers who were passing from the south. One day he was particularly angry. A large number of strangers with their donkeys had come into the town with loads of kola. They were very thirsty and tired and the poor young man saw the girl go and give them all some pito. Now only a short time before when he had asked her for some of the beer she had refused to give it him and had pretended not to hear him. The strangers thanked the girl and took a large pot from the market-place and into this

[1] Beer brewed from millet.

pot each one of them put one kola. Thus her reward was
a rich one.

The poor young man did not know what to do. At last
he bethought him of an uncle who lived some distance away
and who was a rich man. So he went to see him, and he
begged him to lend him some sheep that he might go and
sell them and become rich. The uncle was pleased to do this
and gave the young man twelve sheep. When he had
received them the young man returned to his own village
and sold the sheep so that he had a large amount of cowries.
These he loaded on some donkeys and took the road to the
chief's house. Here he greeted the chief and gave him the
cowries. At the same time he brought some fowls and cowries for the mother of the girl. The chief was pleased and
gave the girl to the young man who took her away.

After a while the young man told his wife to get up and
follow him. She did this and they set out for the bush. When
they were far away he sat down and began to tell the girl all
that was in his heart, how he was angry with her at the way
she used to give strangers plenty of beer, how she used to
refuse to look at him, and all this because he was a poor man.
He ended his abuse by telling her that he was going to kill
her. He then slew the girl.

When he had done this he waited till night came. Then
he picked up the girl's body and tied it all around with old
cloth and set the bundle on his head. He began to follow the
road. After a while rain came, heavy rain, and the roads all
became rivers. While it was still raining he came to a village
where there lived one of his friends. He made his way there
and called out to his friend to come out and help him with
his load. The friend came out and helped to place the load
down in one of the rooms. He noticed that the load was
a very heavy one, but said nothing. The room was very dark
and the rain was falling so hard that no one could speak.

Presently the young man got up and went outside. He

did not return but went off to another village in the rain. Now when the house-owner saw that the young man, his friend, did not come back he looked at the load and wondered what was inside. He knew that his friend was a poor man and could not have much property. Soon he decided to open the load, and when he did so he found the corpse and it was all covered in blood.

He said nothing, but sat for a long while wondering what he could do, for he had recognized the girl as the chief's daughter. At last he fastened up the parcel, and taking his bows and arrows went out with the load to the bush. The rain was still falling and it was impossible to find or see the footprints of any one. So he went into the far bush and threw the body into the river and then returned home.

Time passed, and one market day he met his friend in the market, but they did not speak of the day when the rain fell. But they sat down and drank plenty of beer. They soon became drunk, and then they began to boast of their cunning, and one told how he had killed a girl and left the corpse with a friend, and the other related how he used the rain to hide his steps and then had gone into the bush and thrown the body into the river.

They laughed at their cunning, but their conversation had been overheard and the story was reported to the chief, who killed them both.

But perhaps the most famous and most frequently related stories in which cunning and deceit triumph are to be found in that group of tales which concern the doings of Anansi the Spider or Soamba, Brer Rabbit, which have in *Nights with Uncle Remus* and other tales from the West Indies or Southern States entered our own literature.

When the slave trade was in full swing by far the greater number of slaves imported into America and the West Indies came from the Guinea Coast, between the Ivory Coast and Nigeria. They were not coastal natives usually, but were brought down from the hinterland, from the grass country where the defenceless hare is extremely common. I have seen somewhere that the original of Brer Rabbit is the chevrotain, or water deer, a tiny animal very occasionally found in the forest zone. But as the animal in no way resembles a rabbit, and is not found in the slave-raiding zones, where the hare or rabbit is extremely common, there is no reason to look for a fictitious Brer Rabbit. It certainly seems unnecessary when the real animal is so common in the country whence the slaves came. But yet another point will convince most people. The whole idea in the Brer Rabbit stories is the defencelessness of that animal, which, since it is a hare and lives always in the open, obviously requires great cunning to account for its continued existence, whereas a chevrotain needs no such particular protection, any more than a duiker, for it lives in the thick forest and is almost an aquatic animal; moreover it is not over-common, and lastly, probably never comes into contact with the hyena, the prototype of Brer Fox, which is extremely rare in the forest zone, if not completely unknown, but which in the grass or slave zone is very common.

In all these Brer Rabbit stories the prevailing idea is the same—the triumph of guile over strength, the weak man over the powerful. Aeons of oppression by man and by Nature explain the pathos of this philosophy. It is not a high standard of moral teaching according to our idea, but probably to the proud Roman the doctrine of humility and submission of the Early Church was equally distasteful.

The Brer Rabbit of the grass country becomes the Spider Anansi of the Forest—hence the 'Annancy' Stories of the West Indies. The Ashanti tell how Adankon the Rabbit lost his heritage of tale-owner to Anansi the Spider in a duel of tale-telling where cunning met cunning and a kindly Nyame decided in favour of the Spider who henceforth should be the owner of all stories. That tale is perhaps yet another possible proof that the Twi people came from the grass country. It became necessary for the mothers to choose an animal familiar to their children, and so the rabbit gave place to the spider.

There is no need to recount here many of these Brer Rabbit tales, for they can be found in many a book, especially in the great collections of folk-lore from West Africa assembled by the French. All the old familiar tales are heard in Togoland: how the rabbit borrowed from the elephant and from the hippopotamus, how his two creditors pressed him for payment, how he fashioned himself a rope, how he told either that at the other end was his repayment, and how they tugged at each other till they were exhausted. And so on through the long list. Laughter and much rejoicing greet the success of guile; much more joy at the defeat, especially if it partake of bodily suffering, of the strong. This is why, I suppose, one laughs at Pantaloon when the red-hot poker touches him, and possibly accounts for our delight when the Police or the Government are 'scored off'. The inherited instincts from our ancestors for a moment are apparent.

But a type of Brer Rabbit story—I think of later growth— is also common. Here the listeners have grown weary of the eternal victory of guile, and guile has almost come to be stronger than the strong. Therefore the tales tell how Guile himself is conquered by the duller, heavily-moving Strong. Then by easy roads one reaches the tales where guile meets guile. Such a tale is the story of the *Hare and the Guinea-Fowl*.

In the old, old days Pugo, the guinea-fowl, had cleared the bush and made his farm. But Soamba the Hare heard of this and visited the farm. And he saw it was a fine farm. So he said it was his. And the guinea-fowl got very angry and a great quarrel arose. So they went to the chief.

Now the chief sent his messengers to see the farm and they asked the two where was the path to the farm. The hare showed them his road but the guinea-fowl could not, as he used to fly there. So the chief gave the farm to the hare.

Shortly afterwards the hare had business in Salaga. (N.B. To go to Salaga meant a long journey for the northern people and was the limit of such a journey southward, for Salaga was the great entrepôt of Twi and Moshi until both came under European dominion.) And the guinea-fowl heard of this and waited till the hare was near home on the journey back. He then went to meet him, greeted him as a long-lost friend, and offered to carry his load of merchandise for him. The hare, delighted at this kind offer and weary from the long journey, gave the guinea-fowl his load to carry. So they came back home. But the guinea-fowl refused to give up the load. They quarrelled and went again to the chief, who heard the case.

Both claimed the merchandise, and the chief knew not how to decide, when the guinea-fowl cried out 'Chief, here is the proof. My head is bald from carrying the load'. (N.B. Carriers after long journeys grow bald and the wild guinea-fowl differ from the domestic variety by having no comb.) Whereupon the chief gave the load to the guinea-fowl.

Not exactly a moral story according to our standard, but absolutely native.

So much for the Brer Rabbit tales. Those concerning other animals are similar, with always the same theme, namely, the eventual triumph of the weak. It must be remembered, however, that a child not only learns to be wily, but at the same time is thereby taught to think how to circumvent what seem insuperable difficulties and not to be discouraged by apparently overwhelming opposition.

Anansi or Soamba may possibly have originally, in many of the Brer Rabbit tales, been a real man, whilst in others use of the animals was purely allegorical. Perhaps this Dagomba story may contain traditional history:

In the old, old times there was a great chief. His town stretched all over the land and he had thousands of people. But there was a certain man of the town who declared one day publicly that he was a man of more power and magic than the chief. The latter heard of this and sent for the man and asked him if what he had heard was true. And the man answered that it was and that he did possess more sense than the chief.

Then the chief grew angry and told all his people that he would show this proud man that he was wrong and that he, the chief, had more magic than he.

For a week the chief thought what he should do. At last he decided to dig a deep well in his compound. So he called his young men and told them to make a well in the court-yard where the chief was wont to sit and hear cases. For a week the young men of the house set to work and dug a deep, deep well.

But the man heard of this and he too dug a deep, deep well in his house leading from his compound to the chief's.

When the chief saw that his own well was a deep one he was satisfied, and he ordered all the women to boil water the next day, to boil it properly and to have plenty.

Then in the morning he covered the well's mouth with a skin and placed on the skin a cushion. Then he sent for his rival, and when the latter had come he greeted him and pointing out the cushion told him to be seated so that they could try and see who was the cleverer. At once the man sat down and fell right through to the bottom of the well.

Quickly the chief called the women with the boiling water and told them to empty it down the well and so kill the man. When they had done this he told his young men to cover up the hole with earth. When all was done he sent a crier to call all the townspeople together.

In a short while every one was there and the chief told them that he had taught the proud man who was master and had buried him in the well. And the chief laughed.[1]

But one of the townspeople arose and said: 'Chief, I beg

[1] Cf. *supra*, p. 43, Edubiaku; p. 129, Antiakoti; *et infra*, p. 246.

you to forgive me, but are you sure that the man is dead?' and the chief answered that he had only just finished burying him. But the man persisted and said that even on his way coming he had seen the fellow outside his own compound.

The man was so sure that the chief said he would send a messenger to find out although he knew of a certainty that it could not be so.

The messenger left and came back with the news that he too had seen the fellow. So the chief sent for him and the man came. The chief asked him how it was that he was not dead and the man answered: 'Chief, did I not tell you that I possessed more sense than you? How then can you expect to kill me like this?'

Then the chief was very angry indeed. He dismissed the people and sat down to think. For a whole week he kept to his house and would allow no man near him. Then he sent a messenger to the boastful man, and when the fellow had come he said: 'I want you to go down to the large pond near my town and bring me back the medicine which lives in the middle.'

Now in that pond there dwelt a python of an immense size. It hated the sight of men, and whenever it saw a man or a woman or a child near the banks of the pond it would come out and at once catch the person and eat him.

The man knew this and thought how he should get over the difficulty. At last he decided what to do and went to see the chief and told him: 'To-day I shall go and get your medicine from the pond.'

The chief then gave him two men whom he had told beforehand to see what was done and to report to him.

When the three came near to the pond the man told the others to await him for a while and went into the grass. Hurriedly he raced to the pond and threw in a stone. At once the python raised its head and the man begged him saying, 'Master, the chief wants you.'

Then he ran back to the others who, when they saw the python coming, ran back to the town. The three managed to reach the chief's house just before the python, and the man told the chief that he had brought the medicine. The chief asked where it was and the man answered, 'Look'.

Now the python was very angry and had made its way straight to the chief's house, where it had twisted itself right round the compound so that no one could come out and had raised its head above the outer wall so as to look inside. It saw the chief and cried out: 'Here I am. You wanted me and I have come.' But the unfortunate chief swore he had not called him. But the python said that that was a lie, for he had just heard the conversation with the man. Then the chief begged the monster to return to its pond, but it refused to go and demanded three of the chief's children to eat.

Then indeed was the chief beside himself with worry. He did not know what to do and began wailing his ill-fortune. The noise he made caused several of his young men and women to come out, and as soon as ever the snake saw one he folded himself over him and carried him outside. Thus he took seven. This satisfied him, and he called out to the chief: 'I have taken seven of your people. You need not bother any more. Now I am returning to my pond, and the next time you want me remember I shall want payment.'

Saying this, the snake made off.

The chief shut himself up for many days and refused to show himself at all to the people. He was overcome with rage against the man who had twice circumvented him and more than ever was determined to ruin him. However, he did not dare to kill the fellow openly, but determined once more to resort to a ruse. To this end he kept apart thinking for seven days and at last was satisfied that he had hit on the right plan.

He called for six of his best soldiers and told them that he wished them to go out and hide themselves near the town and when they saw his favourite horse galloping towards them they were to shoot their arrows at it and its rider and kill them both. The men went off and laid themselves up in ambush. Meanwhile the chief sent for the man he hated and told him that he wished him to take his favourite horse and don his, the chief's, best apparel and to take the horse out of the town and then, when he had gone some way, to return home at full gallop so as to give the horse exercise and to amuse the chief. The man at once agreed and went and saddled the horse and put on the chief's best clothes. But as he came before the chief he said: 'Oh, Chief, the horse will not race back quickly if he goes out alone. Give me therefore another to ride and race with me.'

The chief saw that there was sense in this and called for his favourite son and told him to make ready to accompany the other and to take with him one of the small ponies. By this he made sure that the horse would be well ahead and that the waiting soldiers would make no error in their shooting.

The boy did as his father told him and the two rode together out of the town. When they had gone a long way the man said to the boy: 'Why has your father put this shame on you? Here are you the favourite son of the chief and yet you are going to race with me. You are dressed like a slave and I am clothed like a chief. I have the best horse in the kingdom and you are on a pack-pony. Tell me how you have angered your father.'

But the boy could not answer and then the man said: 'It is not meet that this should be. You are my master. Come, let us change horses and clothes.'

The boy agreed at once and they soon effected the transfer. Then the race began. At once the horse took the first place and came galloping towards the town. When it reached the ambush the soldiers arose and shot their arrows and killed both the horse and its rider.

Then the man arrived on the pony and went at once to

the chief's compound and reported his arrival. The chief did not know what to say or do, for he at once realized that the soldiers must have killed his favourite son as well as his favourite horse. And this he soon learned was true, for the men came in and told him that they had done what he had told them and as proof rolled on to the ground the head of the horse's rider.

For a long time there was silence. Every one was afraid, for the chief's grief was terrible to see. Then the man stood up and said: Oh, Chief, I see that you are determined that I shall die. You will never forgive me for this day and it would be foolish for me to await your vengeance. I know that it is useless for a poor man to fight against a chief, but I have shown you that a poor man may have more sense than a big chief. I do not want to go away from my country and my fathers. Therefore I shall change myself.'

Saying this he changed himself into the spider which everywhere is known as Anansi, and that is how Anansi, the cleverest of all men, became a spider and yet lives still in the houses of Man.

Chapter Seven

WHICH TELLS HOW ANANSI BECAME A SPIDER

WHO IS ANANSI?—HERO OR ANIMAL—INFLUENCE OF TWI
LITERATURE SPREADING—THE STORY OF THE DRESS THAT
SANG—TERROR OF SHAME—HOW ANANSI ASSUMED HIS
PRESENT FORM—GREED AND DISCOURTESY ARE MATTERS
TO BE ASHAMED OF.

FROM the preceding tales and the following ones it seems
that Anansi has become the hero of two totally different
types of narrative. In one set he would almost certainly seem
to be a name for some former hero or sovereign of these
negro people, and in the second type he assumes the character more of a spider or is more animal than human. I venture
to suggest that Anansi was either a hero or a name given to
represent the man-in-the-street or serf, and that eventually
owing to his name being the same, whether by design or
not does not matter, as that of the spider, the latter came
to represent in the animal world the insignificant beast
triumphing over the mighty.

This may, I think, account for the fact that in the tales
told by the northern tribes the poor man so often bests the
chief or king, who is of alien stock and cannot be deposed,
whilst in the stories related by the tribes influenced by the
Twi-speaking Ashanti, who are almost republican and have
chiefs who can be deposed, the weakling hero, Anansi,
defeats not the Omanhin or King but God himself. The
negro race has from time immemorial, with only here and
there occasional exceptions, been ever the downtrodden,
the slave, the under-dog. It might be expected therefore that
he would have had to devise some form of consolation,
some means of somehow defeating his superior. He could
only manage that for a short while; he could not remain for
ever master. Thus the poor man might momentarily

triumph; the chief must inevitably regain his chieftainship. It is the folk-lore *par excellence* for the individual who finds himself for ever up against odds too powerful for him to compete with, and therefore one finds that he must resort to some form of sharp practice or wiliness in order to gain the victory over his far stronger opponent.

This is much more apparent in the tales of the northern tribes than in those of the tribes whose form of government approximates that of the Ashanti or Fanti tribes. In these latter countries the King or Omanhin is a personage raised almost democratically to his high position. In his youth he plays with the sons of the generality of the town; his position is only that of a possible ruler; he will not in any case even inherit the divine right in which he can do no wrong. Moreover he is of the same race and tribe as his subjects; he rarely needs to use the ruthlessness of a tzar.

Among the northern tribes it is quite different. There the monarch in all the great states—in Dagomba, in Mamprussi, in Wala, and in Gonja—is an alien. He is in a similar position to that of Norman William in Saxon England; his sons and heirs do not mingle with the common herd; they do not toil in the fields or work in the smithy; theirs is the chase and the noble sport of war. If they do happen to find nothing to do it is easy for them to form robber bands to prey on the passing stranger or raid some village of the despised peasantry. Often in the past they have formed kingdoms of their own, carved them out as it were from the mass of savage tribes who have not yet risen to a form of government sufficiently advanced to resist a determined and united band. Thus it was that all the four great kingdoms of the Moshi were formed, and however deplorable one may consider despotism yet one must admit that through their firm government peace was established and maintained for centuries throughout the whole area of the Niger belt and was commented on in no uncertain tones by that great explorer Barth.

He had traversed most of Northern Nigeria, and when he touched on the borders of the Moshi kingdoms he expressed his greatest astonishment to find a land where there was every sign of a firm and kindly government; for the first time in all his travels he passed through a land where the peasant was to be seen in his fields unarmed and obviously confident that no man would dare disturb him.

The Northerners therefore in their stories will tell how the peasantry bettered the chief, while the southern worker will relate how he triumphed over his god.

As for the tales told about Anansi the Spider one finds in the north the same or similar tales told concerning the doings of the hare. In either case there has been chosen a common object to be seen almost daily, one that is so evidently insignificant in size and strength, one that is surrounded by scores of most powerful masters, and yet one that not only survives but actually seems to thrive. He apparently can only survive through guile and wiliness, for he is the most powerless of animals.

It is, however, to be noted that Soamba the Hare does not figure as Soamba in the stories told by the northerners concerning the triumphs of the serf over his chieftain. In this a great difference is to be noted, for Anansi, as I have pointed out, is the name for both the animal and the human hero in the folk-lore of the southerners.

Another remarkable fact is that Anansi as the hero of the animal stories is spreading northward from the Ashanti country. He is to a certain extent usurping the position of Soamba and is appearing as Patin'naraga in the Dagomba stories. The influence of the Ashanti has never yet been properly gauged. It would seem that he is now imposing his literature and literary style instead of his sovereignty over neighbouring people.

The opening up of the country by European occupation may to a large extent account for this, for the Dagomba and other northern tribes are now able without any fear of being enslaved or murdered to visit in safety the Ashanti and Fanti centres. Indeed, without the men of the north the Ashanti and Fanti to-day would be in a sorry plight, for not only the railroads but all the motor roads are constructed in the event by labour from the north, and at the same time the source of wealth, which is cocoa, depends almost entirely on the labour of the men from the north, who migrate southward each year for the various labouring seasons in their thousands in search of work.

The unexpected wealth that the cultivation of cocoa introduced into the favoured forest zones naturally caused the local native to turn more and more to clearing his forest and planting cocoa-orchards. Then came the time when the orchards became too large for him to handle. Labour had to be introduced, and the only people willing were those of the north. More recently the forest native, having devoted all his time and labour to cocoa cultivation, is now beginning to find himself almost foodless. This means that he has to make more clearings, and as he himself has all his time filled in his cocoa-orchard and other business matters relative to cocoa sales, &c., he must engage outside labour. And the only labour is that of the men from the northern parts outside the cocoa zone. He cannot engage local labour as all his friends and fellow villagers are in exactly the same position as he is. They have more orchards than they can, unaided, handle, and are running each year shorter and shorter of food farms. Thus the freemen of the north come down in their thousands and sojourn for a while in the Ashanti or Fanti villages.

This has been going on now for twenty years or more. It is inevitable that this returning labour brings back with it a store of folk-tales as well as money. All the easier is this since the tales are very similar and the method of thought is absolutely so.

But the influence of the Anansi devotees has been recognized for a much longer period. It has to a large extent coloured the tales told by tribes of such standing as the Hausa. How far this adoption of Anansi is real, and how far Anansi has been made the hero especially for European listeners—for all the negroes know we expect the spider to be the hero—cannot now be determined, but when one considers the natures of the two animals it would be difficult to imagine that Anansi would have been adopted spontaneously by the northerner.

In the Ashanti story of the human Anansi I have pointed out that it was God himself, Nyame or Wulbari, that he found himself pitted against. His animal opponent does not seem to have taken any particular form. Anansi was against all animals, and he had to score off them all in turn. But in the Hare stories of the north, Soamba or Brer Rabbit finds himself pitted against one foe in particular. This is the hyena, who is naturally enough translated into Brer Fox by the slaves of the Southern States, just as the English-speaking natives will interpret hyena 'fox' in West Africa to-day.

But the Ashanti or Twi-speakers in their tales always insist on the fact that once Anansi was a man. Indeed, I rather think that the native mind considers all the animals at one time to have had our outward shape and form just as they still think that all have our senses and faculties. Thus in the Krachi area the tales concerning Anansi and how he came by his present shape are many and of course almost identical with those told by their Ashanti brothers. The northern tribes do not insist on the fact that Soamba was a man, but they do tell many tales as to how he grew such long ears and how his tail came to be so stupidly small.

In a foregoing chapter the human Anansi has appeared in his role as right-hand man to Wulbari, the Captain of his Host. A connecting story has been devised to account for his changing into his present form of spider.

This is told by the Dagomba [1] concerning Patin'naraga, who is Anansi:

In the very old days there was a certain king who had amongst his other possessions a wonderful sheep. It was larger and taller than all other sheep and the king was very fond of it. And he gave orders that no man was to touch his sheep, no matter what it ate or where it went. If any one did touch it or hit it, that man should die.

Now Patin'naraga, whom the Ashanti people call Anansi, lived in that town and he knew of the orders of the king.

One day Patin'naraga made a large farm and planted therein a crop of guinea-corn. When the rains began to fall he went to see how the crop was getting on and he found that it was already as tall as his waist. For at that time you must know Patin'naraga was not small as he is to-day but as big as a man. He was very pleased and walked around the farm. Presently he came across a part where all the corn had been eaten, and there still eating it was the king's sheep.

Patin'naraga was very angry and threw a stone at the sheep. It was only a small stone, but it hit the sheep which fell down dead.

Patin'naraga did not know what to do. And while he was wondering how to get out of the mess a nut fell on his head from a shea-butter tree. He picked it up and ate the outside flesh. It was very nice, and when a second nut fell down Patin'naraga had an idea. He picked up the nut and put it in his pocket. Then he took up the dead sheep and carried it into the tree, where he hung it up.

Then he went away from his farm and came to the house of the big spider called Kusumbuli. He found his friend at home and made conversation with him. After a while he offered him the shea nut and his friend thanked him and asked where such fine nuts came from. Patin'naraga said

---

[1] Cf. the previous Dagomba story, p. 140 et seq.

he would show him, and together they went back to the shea-butter tree.

Patin'naraga then told his friend to climb the tree and shake down the nuts. Kusumbuli did so, and at the first shake shook down the dead sheep.

'Oh, my friend,' cried Patin'naraga, 'what have you done? Look, here is the sheep of the king and you have killed it.'

Kusumbuli was very much upset and asked for advice and was told that the only thing to do was to go straight to the king and tell him of the accident and to hope for the best. This Kusumbuli thought was good advice, so he picked up the dead sheep and started off for the king's house.

The road lay past Kusumbuli's house. So he told Patin'naraga that he would first go in and say good-bye to his wife as he did not know how the affair would turn out.

The two spiders went in and left the dead sheep outside. Patin'naraga stayed in the entrance hut while his friend went in to see the woman.

Now the woman at once saw that there was some trick in this matter, for she said to her husband that she had seen goats climb trees but never a sheep. She therefore gave him this advice: to go down the road to the king alone and leave Patin'naraga behind with her, that after he had gone some distance he was to rest and then return and report that all was well, and that the king far from being angry had actually given him, Kusumbuli, the meat of the sheep to eat.

Kusumbuli agreed to this and came out. He told Patin'-naraga that he would go on alone and that he would ask him as a favour that if anything came to him he, Patin'naraga, would look after the woman and children. Patin'naraga promised and his friend went off alone.

Shortly after he came back and asked Patin'naraga to rejoice with him as the king had not been angry but had actually given him the meat. At this Patin'naraga was very angry and shouted out: 'What! You have the meat, whilst it was I that killed the sheep.'

Then Kusumbuli and his wife seized Patin'naraga and said they would take him to the king. This they did, and when they came to the king's house they reported all that they knew of the affair whilst Patin'naraga threw himself on the ground and begged for his life.

The king was very angry indeed and kicked Patin'naraga as he lay on the ground. The kick was so hard that Patin'-naraga burst into a thousand pieces, and that is why to-day you will find a Patin'naraga in every house, and that is why he is now so much smaller than he used to be.

But the Krachi relate how Anansi and the Chameleon used to live in the same town. Anansi was a rich man and had plenty of children to help him with his farming, but the Chameleon was only a poor man and alone had to till his farm. Now it chanced that one year the rain fell only on the Chameleon's farm, and on Anansi's there was a complete drought. Thus the spider's farm did not come up at all and the Chameleon's was already well up and a good harvest promised.

This annoyed Anansi, and one day he called on the Chameleon and asked him if he would sell him his farm, but the Chameleon said he would not, as if he did he would not be able to get any food during the dry season. Then Anansi was even angrier than before and swore he would have revenge on the Chameleon.

Now it happens that chameleons do not make any roads as others do. They like to walk over the grass and bushes. Thus there was no path leading from the Chameleon's house to his farm. So that night Anansi called all his children together and told them to clean and make a good path from his compound to the Chameleon's farm. At first they begged their father not to do this, but as he insisted they obeyed him, and in the morning there was finished a clean road and a well-used one leading from Anansi's house to the farm.

Anansi at once went to the farm and began to pull up some cassada. Presently the Chameleon came along and saw Anansi taking his cassada and called out: 'Hi! Anansi, what are you doing in my farm?' Anansi at once replied: 'Go away and do not vex me. Can you not see that I am busy working in my farm?'

'Your farm,' cried the Chameleon; 'why, it is my farm, and every one knows that.' 'Do not be silly; go away,' answered the Spider, 'or I shall get angry and kill you.'

So the Chameleon went away and laid a complaint before the chief. Anansi was sent for, and when both had told him how the farm was theirs, the chief asked for proofs. Then Anansi said: 'That is easy. I have a path from my house straight to the farm, which the Chameleon is falsely claiming. He has no path.'

The chief saw that if Anansi was speaking true then verily the farm must be his. So he sent his messenger to see and the man came back and said that it was so. Then the Chameleon was asked what he had to say, and he said that he did not know anything about the path, that he always used to go there over the bushes and grass. This made the chief laugh, and he at once gave the farm to Anansi, who took all his children with him and gathered the crops.

The Chameleon did not know what to do. He was very poor and had but little food left to keep him alive. So he went to his house and shut the door and refused to see any one.

For many days he remained thus thinking over his wrongs and wondering how to get revenge. Then he began to dig a hole. He dug and dug and dug and made an immense well. It went far down. No man had ever seen such a well. When the Chameleon thought he had made it large enough he made some mud and began to roof the well so that soon only a very small hole was left.

Then the Chameleon went out to see Anansi. He came to the latter's house and greeted him: 'Master, I am only a poor man. May I go to your farm and glean what you have left there?' And Anansi was pleased at the Chameleon's humility and told him he could. But there was little in the farm to gather. Then the Chameleon, who had deceived the spider into thinking that he was properly humbled, again sat alone in his house. This time he amused himself in catching hundreds and hundreds of that great fly which makes so big a buzzing noise. These he tied to some dried yam vines which he had brought back from his farm.

One day the chief sent messengers to all the land to call his people together, and from every place people came into the town. Then the Chameleon arose and covered himself with the dried yam vines and walked slowly like a proud and rich man to the chief's compound, and as he went he kept swinging his strange costume and the flies being shaken buzzed. This was wonderful, and as he drew near the chief, swinging his dress, which buzzed more and more, every one admired it and the chief himself asked to buy it. But the Chameleon refused and went home. Now Anansi was late for the meeting, and when he did arrive every one was talking about this wonderful costume. The chief told Anansi that the Chameleon had refused to sell it, and Anansi said that that was nothing, and that he would buy it and would bring it to the chief.

He went and called on the Chameleon. 'Friend,' he said, 'I hear you have a most wonderful cloak, which wherever you walk sings to you. Is this so?' The Chameleon answered that it was so, and then Anansi asked him if he would sell it.

The Chameleon at first refused, but after a time did agree to sell it if Anansi would give him some food. Anansi asked how much food he would want, and the Chameleon said that he did not require a great deal, merely enough to fill the hole which Anansi himself could see. Then Anansi laughed and said that he would willingly do that, and to show that he bore him no grudge would give him twice as much.

Then Anansi went to his own house and called his children and told them to come with him and each to carry a little food. They all went to the Chameleon's house and began to fill the hole with the food they had brought. But that hole could not be filled. All the family of Anansi worked, and for many days they carried the corn and other food to fill that hole and always the Chameleon reminded Anansi that he had promised twice the amount.

Anansi did not know what to do. He had finished all the food that there had been stored in his own bins and granaries and he had sent out in all directions to buy food. But still the hole was not filled. He sold his sheep and his cows and everything that he had, for he knew that when he did get the cloak the chief would repay him. But he could not fill the hole.

Then when the Chameleon saw that Anansi was no longer a rich man and that he had no food left for himself he called him and said: 'Friend, you have not paid me the agreed-on price. But I am not a hard man and I will now forgive you the rest of the debt. Here is the cloak.'

Saying this he took out the cloak from its box and put it over the shoulders of Anansi.

But the cloak had been a long time in the box and the strings which held the flies were all rotted. This Anansi did not know, and when he went outside and began to swing the robe the flies all buzzed, but suddenly there came a strong blast of wind and shook the cloak too much. All the flies were released and flew away and left Anansi dressed only in the dried vine stalks of the yams.

Then all the town laughed, and Anansi grew so ashamed that he began to hide himself from that day away from the sight of man and does not walk in the streets.

Shame is ever one of the most detested things that can

happen to men. The natives all hate to be found out doing something discreditable which causes other men to laugh at them or to try to be too clever and fail. Often suicide will result, and more often a man will migrate to a country far from his own people. Not long ago I had a case of suicide to inquire into. The man had hanged himself after the other villagers had found out that he was in the habit of sleeping with his own daughter. The immorality of this was not so shameful as the fact that it was such an unnecessarily uninteresting thing to have done. He was afraid of the laughter rather than any payment he might have had to pay to an outraged earth-god.

How Anansi came to assume his present form is the theme of many a tale. The Krachi explain that Anansi was always boasting of his knowledge and sense, and at last Nyame decided to teach him a lesson in modesty. To that end he sent for Anansi and told him to come and see him the next day as he had some important matter to show him.

The following day Anansi started from his house to visit Nyame. But the latter had made the Sun very hot indeed and Anansi was unable to walk along the road. So he put on his sandals, but Nyame then made a bush fire and Anansi began to burn. He ran up a tree, but that was no good, and then seeing that the fire was going towards his home he raced off and managed only to reach the house in time to save his pillow. All his wealth had gone, but Anansi said that that did not matter so long as he had his pillow. Nyame agreed to that, and that is why the Spider has only his pillow for all property to this day. That is the white nest we see on the walls of the house.

A Dagomba story accounts for the shortness of his neck in this way: They say that in the olden times the elephant was a boastful person. He was lord of the bush and had a very fine cow. Of this cow he was very proud, and he called all the animals together one day to see the cow. They all

came and admired it. And the elephant, boasting, said:
'I will give this cow to any one of you who will allow me to
give him one, only one blow.' But no one dared.

However Anansi heard this, and being very hungry said:
'O Lord of the Bush, I will take your cow and you may give
me one blow.'

So the elephant gave Anansi the cow and said that on the
following Friday he would come and give him the blow.
And Anansi then went home with his cow and killed it and
gave the meat to his wife and children.

But when Friday came Anansi remembered the promise
of the elephant and was afraid. He did not know what to do.
But at last he called his wife and told her that if any one were
to come to see him she would have to say that he had gone
to his farm. Meanwhile she was to get a ground-nut and
take out the nuts. When she had done this Anansi climbed
into the shell, and he told his wife to cover him up with
the rest of the shell and to throw him outside. This she did,
and threw him away into a corner of the yard where a fowl
at once ate the shell with Anansi inside.

Soon after the elephant arrived and asked the good wife
where her husband Anansi was. She told him that he had
gone to his farm, but the elephant refused to believe this and
grew angry: 'Fetch me', he cried, 'the bakologo man,[1] the
revealer of hidden matters.'

Trembling, the woman sent one of the children to fetch
the man, who happened to live not far off. He soon came,
and the elephant told him that he wanted to find out where
Anansi had hidden himself. Bakologo set out his mysteries
and soon learned that Anansi was inside the ground-nut shell
inside the fowl.

[1] This is a northern word for a man who by magic reveals to his client
the reason for things. Krachi, although of a culture akin to that of the Ashanti,
has so long been in touch, chiefly through their slaves, with northern customs that it has adopted this form of divination. Among the Dagomba
its practice is universal and imperative on every occasion.

The elephant at once seized the bird and killed it. He found the ground-nut inside the crop and breaking it took out Anansi. The latter was sore afraid and began to beg for his life, for he well knew that if the elephant were to give him one blow he would perish.

The elephant at last agreed to listen and asked why Anansi had deceived him. The wretched spider explained how he had been hungry and had wanted to get the cow to eat and had hoped to escape by his wits from the promised blow.

Then the elephant was sorry for Anansi and said that he would not give him a hard blow, but would give him twelve taps, and would come on the following Friday to give the second. At that he gave Anansi a tap. But the tap of an elephant is no small matter, and this one was so hard that it drove Anansi's head down into his shoulders, so that to this day he has no neck.

When the following Friday drew near Anansi was in a great fix. He did not know how to escape the elephant, but decided again to risk the ground-nut hiding place. He then called his wife on the Monday morning and told her that he expected the elephant again on Friday, but that he was afraid, and she was to tell him that he, Anansi, had gone right away. He then got inside the shell of a ground-nut and told his wife to throw him this time far away.

The woman picked up her husband and threw him well away into the bush. But again a fowl found him and ate him. That night a civet cat came to the fowl house and ate the fowl, but in the morning a dog came along and saw the civet cat, which he ate. In the night a hyena found the dog and ate him too. But as the hyena was returning home a lion came along and ate him. Then the lion went down to the riverside to take a drink and as he leant over the water a python swallowed the lion.

On the Friday morning the elephant presented himself at

the door of Anansi's house and asked where the spider was. Anansi's wife answered as she had been bidden, that he had gone right away and that she did not know when he would return. The elephant was really very angry this time and shouted for the Bakologo man. The latter had heard the noise and had hastened up with his magic bag. The elephant at once told him what he wanted and the Bakologo man said that he would surely be able to find out where Anansi had hidden himself, and at once set himself down to discover the place with his magic. He soon learned where the spider had gone and told the elephant to follow him. They went down to the riverside and the Bakologo man showed the elephant the python and told him to kill it, and the elephant did so and found the lion inside the stomach of the python. He cut the lion open and found the hyena; he cut the hyena open and found the dog; he cut the dog open and found the cat; he cut the cat open and found the fowl; he cut the fowl open and found the ground-nut; and inside he found Anansi.

The elephant then said that now he would of a truth give Anansi a blow. 'Do you think that I, an elephant, Lord of all this Bush, should go about following a Bakologo man? What have you got to say for youself before I give you the blow?'

But Anansi had nothing to say. He begged the elephant for his life, but the elephant would not listen. Then Anansi was afraid and begged harder. The elephant, who was not a bad animal, asked Anansi if he had any friends at all who would come and speak for him. But Anansi said he had none excepting the little Red Duiker, Bambua.

So the elephant called Bambua to come. And when the Duiker arrived Anansi asked him to beg for him. But Bambua replied that this he could not do, for the trouble had come to Anansi from his own acts, that he deserved to die for his deceit, and that in any case why should he,

Bambua, support him, for Anansi had not given him even a small piece of the cow's meat.

By this time the anger of the elephant had cooled and he began to be sorry for the spider, who was so miserable a being. So he said that he would do nothing and gave him a kick, saying: 'Get out, you are too wretched for me to bother about.'

But the kick of an elephant is no small matter, and Anansi was hurled against a tree, and that is why he is now quite flat, for in those days he was much fatter.

And the elephant turned to the Duiker and said: 'You have spoken with sense and justice. I am master of the bush and I will make you second to me. You are only a small weak animal but you shall have much magic and all men will fear you as they fear me.'

And that is why Bambua the Red Duiker is feared by all hunters.

Another story of how Anansi came by his shyness is told by the Dagomba, and once again the horror of feeling ashamed is apparent.

In the very old days Anansi and his family used to live in the same compound as a hunter and his family. They were firm friends and neither interfered at all with the work of the other.

Now it happened that hard times came to the household and food was very scarce. The hunter in vain went to the bush; he could find no meat, and day after day he returned empty-handed. Anansi had no better luck, and all the grain in the house was finished.

Then the hunter said that he would go into the far, far bush and try once more his luck. So he fared forth and went a great way into the bush, where he had never been before. But of meat he saw none. At length he grew weary and was forced to rest. A large tree gave him shade and he slept there through the heat of the day.

M

Suddenly he was awakened by the sound of something falling, and he looked around and saw on the ground a small sheepskin such as are used by children to sleep upon. But the hunter did not move. He just watched. Then he saw fall from the tree a tiny pillow, which came to rest on the sheepskin. Then there came down from the tree a little, little man, whom the hunter at once recognized as a chichiriga or Kulparga.

The dwarf saw the hunter and greeted him and asked him if he had by any chance any food on him as he, the dwarf, was very hungry. The hunter explained that he had but little; however, he would share what he had. They then both sat down together and made a meal. When it was finished the chichiriga asked the hunter to lift him up and carry him down to the river as he was thirsty.

The hunter agreed to this and placed the little fellow on his shoulder. Then they went down to the riverside, where the hunter put the dwarf down.

Having finished drinking the dwarf said to the hunter: 'Do you like fish?' To this the hunter replied that he did, but that he had no means of catching them. Then the chichiriga said: 'I have a mouth which can swallow all the water that is in this river, and when it is quite dry you can throw on the bank all that you require.'

Immediately the chichiriga opened his mouth and swallowed all the water so that the river-bed was quite dry. The sand was all covered with fish and crocodiles and hippopotamuses. And the hunter ran into the middle and began to throw out on to the bank all the fish he thought he and his family might require.

When he had thrown out an immense number the chichiriga called to him to be quick as he could no longer hold the water. The man came out of the river and the dwarf opened his mouth and all the water flowed back again into the river.

Then the hunter picked up the chichiriga and carried him back to the tree and thanked him. The latter said that he would always remember the hunter's kindness, and if at any time the hunter was in need of food he need only come to the tree and he, the chichiriga, would help him again.

Then the hunter returned to the river and picked up as many of the fish as he could and went home, where he collected his family, and they all went and brought in the rest of the fish.

The next day Anansi noticed the vast quantity of fish and asked his friend how he had come by so many fine fish. The hunter replied that if one goes to the bush one will often there see wonderful things, and that he had been given the fish in a wonderful way. Then Anansi, who was always quick-tempered, grew angry and abused his friend, and asked him why he, a mere hunter, had not come to him, Anansi, whom every one knew to be a great fisherman, and so they would have been able to have brought home even more fish than had already been done.

To appease Anansi the hunter agreed to take him into the bush and show him the wonders which he had seen there. So in a few days, when all the fish were eaten, the two departed for the far, far bush. The hunter looked everywhere for some meat to kill but only managed to get a small duiker. They carried this to the big tree and sat down.

While they were cooking the meat the skin fell down just as before, but the hunter took no notice. Anansi on the other hand jumped up in fear and cried out: 'What is that?' He was scarcely reassured by his friend than there fell down the pillow. Anansi was thoroughly alarmed, but his friend quieted him, and then the chichiriga himself came down the tree. Now Anansi, seeing only a dwarf, became very insolent to the stranger, and when the latter asked for some of the meat they were preparing refused to give any. It was the hunter who calmed matters and gave the chichiriga some of the meat.

M 2

When the meal was over the chichiriga asked the hunter why he had come again so soon, and the man replied that his family was a large one and that all the food was finished and that he had remembered the promise given him by the chichiriga and so he had come with his friend Anansi.

The chichiriga said that as Anansi was the hunter's friend he would overlook his discourtesy and that he would give the hunter as much fish as he could carry. So they went down to the river, the hunter carrying as before the chichiriga. Anansi laughed at this and said that any way he was not a slave to carry misshapen dwarfs.

When they reached the river they quenched their thirst and the chichiriga swallowed all the water. Anansi was astounded, but when he saw there the large crocodiles and hippopotamuses he neglected the fish and threw on to the bank all the meat he could see.

But the hunter collected the fish.

After a while the chichiriga said that he could no longer hold the water and the two came out on to the bank and the water flowed back into the river from the mouth of the chichiriga. Then the hunter thanked the dwarf and carried him back to his tree. But Anansi stayed with his meat.

And while the hunter was away Anansi made plenty of rope to tie up his meat. But as soon as the former returned the crocodiles and hippopotamuses got up and returned to the river. The fish, however, remained. Then Anansi was very sorry, and he knew that he had done wrong in being so discourteous to the chichiriga. So that when he came back home empty-handed whilst his friend had abundance he was so ashamed that he withdrew into the dark places of the house, and that is why to this day Anansi always hides himself and keeps in the corners and holes and behind skins and things in the houses of his friend, Man.

Chapter Eight

WHEREIN WE LEARN THAT THE SIMPLEST OF THINGS MAY HAVE THE MOST ELABORATE OF CAUSES

THE WONDER-CHILD'S WISDOM—HOW BLINDNESS CAME—
'JUST-SO' STORIES—ANANSI AND THE SPOKESMAN OF GOD—
MASON WASPS AND HUNTERS—AN UNFORTUNATE MOTHER—
THE GOAT LEAVES THE BUSH—DOGS COME TO MAN—
CUMULATIVE STORIES.

PERHAPS no story illustrates better than the following one how the natives wrap up a simple fact in the most elaborate of garbs which seem not only unnecessary but almost incomprehensible to us. It was communicated to me by Mr. Tamakloe and is a Dagomba yarn.

In the olden days a certain man had a cow. He informed the world at large that he would give this cow to the person who would give him three extraordinary answers. ('Sayings' is the word used.) For a long time no one was able to satisfy him, but one day he chanced to arrive in the courtyard of a house where a woman had just given birth to a baby. She had laid it down on her couch and had gone to get some water whilst the father had gone to his fields. The man therefore was able to find no one at home. So he called out: 'Is there any one here?' The baby heard the call and turning himself into a boy came out and asked what he could do for the stranger. The man replied that he wanted some water to drink and the boy re-entered the house. There he lay down again on the couch.

The man waited for long enough and at last called out: 'Is there no woman in the house?' The baby at once got up and came to the man and said that he had been delayed because owing to his mother and the other wife of his father having had a quarrel their water had got mixed together and he was sorting it out.

Then the man exclaimed: 'Here of a truth is one extra-ordinary saying.'

Shortly after, he told the boy to go and get him some glowing embers so that he could light his pipe. The child arose and went into the house, where he again lay down on the couch and waited.

Presently the man called out to know where he had got to. The boy at once returned, and when he was asked why he had been so long he replied that owing to the quarrel between the two women their fires had all got mixed and he had been trying to sort them out.

Then the man exclaimed: 'Here of a truth I have heard a second extraordinary saying.'

Shortly after the man asked the boy where his father had gone to and the boy replied that he had gone to his fields. Then the stranger told the boy to go and fetch the man as he wished to speak to him. The boy at once went out of the compound and climbing the wall regained the room where he had been born and resumed his lying down on the couch. The stranger waited and waited. At length his patience began to give out and he began to shout and call for the boy. The latter did not move for some time, but at last he got up and, climbing over the wall, returned through the main gate of the house, panting and breathless as if he had been running from afar. The stranger asked him where he had been and if his father was coming, and the boy replied that while he was going to the fields where his father was at work the road had broken in half like a bit of string. He had tried to join it again when he heard the calls and had run back to see what was the matter.

Then the stranger exclaimed: 'Here of a truth is the third of the extraordinary answers.'

So he called the boy and gave him the cow he had announced to the world at large that he would give to whomsoever would tell him three wonderful sayings. He then went away.

The boy looked at the cow and decided that the best thing he could do with it was to take it to his grandfather's house, where he knew there was a bull, and then when he had grown up he would be able to claim it and the herd which would by then be its offspring. So he went out and drove the cow to his grandfather's and then returned to his house and lay down on the couch, where his mother returning from the watering-place found him.

In due course the babe grew up to be a youth, and one day returning from the fields with his father he asked the latter if they might pass by the way of his grandfather's as he wished to collect his cattle.

The father was astounded and said the boy was a liar, for how could he have got any cattle. Then his son told him all that had happened on the day he was born and how he had obtained the cow. So the father consented to go along to the grandfather's compound, where the boy asked for his cattle.

Now the grandfather selected all the best of the young stock and said that they had been born from the bull and gave the others together with the old cow to the boy. The latter said nothing, but drove off the animals which had been given him. After he had gone some way down the road with his father he stopped and said that he would go back for the rest of the herd out of which his grandfather had cheated him. The father he bade stop on the road with the cow and the other cattle.

Then the boy took a calabash and returned to his grandfather's house. There he met the old man, who asked him what he wanted, and the boy replied that his father had just had a baby on the roadside and he wanted some water to wash him with. The old man grew very angry and said: 'What do you mean by this lie? You are making a fool of me. Whoever heard of a man having a baby?' To which the boy replied that if his grandfather's bull had been able to have calves then there was no reason why a man should not have a baby.

This answer pleased the old man, who said that his grandson was wiser than he and therefore he would no longer try and keep the calves which belonged to the youngster. So he gave the rest of the herd and the boy drove them off.

He soon reached the place where he had left his father and there to his horror he found that the old cow had gored his parent to death. He began to weep and cry, and then as the sun was setting he asked the sun to tarry awhile in the sky as he wished to bury his father. But the sun refused and went to rest. Presently the moon arose, and the boy begged it to stop in its course so that he might bury his father. The moon consented, and the boy dug the grave, and after burying his father slew the old cow and placed its meat on the newly-fashioned mound in sacrifice to his parent's spirit. He then went home.

In the morning he arose and went early to the place where he had left his parent. There he found the sun sitting on top of the grave eating the meat which he had left for his father. He approached stealthily and caught the sun and placed it in his bag. (N.B. All these northern people carry a leather bag with them. It is made from goat hide and is slung across the shoulder.)

The sun thus imprisoned was unable to appear next morning so that there was no daylight. For three days matters remained thus. No sun appeared at all. The elders of the country were much distressed at this and decided to see their king about the affair if he could devise some way out. Accordingly they all repaired to the king's compound and with them went the boy.

After every one had spoken and made suggestions as to how to get the sun back the boy wished to speak. But he was refused a hearing and told not to meddle in men's affairs. However, the eldest wife of the king rose and told them that they should listen as after all the boy could do no harm.

He then related how the sun had come to disappear and all the troubles and adventures he had been through. The king asked him, moreover, to allow the sun to go free, and the boy agreed but first he warned the people gathered there to shut their eyes as otherwise they would be blinded by the brightness of the sun when he released him. Some of the people closed their eyes, but others only closed one whilst still others merely put their hands in front of their faces and gazed through their fingers. The sun was released, and so brilliant was his light that all those who saw him were blinded, those looking through their fingers in both eyes and those who closed one eye blinded in one eye.

Thus blindness came to the world.

A very similar story of how blindness came is related above (*vide* p. 21). It is a common theme amongst story-tellers, for blindness is one of the most common of ailments in the country and naturally one of the most dreaded. The Krachi relate the following to account for the frequency with which this unfortunate infliction is encountered.

There was a certain old woman who was blind. She had been born so, but always she longed to have eyesight and to see the world. Her home was under the shelter of a tall shady tree. Now one day there flew along the eagle called Abroma. He saw the tree and thought it a most suitable one for his home. He therefore asked the old woman if she would mind if he made his nest there. She replied that he could do so and asked if he could manage to give her her eyesight. He said that he could, but that if he did do so she and all hers were to be good to eagles and never kill them. To this she agreed, and not only was she able straightway to see, but she found herself rich beyond her dreams with a fine village and hundreds of children. The tree stood as it had stood before and became the village shade tree where the children could play in the daytime and where the elders could meet and discuss matters in the evening.

One day some of the children noticed the nest of Abroma and saw that there were several young eaglets there. They were very anxious to see the young birds nearer, and though their mother had often warned them to leave Abroma and his family alone, they decided to get the young birds. They therefore cut down the tree, and when the giant fell down the nest fell as well and the eaglets were killed. At that moment the father eagle came back. He saw what had happened and at once withdrew the medicine he had given the old woman.

Away went the children and away went the village. Blindness fell once more on the old woman. Even then the eagle's anger was not appeased and he cut the old one up into a thousand thousand pieces and scattered them all over the world. Thus it is that so many people are blind, for those who are unfortunate enough to pick up a piece when they collect their medicine become blind for all time.

All the natives are fond of listening to and repeating stories classified by Mr. Kipling as 'Just-So' stories, and in their mass of tales these figure to a vast extent. One could without difficulty fill many volumes with them, but the following will suffice to illustrate the type and show the great simplicity of the native mind. At the same time the power of imagination seems pretty lively and the power of ingenuity extreme.

A Krachi tale tells how Nyame in the olden time had a cow. It was a wonderful cow of an immense size, and Nyame was very proud of this cow. He had told every one that this cow was to be kept until the time came when his mother-in-law should die and that then he would sacrifice it to her. But Anansi heard this and he wanted badly to eat the cow himself. So he repaired one day to Nyame's house and after some talk mentioned the cow, and Nyame explained what he intended to do with it. Then Anansi said:

'Nyame, you have no respect for your mother-in-law.
A cow is only a common thing and yet you want to offer it
to her when she dies. That is wrong. Only a man would
suffice, and you had better think the matter over.'

Nyame was ashamed then and said that Anansi was right,
but that he did not know where to find a man to sacrifice.
Anansi at once offered himself [1] on the condition that Nyame
would give him the cow. Nyame agreed, and Anansi went
away with the cow which he at once killed and ate.

Then Anansi began to realize that he had done a foolish
thing and that Nyame would certainly ask for full payment
when the old woman died. He therefore made his sons dig
a great hole leading to Nyame's house and then covered the
entrance. The hole led right up the yard where Nyame was
wont to hear complaints and other matters, but it did not
pierce the surface.

Shortly after the old woman died and the news came to
Anansi. Quickly he ordered his sons to go down the hole and
to take with them his talking drums. He had told them what
to do. Then came the messengers from Nyame and took
him away to Nyame's house.

Nyame greeted him and told him the news and that he was
now about to take the promised payment. At once the man
who did the killing came forward and seized Anansi, who
began to cry out. At the same time there sounded the drums,
and every one was astonished and asked what they were
saying. And Nyame heard them and knew what they sang—
how that Anansi was about to die but that he would not
die alone, for as soon as he was dead Nyame's wife would
die and accompany him, and then Nyame's son would follow,
and last of all Nyame himself.

This made Nyame afraid, and he called to his counsellors
and asked if they too had heard the message of the drums.

[1] A common enough practice formerly. Such men were known as 'King's
souls'.

And they begged him and told him that they had heard. Then Nyame sent for Esono the Elephant who knew all about drumming and asked him to interpret the words of the drums. And the elephant interpreted. He said they sang that when Anansi died much sorrow would come to Nyame and that all would follow Anansi to the grave, even Nyame himself.

Then Nyame released Anansi from his promise and the latter ran back to his house and called to his sons to come back with the drums. Just as they were coming out of the hole Cotere the House Lizard, who was the linguist to Nyame, came in and saw the deceit which had been practised. He was very angry and said he would go back at once and report to Nyame. But Anansi begged hard for his life.

It was of no use, however; and when he had promised to go back to Nyame and tell all if the lizard would let him have one night more to allow him to make a big dance for his own funeral custom, the linguist agreed and sat down to watch the spider.

Anansi himself made great preparations. He sent his wife out to get food and drink. He made his children clean up the yard and then began to make himself ready in his best clothes. All this time the lizard sat quietly in the yard. Then Anansi said to him: 'Friend, this is my last night. You must rejoice with me. Let me help you to make ready.' And the lizard agreed, and then Anansi told him to open his mouth so that he could clean his teeth for him and scrape his tongue. The lizard agreed and immediately Anansi cut off his tongue.

Then the lizard ran back to Nyame to tell him all that he knew but he found he could not speak. All he could do was to nod his head. He still nods his head to this day.

And this story will tell how the Mason Wasp came by his waist:

There was a certain hunter named Wainyare. He used to

go every day into the bush and bring back meat for himself
and his wife. One day the woman said to him that she was
tired of having always the same meat and told him to go out
and kill some animal which she had never before tasted.

Wainyare wanted to please her and went forth, but he
could find no new animal. He hunted everywhere and
searched far and wide, but still he could not see this new meat.
But one day he did see a large antelope which he had never
seen before and whose name he did not know. He hunted
it very carefully and managed to come near enough to shoot.
But, alas, the bullets did not kill the animal, but merely
wounded it in a part that was very painful to it.

Immediately the animal turned on Wainyare and chased
him home. His wife called out to him and asked why he was
running so fast and the man replied he could not stop as her
new meat was after him and was very angry.

Presently in his flight he came to a place where some young
men were roofing a hut. He called to them to give him
shelter in the thatch and they agreed. Presently the animal
came up and asked the men if they had seen the hunter. At
first they replied that they had not, but when the antelope
explained that he did not mean them any harm but merely
wished to catch Wainyare, who had wounded him in a very
tender spot, they told him where the man had hidden.

Wainyare heard all this and escaped just in time. He ran
faster than ever and the antelope came after him. At last
Wainyare could run no more, but by good fortune he reached
the house of a mason wasp.

'Wasp,' he cried, 'help me. I am being chased by an
angry antelope which I have wounded. If you will hide me
in one of your cells I will always give you and your children
shelter in my house.'

The wasp agreed and quickly sealed the man up in one of
his cells. Just then the antelope arrived and asked the wasp
if he had seen the hunter. The wasp said he had, and the

antelope asked him to give the man up as he had for no reason done him an evil thing. But the wasp refused and then the antelope said: 'You and I have no quarrel, but if you take on the troubles of this man then you and I will have to fight.'

The wasp refused to give up the man and they began to fight. And the antelope swallowed the wasp whole. But as the wasp was only a small thing it soon escaped from the body of the antelope and then tried to swallow the antelope. When the antelope was right down inside the stomach of the wasp, the latter cried out to the man to come quickly out of the cell and get some string. This the man did, and obeying the orders of the wasp he set to work and tied up the waist of the wasp so that the antelope could not escape.

That is why the mason wasp has so narrow a waist and why hunters never destroy the cells of these wasps.

The above story can be compared with the following 'Just-So' story which was communicated to me by Mr. Tamakloe and is of Dagomba origin. It seems to me to show signs of having once been a sort of cumulative story to account for all the animals in the bush behaving as they do, each in its own peculiar fashion, but only the three cases herein related were sent me. At the same time to us an explanation is required as to why the old woman should have been so badly treated. Her annoyance at being called a witch is understandable when one remembers that all these natives are extremely sensitive on certain points. One can abuse them to almost any extent, but there are certain epithets that must never be used. One of these is undoubtedly that of 'witch'. The memory of the not distant days when witches were cruelly killed is naturally still quite green; the belief in their existence and the awful evil that they make and do is almost without exception as strong as ever.

The story runs that once upon a time there lived a certain old woman in the same house as her daughter. One day the latter wished to go down to the waterside to fetch some water. She called her mother and asked her to sweep out the compound whilst she was away and then set out.

On her return the girl asked her mother to help her to take the calabash of water off her head. The old woman made no reply so the girl said angrily, 'Help me with the calabash, you old witch.'

This epithet so enraged the old woman that she threw down her broom with which she had been sweeping out the yard and it changed immediately into a black horse. The girl, in no way dismayed, threw the calabash from off her head. It broke into a hundred pieces, and out of the fragments there arose a white horse.

Frightened at her mother's anger the girl mounted at once her white steed and sped away into the bush, her mother on the black horse in hot pursuit.

Galloping thus the old lady kept time to her horse's hoofs, singing for all the world to hear:

'My father and mother gave me birth.
They never called me a witch.
And I, I have born me a child
Who this day has called me witch.
Oh ye evil rocks and stones,
Oh ye evil roots and branches,
Ye that lie athwart my path,
Give me free unhindered passage,
That I may learn why mine own calleth me a witch.'

This somewhat pathetic song had no effect on the girl, who fled faster and faster until at last she met an elephant who asked her: 'Whither fleest thou so fast?' The girl replied, and the elephant made her sit down, saying that he would save her.

Presently the mother drew near and the words of her song came down the breeze to the elephant, who exclaimed:

'Alas! this matter is beyond my power. It is no affair of mine; go you your way and I shall go mine.'

Saying this he fled into the bush, uprooting all the trees and bushes that were in his path. That is why to this day all elephants pull up the trees and bushes for no reason at all.

But the daughter fled on and on, always with her mother not far behind. Soon she came to a lion, who asked from whom she fled. The maiden made reply: 'You cannot save me from the direful thing that follows.' But the lion told her not to fear, that he would take care of her. Hardly had he spoken than he heard the words of the pursuing mother:

' My father and mother gave me birth.
They never called me a witch,
And I, I have born me a child,
Who this day has called me witch.
Oh ye evil rocks and stones,
Oh ye evil roots and branches,
Ye that lie athwart my path,
Give me free unhindered passage,
That I may learn why mine own calleth me a witch.'

At once he cried that this was no affair of his, and telling the girl to make off in her own direction he betook himself as fast as he could into the remote bush where he still lives to this day.

The girl raced on on her white steed. She galloped and fled until she came to the home of the great hornet that weaves its cells on every roof. He called to her to stay her course, but she called back that he could do nothing against the dreadful thing that pursued her. However he made answer that she should rest and that he would save her. So she stopped her flight and sat down by his side.

Presently her mother appeared still singing:

'My father and mother gave me birth,
They never called me a witch,

And I, I have born me a child,
Who this day has called me witch.
Oh ye evil rocks and stones,
Oh ye evil roots and branches,
Ye that lie athwart my path,
Give me free unhindered passage,
That I may learn why mine own calleth me a witch.'

The girl got up to try and escape, but the wasp told her not to fear but to sit down again.

Then the old lady arrived and a mighty fight began between her and the wasp. At last she swallowed him whole. In vain. He merely passed right through her. Moreover he countered her move by swallowing her, and before she had time to do anything called to his sons to come quickly and tie him up tightly by the waist. They did this, and the old lady was unable to move backward or forward. Indeed she has had to remain there ever since, and that is why we see the hornet with a swollen forward and an equally swollen afterward. Moreover, as the old lady had gone in head first her sharp tongue has become that snappy thing we know as the sting.

A simpler story from the Dagomba, who as a rule seem to tell longer tales than their southern neighbours, the Krachi, is as follows.

There was once a female goat. She had ten children and they all lived in the same house. But one day a hyena came that way and saw the goats. Every night he came and killed one, and at last there was only left the mother goat. She was afraid and left the house and went out into the bush. There she gathered some honey and put it into a calabash which she carried by her side. While she was wandering about a lion came along and asked her what she was doing. She told him all her troubles, and he said he would certainly kill the hyena for her but that he was suffering for more than forty days from terrible toothache. The goat then replied that she knew of a very good cure for that sickness and told the lion to follow.

She led him straight to the house of the hyena, and when she got there she called her enemy to come out. The hyena looked out of his door, and when he saw the goat whom he recognized and with her the lion he was afraid. So he asked what was the matter, and the goat told him that the lion was suffering from toothache for forty days and that the only medicine was a piece of hyena skin and meat. So she had brought her friend the lion along and begged the hyena for a small piece of his skin and meat.

The hyena was afraid and said that he had a fine young son and that he would give that to the lion. But the goat refused and said that the meat must be from an old hyena. The lion then said that he could not wait as the tooth was hurting him too much. So the hyena tore off a piece of his side and gave it to the goat to give to the lion.

The goat at once put it into the calabash of honey and then gave it to the lion.

The lion ate it and said that it was truly a powerful medicine and asked for more. The hyena did not want to give any more but he was too afraid and had to tear out a bit of the meat from his other side. The goat again put it into the honey and the lion asked for more. But the hyena was not willing and tried to escape. He ran off and the lion chased him across the country.

Then it was that the goat decided to leave the bush and to come and live with men. And that is why the goats are always being caught by the hyenas and why the latter are so afraid of lions, who do not eat them but are always chasing them.

And if you want to know how it is that hyenas and dogs are such enemies the following will tell:

In the long long ago the King of the Bush, the lion, had two messengers, Swassa the Hyena and Gani the Dog.

Those are the old names, but since that time all names are changed. And there was great hunger in the house of the lion. So he called Swassa the Hyena and told him that he would go far away into the bush and bring back meat, meanwhile he, Swassa, was to remain with Gani the Dog and look after the house. At the same time he gave him two calabashes to look after until his return.

The lion departed and after a while Swassa got very hungry. So he called to Gani to come and look after the calabashes, while he himself went and turned over the old bones on the ash-heap to find something to eat.

While the hyena was busy doing this, Gani too got very hungry. So he took the two calabashes and followed a road in the bush. He soon could go no farther, so he broke one calabash to pieces and found therein honey. This was no good to him, so he broke the other and found milk. This he drank up. Then fearing to return he continued along the path till he came to a village of Men. They were all eating and he hovered around them, nor did they drive him away, but from time to time threw him a morsel to eat. So Gani the Dog came to Man, and was their friend.

Meanwhile the lion came back, crying 'Hm! Hm! Swassa! Hm! Swassa! Hm! Swassa! Ntocho! ntoch! ntoch! ntoch!' (Here every one repeats this, for properly pronounced these words resemble the growl of the lion.) And Swassa went to find the calabash. But Gani had gone. Rapidly Swassa followed the scent of Gani and coming to the village called out:

'Gani! Ganie! Ganii Ganie!'

(which is, if properly said, the cry of the hyena; and every one repeats this.)

But Gani refused to come out and barked back:

'Tokle! Tosh! wegshe!

Mbaghse! Mbaghse!'

(Every one delights in this for if very carefully said the dog's bark is imitated.)

N 2

And so the hyenas remain the messengers of lions, and dogs and hyenas are enemies to this day.

That is rather a longer tale than is usual, but is a most enjoyable one to listen to. The choruses are so enthusiastically responded to and eagerly awaited; as soon as ever they are due, the audience is on tenterhooks, and once the signal is given renders a very realistic imitation of the animals' cries.

There is a group of these 'Just-So' stories of a different nature. A quite elaborate tale ends in the slaying of an animal or whatever may be the subject-matter of the story. It is then cut or broken into pieces, and these come to life and thus the original is reproduced all over the world. Thus it is that the Ashanti child accounts for the numerous Sasabonsam—or giant-folk who inhabit trees and rocks and other magic places.

The story illustrating this which is the most frequently told is as follows: The spider noticed one day how other people than himself were beginning to use wisdom. This did not suit him at all, as he wanted to keep all the wisdom for himself. So he collected it all and put it into a large gourd that he had hollowed out for the purpose. He then hung the gourd up on the wall of his house. But his fears were not allayed and he decided to hide it right away in the bush where no man could find it. Therefore on the following morning he took down the gourd from the wall, and accompanied by his son went forth into the bush. Presently they came to a tall palm tree, and it seemed to the spider that if he put the gourd at the top amongst the foliage it would be quite safe. So he began to climb the palm-tree. But the gourd was a large one and the spider had slung it in front of him. So he could not make any progress. Always the gourd got in his way. Now the son of the spider had been watching his father's efforts and at last cried out: 'Father, why not sling the gourd over your back?' And Anansi the spider answered: 'My son, you are right: but your words also show to me that it is better for many people to have wisdom rather than one. For alone I should not have thought of that.' So speaking he opened the gourd and scattered the wisdom all over the ground so that he who may want it can gather what he will.

Another series of tales resemble our own *House that Jack Built*. As a child I hated that story, the word malt being especially in disfavour. One lives and learns. I preferred the *Old Woman and the Pig*.

The Moshi version of this well-known sequence is recorded by M. Froger in his study of that language. A man loved his friend and went to pay his respects to the dead man's children, who offer him various presents which, however, do not satisfy him. At last a fowl is given but he declares it to be too old and he calls for some millet, which he gives to the fowl. Then a hawk snatches the fowl, an arrow kills the hawk, fire burns the arrow, water quenches the fire, an elephant drinks the water, a hunter kills the elephant, a scorpion bites the hunter, a stone crushes the scorpion, and the stone rolls, rolls on for ever whilst his friend lies in his tomb.

A more elaborate one is the following Dagomba story: God killed the father and mother of a boy who, beginning to wail, is appeased by God giving him a stick especially made to kill mole-crickets. He kills one and a hen asks for it. (N.B. To ask a thing of a child is the same as to take it, as an infant will never dare to refuse a request from an elder.) He bewails his loss and the hen offers him an egg. He then meets a fire. The fire wants the egg and the child's tears are stopped with a present of some charcoal. Blacksmiths ask for that and give him an axe. He loses this to a river which gives him some fish. He proceeds on his journey and meets some farm people who take the fish.

Then begins the other form of sequence. They offer him millet, he refuses it; fowls, he refuses; and so on until at last they give him a cow. He drives the cow into the village and the butchers take it. They offer him everything, but nothing pleases him. So they kill him, and then are killed in turn by the chief.

These are excellent stories for any one anxious to acquire a vocabulary. At the same time their close similarity to our own versions is worthy of note. The stick, fire, water, drinking, are apparently universal, and they occur in the following Krachi story:

One day Anansi decided to make a farm, and to this end he called all the animals together and asked them if they would help him. First he turned to Akoko the Fowl, and Akoko answered 'I will help you if you agree not to invite Abrebia the Civet on the same day, for Abrebia hates me.'

Abrebia then agreed if he would promise not to ask Wonanka the Snake, for Wonanka hated him.

Wonanka agreed if he promised not to allow Duia the Stick to come on the same day. Duia agreed if Eja the Fire were absent, and Eja expressed his willingness if Nsiu the Water were uninvited.

To all these conditions he agreed. But Anansi got mixed up with their different requests and made the mistake of inviting them all on the same day.

They set to work and made a great farm. Then when the sun was too hot they all gathered under a shade tree and took refreshment. Suddenly Abrebia looked at Akoko and said: 'Now what is the matter with you that you are staring at me? I hate being stared at.' And he began to attack poor Akoko. While so doing he trod on the tail of Wonanka, who hated that, and Wonanka began to attack him. In the scurry Wonanka hit against Duia, who resented it and began to flog him. The flogging made the Fire flare up and begin to burn the tree. This annoyed the water which wanted to keep cool. So the water began to quench the fire, the fire began to burn the stick, the stick began to flog the snake, the snake began to kill the civet, the civet began to eat the fowl, and only the yam profited from all this turmoil.

Chapter Nine

WHICH CHIEFLY DEALS WITH FRIENDSHIP, TRUE AND FALSE

THE STORY OF THE TWO FRIENDS WHO WERE EXACTLY ALIKE——
A BRONG STORY OF FRIENDSHIP BETWEEN MAN AND LION——
FALSE FRIENDSHIP——NEVER INTERFERE IN STRANGERS'
AFFAIRS——THE MOHAMMEDAN, THE SNAKE, AND THE WILD
DOG——RIDDLES.

ONE of the finest traits in the character of nearly all the
Africans I have had the good fortune to come in contact with is their magnificent power of bestowing friendship.
This trait is naturally reflected in their literature. Of such
tales perhaps the following selection will prove of interest:

In the olden times there was a certain village.[1] A wonderful thing occurred there. On one day there were born two
boys. One was the son of a rich man and the other the son
of a very poor man. They were exactly alike, and it was
impossible even for their parents to tell them apart.

At first they did not know each other. The poor boy used
to go into the market and people would greet him and give
him many things. On the following day the people would
see the rich boy and talk of the day before. Thus the rich
boy began to hear of the poor one. So he waited until one
day he met him.

Then the two made friends. They played together and
danced and sang. They went together to the bush to hunt
rats and mice and hares and grass-cutters. When they grew
up they left their boyish games and worked on each other's
farms. They were very great friends.

One day the rich man said to his friend that he wanted to
see the world. So the two made ready and on the favourable
day set forth on their journey.

[1] A Dagomba story.

And it happened that in the course of time the two came to a great town. It was market day. And as they wandered about they heard the people talking of a most wonderful woman, who to look upon was finer than any woman in all the world. But she was seeking for a husband and could not find one, for her guardian spirit had said that she was not to marry any one unless he performed certain things.

This news interested the young men, and the rich one said that he would like to see the girl. The people of the town then took him to the girl's house. And it was true. The girl was the finest girl to look upon that had ever been known. And the rich young man then said that that girl was the girl he would marry and no other, that he would perform any deed necessary to win the girl.

Then the people laughed and said that he did not yet know what had to be done. So they told him that if a man wished to marry the girl he would have to sleep in her hut for six days and nights, and that for all that time he must not touch food or water. That if he took even as much as one drop, then he would be killed. This the chief had sworn and had added that even he would kill his own son if he tried to perform this deed and failed. Moreover, many men had tried and they had failed and had been killed.

But this did not frighten the rich young man. He said he would try.

That night he talked with his friend, who promised to help him if he could.

The following morning the rich young man got up and entered the woman's house. All day he did not drink nor did he eat.

(In the original the details are somewhat crude and realistic.)

When night fell, he placed his bed-mat against that part of the wall which was on the street, exactly as he had arranged with his friend. There were no windows or holes in the hut, only the narrow door. And in front of this the woman spread her mat so that the man could not escape.

When all the town was quiet and the people asleep, the poor young man came to the hut on the outside and made the dried mud wet. He then took out his knife and bored a small hole through to his friend. Into this hole he thrust a guinea-corn stalk and put one end of it into a calabash of water. Thus his friend was able to take water. When he had finished he filled up the hole so that no one could see it and went away.

In the morning the rich young man folded up his mat and left it against his side of the hole so that the woman could not see it.

For five nights this went on and the woman marvelled. She said to the young man: 'I know you must be getting water for before this no man has lasted three days. I shall find out and you will be killed.'

That night she moved her mat to the place where before the man had been sleeping, and when all the town slept she heard the poor young man from outside and then found the stalk and knew how she had been deceived. At once she began to abuse the young man and told him how he would surely be killed when morning came.

She then lay down and began to think how she would be able to prove the case. She took a calabash and filled it with the water which the poor young man was supplying from outside. She then remembered that a calabash might get broken, so she took her cloth and soaked it in the water.

The rich young man saw all this and knew that he was lost. He began to cry aloud against his fate, and his friend heard him. The latter went off, crying bitterly. On his way he met the great house rat, Daiyuga, who asked him what was the matter. The young man told him and begged the rat to help him. The rat said he would do his best and would get the large white ants to help.

So the rat came to the house and made a large hole and went inside. He found the calabash full of water and passed it out to the white ants. Then he took the cloth and gave that also to the white ants, who took them away to their house and destroyed them entirely.

All this time the woman did not wake as the rat is a very clever thief and makes no noise.

In the morning the woman went to the chief and reported what she had found out and claimed that he should have the young man killed as usual. The chief demanded from her what evidence she had, for the tale was a strange one. She told him that she had filled the calabash with water and had soaked her cloth in it as well. She was told to go and fetch the proofs, but when she came to her hut she could not find them. Then the chief was angry and said that she had tried to deceive him. So he gave her to the rich young man, who took her away to his own town and there married her.

The poor young man went with them.

On their return the father of the rich young man was very happy. He gave to the two a magic knife each. These knives were exactly alike and had been made in the very old old time by the giants,[1] who, as all men know, used to live in the land and made iron. He also built for them a fine new house at the entrance to the village. He gave Daiyuga his white tail.

One day the poor young man said to his friend: 'I want to go away again and see the world. Now to-day I shall plant outside your house a silk-cotton tree, and when the tree is as high as this, I shall go away,' and he showed with his hand the height the tree would have to reach.

In due time the tree grew to the height and the poor man called to his friend: 'Come and see the tree. It has now reached the proper height. I shall go away to-morrow. Look always at this tree. If you see the leaves are dried up and

---

[1] Cf. *infra* in the History of the Dagomba, p. 238.

withered, then you will know that evil has come to me or that I am dead. I beg you then to come and seek me.'

The rich young man promised his friend that he would do so, and then called to his wife to make food for his friend to take on his journey.

Next day the poor young man set out, taking with him his magic knife. He wandered far, and one evening came to a very large town. The people were not glad to see him, but were weeping and crying out. He asked what was the matter, and they told him that close to their town was a great river. This river gave the town its water-supply. But the river was always dry and the people were dying of thirst. However, the river used to give plenty of water each time that the people offered it a young girl, one just ready to be married. Now all the young girls were finished and only one remained, the daughter of the chief. On the morrow she would be sacrificed.

Next day the young man made his way down to the river and found it quite dried up. In the middle was seated a young girl crying. He went to her and she told him that in the evening the river would come up and eat her and then the town would get plenty of water. She had been left there by the people and therefore could not return to her home.

The young man was very sorry for the girl, whom he began to love. So he said he would stay with her and see what evil thing would come.

Towards sunset the spirit of the river came out. He looked like an enormous python, and he made straight for the girl. But as he drew near the young man jumped out and took his magic knife and cut off the head of the python with one blow. At once water flowed from the neck, but the body began to slip back into the hole from which it had come. The young man went on hitting the python and cutting it into pieces until it could no longer slide back. Then there was plenty of water and the young man took the girl back to the town.

When the people saw her they began to cry out, but the young man said that there would be plenty of water and that it would even come as far as the town itself and so save the trouble of fetching it. And it was so.

But the people and the chief refused to allow the girl to remain in the village, for they said rightly that they had given her in sacrifice to the river and could not take her back. If the young man wanted her he could have her, that was his affair and not theirs.

So the young man built a house for himself and the girl outside the village.

In course of time the people, seeing that there was now plenty of water, made friends with the young man who had done this thing. And one day they came to him and said they were all going out next day hunting, and they would like him to come.

To this he willingly agreed, and on the next morning went with the others into the bush.

Now it chanced that that day there was plenty of meat. But the meat all ran far from the village to a certain hill. When the people saw this they were afraid and told the poor young man that the hill was a very sacred place, that there lived there some dreadful spirit. They showed him a great rock and said that if any one went near there the rock opened and swallowed him up. Just then a big antelope came running past, and the people forgetting their fears, followed, shooting their arrows at him. Thus they drew near the hill, and suddenly the rock opened and swallowed them all.

The next morning the rich young man came out of his house and gazed as usual at the silk-cotton tree. He saw the leaves were all withered and dried. So he called to his wife and told her that he knew some evil had befallen his friend and that he must needs up and go forth to his help. The woman at once made ready plenty of food for the journey, and next day her husband departed.

The rich young man travelled far that day, asking everywhere for news of his friend. In time he came to the town where the poor young man had killed the python. The people seeing him at once mistook him for their friend and led him joyfully to the house outside the town where the girl was bewailing the loss of her husband. As soon as she saw the rich young man she arose and greeted him, nor did he say that he was not her husband.

That night he told her that he had sworn not to touch a woman until he had restored the lost villagers. She was too pleased at seeing what she thought was her husband to mind, so they kept apart for several days.

At last one morning the young men of the town came and said they were off hunting, and asked the rich young man to join them. He agreed in spite of the girl's entreaties, saying to her: 'You see me here, well, I shall not get lost again.'

So the band of hunters set off, and it chanced that the hunt took the same course as before and the people came to the sacred hill. They warned the rich young man not to go near, but he laughed at them and whilst they sat down to see what they should see, he went up to the rock, clasping in his hand the magic knife his father had given him.

As he drew near to the sacred rock the rock bent over to swallow him, but he smote hard with the knife and the rock fell into two pieces, one part falling to the right and one part to the left. Then all the people who had been buried inside came out laughing and singing.

Thus the two friends met again and all the people were astonished for they could not tell them apart, and when they came back to the town the girl could not tell which was her husband. But the poor young man told her, and she was astonished at the great friendship of the two.

Now tell me which of these two was the greater friend.

Of friendship between man and animals the Ashanti (Brong division) relate the following story:

In the olden time a man went hunting in the far bush. He took with him his wife. But one day the man did not return, and the woman left alone could not find her way home to their village. She therefore built herself a shelter near a shea-butter tree, where not long after she gave birth to a boy child.

Now at the same time a lioness lived quite close to the shea-butter tree, and she gave birth to a male cub; but she was unaware that a woman lived near by. Every day the lioness went forth into the bush to seek for meat, and the woman also wandered away in search of roots and fruits. While they were absent the two children, the man-child and the lion-cub, met and played together and became the fastest of friends, without their parents' knowledge.

One day, however, the lioness lay in wait near the shea-butter tree and sprang on the woman as she was returning home, and killed her and brought the body back to share with her cub. The man-child missed his mother at mid-day, and went out in the evening to play again with the lion-cub. But the latter would not play, but kept looking at his friend who at last said: 'Lion, what is your trouble?' And the lion replied: 'Man, I have had no food to-day; I have bad trouble for you. Follow me.'

So the man-child went with the lion-cub back to the latter's home, and there on the ground he saw his mother lying dead. He began to wail, when the lion-cub said: 'Stop. I have sworn a big oath to-day that as my mother has slain your mother, so shall I be your faithful friend from to-day till my death. I will avenge you and until then I shall care for you.' Having said this he took the man-child back to his home.

For many months after that every day the lion-cub brought a large share of the meat his mother gave him to the man-child. And they grew up together playing and becoming more and more friendly, but each morning the lion-cub called the man-child, and, placing his pad in the pad-mark of his mother, said: 'Soon, very soon, I shall be strong enough.'

At last there came the day when the two fitted exactly, the footprints of the cub and its mother. Then the cub went out with its mother and said: 'Teach me how to catch meat.'

After a few lessons the cub thought he was strong enough for his purpose, and he told the man-child that next day he would avenge the slaying of the woman. The following morning the cub killed the lioness, his mother, and showed the corpse to his friend, saying: 'I have paid the first part of my oath.'

Then for a long time the two lived quite happily together, but at last the lion-cub said to his friend one evening: 'You must return to your brothers and live in the village. There you will get married. But return there alone and on every Friday evening I will come to see you, if you meet me out in the bush. I have seen a very fine girl, the daughter of a chief; she must be your wife. Now listen to my plan. You will go to the village and being naked every one will say you are crazy. Do not get angry (N.B. to call a man crazy is a very great insult indeed, among all these people) but just wait. I will hide myself near the watering-place, and, when I see this girl, I will catch her but I shall do her no harm. Every one will shout out and run away, and if you go to the chief and ask him for his daughter, provided you can save her, he will agree; then come to where I am with the girl and I will give her up to you. Then build your house on the outskirts of the village and we will meet on Fridays as I have said. But remember this, never, never take a second wife, or trouble will surely come.'

The man-child did all this, and married the chief's daughter. The people built for him a house outside the village and every Friday he sent his wife to spend the night with her people in the village, whilst he and the lion-cub played together and exchanged their news.

A long time passed thus, when one day there came to the village a woman of great wealth and power. She had refused every man's offer of marriage and had decided to choose for herself. So she was travelling everywhere throughout the land in search of a suitable husband. She saw the man-child and loved him and asked him to marry her. But he, mindful of the lion-cub's words, refused her. She insisted, so he compromised and took her into his household.

Every Friday, however, he sent her to the village with his wife. The lion-cub foretold trouble, but the man-child explained he had not married the woman, she was merely his.

The latter could not understand why every Friday she was sent off, so one day she hid herself and seeing the lion coming to the house went and told a hunter, who hid himself in the lion's path. That night the two friends made merry, but when the lion left in the morning the hunter shot him and went back to tell the people. The man-child heard the news and ran to his friend's corpse. Seizing the arrow that had killed him, he stabbed himself with it and died. His proper wife arriving saw the body of her husband and his friend. She went straight back to the house, found a rope and hanged herself.

The story, as the preceding one, ends with an abrupt question: 'Now which of the three, Lion, Man, or Wife, do you think did best?' The right answer is 'The Wife.'

Tales of false friendship are a natural corollary, and the Dagomba relate how there was once a chief of a very large town who had only one son, to whom he gave everything he asked for. Now the boy wanted a friend and could not find one. But one day he met in the market-place a boy of his own age who was the son of very poor parents, so poor indeed that they could not even afford a loin cloth for their son. And when the chief's son saw this unfortunate youth he loved him and decided to make him his friend. He sent him presents of every sort, and when his father, the chief, gave him a horse he asked him for one also for his friend. Thus the two became the greatest of friends and the chief's son took pleasure in giving half of everything he had to his poor friend.

Thus it came about in the course of time that the two of them owned many women and slaves, and had horses and cattle and sheep and many followers. Each had the same as the other. Then there came into the head of the chief's son a desire to travel over the world and he told his friend. The latter agreed to this and both of them set to work to collect as much food as they could for their approaching travels.

When sufficient had been gathered together the two friends bade the townsfolk farewell, and set forth with all their possessions to see the world and possibly to found somewhere a new country.

The first evening came, and the poor man asked his friend if he did not think it better for only one of them to open his bags and feed the people, and the chief's son agreed to this and said that as they both had the same number of people and cattle and also had brought the same amount of food, he would first get rid of his stock. Thus they carried on for several months and then the end of the chief's son's provisions came. That night he asked his friend to provide the food, but he refused, demanding payment. The chief's son had to agree to give his friend his wives and then received enough food for that day. The next night the poor man demanded his cattle and next his slaves, then his horses, and lastly his clothes. Then were all the people sorry indeed for the unfortunate youth who was thus so sorely requited for the good he had done. But still the one-time poor man was not satisfied and demanded the chief's son's eye for the next meal and then the other eye as well.

Naked and blind, without followers or wives, the chief's son was left behind next day in the middle of the bush. He managed to find a tree for shelter and sat down under it to await death. While he was thus resting, bewailing his hard lot, a bird came into the tree and spake to him and asked him to tell all that had befallen him. Then the bird was indeed sorry and said he would help him. If the chief's son would ride him he would take him to a great city and there he would know what to do, for he, the bird, had a magic medicine which would restore to him his eyes. This medicine he would willingly give the unfortunate youth.

The chief's son thanked the bird and climbed on his back, and the bird flew far away and fast, and at nightfall set him down near the watering-place of a large town. There the bird restored sight to the youth and gave him some of the magic medicine. Then it flew away.

The women came down to get the water and the man hid, being naked, but when they started on their way back he followed and so reached the town. Now if his father's town had been large, this one was immense. Never had man seen so great a number of houses in one place. It stretched from Yendi to Tamale and from Karaga to Kpabia. The people were wealthy and their horses and cattle were without number. So the chief's son sat down quietly under a tree and there he heard that the chief of the place was very unhappy in spite of all his wealth. A boy passed by with grass for one of the chief's horses, and the boy was crying, and when the youth asked him what was the matter he replied that he cried because his master, who was a very good man, could no longer see, both eyes having lost their sight. Then the chief's son rose and said he would cure the chief. So the people took him before their king and told him that they had found a naked stranger who had said he could cure the blindness. Then the king rejoiced and said that if he did succeed there was nothing he would not give him. Then the youth took the medicine the bird had given him and at once restored sight to the king.

The latter was overjoyed and at once gave food and clothing to his healer. The next day he divided the town into two halves and gave one to the youth. He gave him wives and slaves and horses, and all that he had he halved with him. And the two ruled in that place happily.

Some months later the unfaithful friend arrived with all the cattle and horses and slaves. They passed through the town and came to that part where the chief's son ruled. Now the latter chanced to be outside his compound when the procession passed by, and only the favourite wife of the chief's son recognized her whilom husband. That evening she came to him and verified her discovery. He asked her to say nothing about it but she went back and told her people, for they all loved him. Then the unfaithful friend came to hear of the news and he would not believe it. He decided to go and see for himself.

When he presented himself at the compound door he suddenly met his erstwhile friend. He was overcome with shame, and when the latter began to abuse him he grew so frightened that he changed himself into a hartebeeste. The chief's friend then grew angry and changed himself into a lion. That is why to this day lions hate hartebeeste more than any other animal in the bush.

Stories of false friendship and stories of which the theme is that one should never go out of one's way to help others in distress are somewhat similar. This story was told me in the first person by a Dagomba.

'I was coming along the road one day with Salifu. We were friends. As we came near the village there was a bush fire across the path. We hastened. As we came near a shea-butter tree we saw a chameleon trying to escape the fire. But as you know chameleons are strange animals. This one was pushing out its head and drawing it back, and if it did not hurry it was sure to have been killed by the fire. Now Salifu tried to push it back into the flames. But I told him that that was not good, so he let me pick it up and I put it in a hole in the tree where the fire could not get it and would pass by.

'We went on to the village.

'Some days later Salifu and myself were again on that path together. When we reached the shea-butter tree we heard a voice coming from the hole calling us by our names. We answered and asked who called. The chameleon then said it was he and asked if we were his friends who the other day had passed that way. We told him yes. He then asked which of us was the one who had placed him for safety in the hole. Salifu told him, and he then told Salifu not to fear although he had tried to kill him, but to put his hand into the hole and he would see what he would see.

'Salifu did this and he pulled out his hand and he found that it was full of gold.

'Then the chameleon said to me: "Now it was you who helped me. Put in your hand and you will see what you will see."

'I did so, and the chameleon bit off my hand. When I cried out the chameleon said: "It will be well with you. You will not die. But go into the village and tell all men what I have done to you both. Thus shall men learn not to help strangers in distress".'

The tale of the Snake and the Mohammedan is on a similar theme. It is also a Dagomba story.

In a certain country there lived a bad snake. It was a very bad snake and killed many people. At last the men came together and decided to ask a hunter of great repute to come and kill it. The man agreed to their request and came to live for a while in the village, going out every morning to see if he could come across the snake.

One day he found the tracks and began to follow hotly on the trail. Now it chanced that the snake knew this and he hurried as fast as he could away from the hunter. But the latter gained on him. The snake did not know what to do.

Perceiving, however, a Mohammedan on the roadside praying, he hurried to him and asked him in the name of Allah
to save him. 'Since it is in the name of Allah that you have
asked me, I cannot refuse,' said the Mohammedan, 'get up
my trousers and you will be safe.'

The snake did so and scarcely had he done so than the
hunter arrived. He looked around everywhere for the snake
and could no longer see its trail. He asked the Mohammedan,
but could learn nothing. Then ensues a long conversation
between the two men, but the Mohammedan refuses to
betray the snake, and at last the hunter goes away telling the
former that surely he will repent for having given the snake
the opportunity to escape.

The Mohammedan finishes his prayers and wishes to get
up off the ground. But the snake asks him if the road is clear
and being so informed then says: 'Before I leave your
trousers I must first bite you.' 'What,' cries the Mohammedan, 'after all I have done for you?' 'Yes,' replies the snake,
'for such is my nature and it would be a bad thing for me to
let you escape.'

The argument continues for some time and the snake
refuses to let his befriender go. While they are still discussing
the matter a wild dog comes along the road, and, hearing the
dispute and seeing only the man, asks what the matter is
about.

When he has been told he says that if the two will agree
he will hear the case and give judgement. To this both assent,
and the Mohammedan first states his case. The snake is then
asked to give his version. The dog pretends not to hear
properly and eventually persuades the snake to stretch out
its head from the trousers. As soon as ever he does this the
dog at once bites the head off and so kills the snake.

The Mohammedan does not know how to thank the dog.
At last he persuades him to come back to the village and
there to receive at least some small reward. Now, the dog

was not friendly at the time with men, and when the village came into sight he stopped and told the Mohammedan that he could go no further but would hide himself in a bush which he pointed out, and would there await the return of the Mohammedan with the promised reward. So the Mohammedan went on alone to the village.

Now it so happened that while the Mohammedan had been absent from his house his wife was giving birth to a child. But the labours were difficult and the people of the household had called in a sorcerer. As a result of their consultation with him it was learned that the only thing that could save the life of the woman was to make a soup from the skin of a wild dog. But the people did not know where to look for the skin since the sorcerer had also informed them that the skin had to be a fresh one.

It was at that moment that the husband returned. He was immediately told what the sorcerer had said, and as soon as he saw his wife dying he began to lament bitterly. But after a while he remembered the wild dog that was awaiting him, and, thanking Allah for his goodness, he told the young men where they could find a wild dog at once, and they all set out with their bows and arrows and spears.

But the dog had always been a careful beast. And when the Mohammedan had left him he immediately changed his hiding place. When he saw the people coming to the bush he had shown the Mohammedan he stole quietly away and returned again safely to his home in the bush.

Men were at one time quite often very friendly with the animals, as this Krachi story will show:

A certain hunter once went into the far bush. He no longer wanted to live in his own village, but had decided to make for himself a little home in the bush. He therefore searched for a nice place and there built a small house and made a little farm of yams and cassada. But he had lost his gun and was unable to get any meat.

One day he returned to his house and found there a young lion, who said to him: 'My friend, I have come to see you. This is my country, but I like you and we two will share this house.'

The man did not mind at all and agreed that the lion should sleep in the house. Now every day the man went out and looked at his farm and watched the crop growing, whilst the lion went away into the bush and killed meat which he brought back and shared with the man.

Thus they became fast friends.

But one day the lion said to his friend: 'Now, you men, how do you kill meat? You told me you were a hunter, and yet all this time that we have been together it is I, not you, who have killed our meat.' Then the man told the lion that men killed their meat with guns, and the lion said nothing.

However, he set forth and came near the dwelling-places of Man. He watched them at work and one day saw them come out to a farm in a band and all begin to hoe the field together. First they had set their guns against a tree. Then the lion rose up and went to the tree and took away one of the guns with all the little bags of powder and medicine attached to it. These he carried home and gave them to his friend the man.

Then the hunter went out every day and killed meat until they were both tired of it. Then the man said that it was now time for him to leave the bush and return back to the villages of men. The lion said he was sorry but that Man knew best, that he, the lion, would never forget him and would remain his friend so long as he never told other men that he had as a friend a lion. The man promised and left the bush and settled in a village where he married and had many children.

One day the lion remembering his friend decided to visit him and to find out if the man were still faithful to their friendship. He therefore came down to the man's farm and hid himself near some rocks, making pretence that he was

dead. Now when the man and his children came to the farm
one of the youngest saw the lion and told his father to come
quick and kill it. Then the man went to see, and when he
saw it was a lion he remembered his friend and said: 'Maybe
it is my friend. I will not take its skin but rather make a
funeral custom and bury the poor animal, for it may perhaps
be my own friend. Come, therefore, children, and dig a large
hole so that we may bury the Lord of the Bush.'

So the children did as their father bade them. But the lion
got up and thanked his friend and said that now of a truth
he knew that the man was his friend and that he would go
back happy.

Now, not long afterwards, the lion again wished to visit
his friend and show him his eldest son. So he took the cub
with him to the farm and again hid himself, pretending to
be dead. But this time he did so in a different place. The cub
was told to keep away in the grass and to watch how his
father's friend was a good man.

When the man and his children came to the farm, one of
the boys saw the lion and told his father that there was a meat
lying there. The man then took his gun and going to the
spot saw that it was a lion, and thinking that it was not his
friend since he had chosen a different place to hide himself
in, shot the lion and killed it.

Then he saw that he had killed his friend and he began
to weep. But the lion's offspring, who had seen the whole
affair, was angry. He swore that from that day onward he
and all other lions would never look on the face of hunters
again with pleasure, and that they would kill them whenever
they had the chance.

That is why from that day to this hunters and lions never
agree and hate each other. And through man so often
betraying his friend the animal, the latter has mostly decided
to live in the far far bush.

It will have been noticed that in many of these stories the

relator turns to his audience and asks which of two fine acts was the finer. This problem-setting device is a common one, and in many of such tales the ingenuity and power of imagination is very great. The following are told by the Krachi:

Two men had a dispute as to which of them had the most sense. Each decided to show the other that he was the greater man. So they went to a deep pond. The first one threw in a needle and then he threw in a thread and fetched up the needle properly threaded. The second admitted that that was certainly a very clever thing to have done, but said that he, too, could perform wonderful things. Whereupon he threw into the pond an empty calabash bottle. Then he fetched some palm oil and threw that in as well, and then, taking out the calabash, he showed that he had succeeded in filling it with the palm oil. To this day we do not know which man had the more sense.

Or again: There were once three men travelling together and they came to a deep and wide river. None of them knew how to swim and they sat down to discuss the matter. Then one got up and said that it was not a very serious affair after all since he had a pair of sandals which would allow him to walk dry foot across the water. The second then said that he could do even better than that, for he possessed a cutlass which was so magicful that he could cut the water in half and leave a road for them to pass over. The third said that that was too much trouble and that he had a thread so magicful that if he threw it across the river they could all pass over along it. Now it has never been decided as to which of these three men possessed most power.

A third story of this character runs:

An old man had three children. They were all boys. When they had grown up to manhood he called them together and told them that now he was very old and no longer able to get food even for himself. He ordered them to go forth to obtain food and clothing for him.

They all set out together, and after a while came to a large river. The journey had lasted many moons, and they decided to cross and there separate. The eldest told the youngest to take the middle road, and the second to go to the right, whilst he himself would go to the left. They were all to meet at the same spot in a year's time.

So they departed, and at the end of a year as agreed upon they found their way back to the riverside.

The eldest asked the youngest what he had obtained during his travels, and the boy replied: 'I have got nothing except a mirror. But this mirror has wonderful power, and if you look into it you can see all over the country, no matter how far away.'

The eldest then turned to his second brother and asked him what he had obtained. And the second replied: 'Nothing, except a pair of sandals which are so full of power that if one puts them on one can walk at once to any place in the country at one step.'

The eldest then said: 'I too have obtained but little. A small calabash of medicine and that is all. But let us look into the mirror and see how father fares.'

The youngest produced his mirror and they all looked into it and saw their father was already dead and that even the funeral custom was finished. Then the elder said: 'Let us hasten home and see what can be done.' So the second brought out his sandals and all three placed their feet inside them and at once they went straight to their father's grave. Then the eldest took his bag and shook out his medicine. This he poured over the grave and at once their father arose, just as if nothing had been the matter with him. Now which of these three has done best?

Or the Dagomba will tell:

There was once a man who had three wives. It happened that they were all about to bear him children and they asked him for permission to return to their homes. He agreed to this, and on the appointed day set out with them to lead them on their way.

Presently they came to a cross-roads where there were three roads branching out. Here the man turned to his women and said: 'Here I will leave you, as here it is that you will each take your different roads.' As he said this he fell dead.

Then the women began to make a great ado, and the first woman said that she would not leave her husband like that but that she would follow him, and then she went and hanged herself. The second woman said that she could not leave her husband's body for the vultures and hyenas to devour, and she sat down by the corpse and kept everything away from it. The third ran into the bush wailing her man's death, and there she saw a Kulparga who asked her what was the matter, and when he heard he said that he would help and returned with the woman to the cross-roads. There he took his magic cow's tail and tapping the dead woman and man raised them both from the dead and gave them back their life.

Now which of those women is best?

And lastly, one from a Grunshi source.

There was once a girl. She was the chief's daughter. She was finer to look upon than any other girl which men had seen. But there was no one whom she would agree to marry.

Men came from all the countries but she would not take them. And all the land heard the news of this girl and that though she was of marriageable age she would take no man.

It happened that this thing was heard by a snake. He was a large python and dwelt in a vast lake near by the river. When he heard about this girl he decided that he would marry her. So he changed himself into a man and came to the village of the girl's father.

As soon as ever the maiden saw the young man she was delighted and said she would marry him at once. Every one was pleased and that night they took the young man and the girl on to the roof of the house, for the Issalla houses have flat roofs, and there they left them.

Now during the night the snake licked the girl all over and swallowed her, and changing again into his snake form made off to the great lake.

Next morning people came to the house and called to the girl and her man to come down. There was no answer and the chief told the people to climb up and see what was the matter. This they did and reported that the girl and the man were missing.

The chief was very angry and at once ordered all the people to make ready to follow the girl and her lover. But when they began to search for their tracks they could find none. Then they called for a man who could smell everything. He at once smelt the girl and followed a trail down to the great water. There he could do nothing. The people, urged on by the anger of the chief, then called on a man famous through all the country for his thirst. Him they told to drink up the lake. This he did. But still there was no sign of the man or the girl. Then the people called on a man famous for his power of working and told him to take out all the mud of the lake. This he did and thereby revealed a hole. But it was so long that no one could reach the bottom until they remembered that there was a man with an arm which could stretch over all the Dagomba land. They told him to put in his arm and pull out the girl. He did so and pulled out the great python, which was immediately killed. And when they had cut open its stomach they found the girl inside. But she was dead. Then the people remembered a man who had much medicine and was able to raise the dead. He came and at once restored the girl to life. Now which of those five men did best?

To which question the answer is that they were all as good as each other, and the girl never married again.

Allied to the problem tale is the riddle, of which the follow-

ing is one. Its source is not without taint. I heard it first in
Ahafo, where there was at that time no local means of literary
corruption, but afterwards from a Mission-trained youth.
It is a riddle of a type which, however, is very popular, and
this would account for its travelling far afield. I give it merely
for this last characteristic.

There was a certain man who was running away from his
village and he was taking with him all his property. This
consisted of a leopard, a goat, and a yam. Now he came in
time to a certain river where there was only one canoe. This
was so small that it was impossible for him to take more than
one part of his property with him at one time. Now how did
he succeed in doing this, for if he left the yam with the goat
or the leopard with the goat, the goat would eat the yam or
the leopard devour the goat?

The answer is: He took the goat over first and then the
yam. He then recrossed the goat and ferried over the
leopard, returning a fourth time for the goat.

Chapter Ten

WHEREIN MEN LEARN CONSOLATION IN AD-
VERSITY AND ARE WARNED AGAINST WOMEN

CHILDISH NATURE OF MANY STORIES—MORALS TOLD TO THE
YOUNG AND OLD ALIKE—DISTRUST OF WOMEN—NOT
EVERY ONE HAS GOOD LUCK—EVIL STEP-MOTHER TALES.

A CHILDISH story is told of a certain Mohammedan teacher who had determined to make a journey. He carried with him for food one fried cake of millet flour. On the way he grew hungry and was about to eat the cake when a hyena came along and said to him: 'Be quick, Man, and eat the cake so that I may devour you.' The unfortunate fellow was very frightened, but just then a leopard came along and said to the hyena: 'Be quick and eat the man, Hyena, so that I may eat you.' It was now the hyena's turn to be afraid. However, at that very moment there came along a lion which said to the leopard: 'Be quick and finish the hyena, Leopard, as I want to eat you.'

At this critical moment a rat appeared and cried to them all: 'Wait there, all of you, for I am hungry and wish to feast on the lot of you.'

This so frightened them that the hyena ran away, followed by the leopard and the lion, leaving only the rat and the man. The former then turned to the latter and asked if he, too, would not flee, but the man replied that he would not but was at the mercy of the rat, who told him to go away and continue his road in peace.

To this day there is a great friendship between Mohammedans and rats, and we see this particularly in the fact that the rats are wont to leave the books of the Mohammedans alone and do not eat them, and that those books are always carefully wrapped up in rats' skins.

The childish character of so many of the stories told by

these natives is nowhere so prominent as among the vast series of tales which are told presumably by way of education to the young. But even these are listened to with the greatest interest by the grown-ups, and I think it quite possible that many of them are not traditionally handed down but are actually made up impromptu. Of such simple stories the following is typical. It is a Dagomba version of the well-known story of how the hare borrowed a cow from both the elephant and the hippopotamus and repaid them by tying each to the other at the end of a long rope. It has the addition that when the elephant had realized how he had been done by Soamba he agreed with the hippopotamus, his fellow dupe, that they would refuse to allow the hare any grass or water.

This news reached Soamba and he was in a great fix. Whilst pondering over this new difficulty he met a kob to whom he related his troubles. He asked the latter if he would lend him his horns for a short time, and when the latter agreed he took them and placed them on his head. Then Soamba went and sought out the elephant, who asked him what sort of sickness had come to him that horns should grow from his head. Then Soamba began to spit all over the place and explained how the sickness came from his mouth and that his spittle was dangerous. The elephant was very frightened lest he, too, should get this bad illness and ran away. The same thing happened with the hippopotamus, and thus the hare was once more able to procure water and grass. From this story we are supposed to learn that even the smallest of men may overcome the greatest of opponents.

That is a moral which we could draw from most of the Brer Rabbit tales as the following will show:

The snake, the leopard, and the lion used formerly to live in the same compound. They were the greatest of friends. Each of the two animals would take turn and turn about to provide meat, and the snake for his part would procure them firewood. As their friendship grew apace they exchanged confidence such as only the truest of friends are wont to do. Thus one night the leopard explained that there was only one thing in the world that annoyed him, and that was when dust was thrown into his eyes. The lion said that he hated any one staring at him, and the snake that only one thing really made him angry and that was when some one trod on his tail.

Now it chanced that the hare was outside the compound and overheard this conversation. He went straight to the mole cricket and told him that near the outside shelter where the three used to sit for shade there was excellent feeding, and the cricket went there the next day. He began to dig a hole, and in doing so threw dust into the eyes of the leopard who, thinking it was the lion, began to stare at him. This made the lion angry and, as he began to fight with the leopard, the two of them trod on the snake's tail who promptly killed them both. The snake then rested, and the hare coming along asked him what he was going to do with the meat. The former said he was going to cook it and eat it and told the hare to go and fetch some firewood. The hare set about the task, but the snake was lazy and kept on telling the hare to look inside the pot and see how it was getting on. The hare grew weary at last and told the snake to look for himself. When the snake did so the hare pushed him into the pot and, quickly putting on the lid, cooked him as well.

The northern tribes are, as a rule, fonder of keeping more to human heroes, and they tell as follows:

There was a certain chief who was very jealous of his youngest brother, for the latter had, after many years of trading, amassed great wealth whilst the chief only had six cows. He therefore sent for him and bade him kill a cow by merely looking at it. The youngest brother was very upset at this as he knew he could not succeed. So he went out into the bush crying and there met a monkey who asked him

what was the matter and he told him. The monkey replied
that he would help him, but he would have to wait for the
new moon.

The youngest brother went back and told the chief.

Now it happened that the favourite son of the chief was
a leopard, and when the new moon came the leopard was
sleeping in the house. Then the chief told his elder son to
open the gates and let out the cows. The boy did this and
the monkey bit him so that he died. As each cow came out
he did the same and all the cows died. Then the chief himself came out and when he saw the disaster began to bewail
his lot. But his younger brother said there was no need to
make so much fuss as all that was necessary to resurrect them
was to sprinkle a little of the blood from a leopard's tail.
He then went into the house and slew the leopard, and taking
some of the blood sprinkled it over the dead boy and the
cows and they were immediately restored to life. But the
blood would not resurrect the leopard, and thus the chief
lost his favourite son. By this we learn that chiefs should
not trouble their younger brothers, and how sometimes the
weaker wins.

Great ones also can learn from their subjects, as this tale
explains :

Once upon a time an old man lived alone with his wife,
and they were so old that it was no longer possible for them
to do the necessary work to live. So they sent for their
nephew, who came and worked for them. One day the old
man became quite blind and told his nephew to take three
beads and go forth and sell them. But he was not to part
with them until the would-be purchaser had said: 'May God
help you.'

The boy departed and soon came to a market where a man
offered him ten cows for the beads, but as he did not add
the magic words the deal was not carried through. Shortly
after an old woman offered him a goat and a bundle of grass,

and as she added: 'May God help you', the deal was put through and the nephew went back home.

He told his uncle what had happened and the old man was very distressed at the way matters had turned out. To console himself he asked for his tobacco and then wanted fire with which to light it. This was procured from the bundle of grass, and as soon as ever the tobacco had caught, the old man's sight was restored.

Overjoyed at his good fortune he went and told the village chief, who was also blind, and the latter offered him a hundred cows if he could get back for him his sight. The magic grass was brought, and lo and behold the chief also could once more see.

Every one was so struck by this wonderful event that it was decided from that day forth men should never be separated from that grass. Thus it is that men make their bedmats from that grass.

There is more lore in that story than at first sight is apparent. The particular grass used for making the bedmats is that one which formerly was used to make fire from by friction, before the newer stone and tinder. Moreover, in nearly every tribe man is buried in his bed-mat or the mat is taken to the graveside and either left to rot there or is burnt.

The hare, which is generally depicted as rather a nasty type of fellow, using his greater common sense to serve his own greediness, sometimes appears in a better light:

There was a certain hunter. He had only one child, and that was a girl. Now when he had made his farm and the corn was growing up, he sent the girl there to keep away the birds from the grain. Now it chanced that while the girl was in the field a lion passed by. He was hungry, so killed and ate the girl.

When the child did not return the hunter went out to the field to see where she was, and he came to the place where the lion had killed his daughter, and the man knew that evil

had befallen him that day. So he went back to the town and
cried out that this bad thing had fallen on his head, and the
people came out and brought back the body of the child,
for the lion had not eaten it all.

The next morning the hunter arose and went to his farm
and began to track the lion. He followed quickly, for he
was a good hunter. The lion soon heard the man coming
and began to be afraid. For he knew he had done an evil
thing and that the hunter would surely kill him. So the lion
ran away. But the hunter came after and was always getting
nearer and nearer.

The lion, sore pressed, came to the path not far from the
village. There he espied a Mohammedan busily engaged in
bowing and making reverences. He saluted the man and
asked him if he could help him. The Mohammedan agreed
and took his bag and made some writing and changed the
lion into a stone, which he put into his bag.

Scarcely had he done this than the hunter came up, and
finding that the footprints of the lion ceased at the Mohammedan, he asked him if he had seen the lion. Now the
Mohammedan had promised in the name of Allah not to
betray the lion, so he answered that he had not, and after
a time the hunter was forced to return home without taking
his revenge.

Meanwhile the Mohammedan, as soon as he saw that the
hunter had gone, took out the stone and after making some
writing changed it back into the lion. Then the lion said
that the changing had made him very hungry and proposed
to eat the Mohammedan. The latter began to be afraid and
begged the lion to leave him. While they were disputing an
old woman came along, and the Mohammedan suggested
that they should tell her the case and let her decide what
they should do in the matter.

The lion agreed, and when the old woman had heard the
complaint of the Mohammedan she made answer that the

affair was no concern of hers, that she was a very old woman now and that men no longer troubled themselves about her, so that she cared nothing for men and that the lion could eat this one if he liked. Saying this she went on her way and the lion made ready to eat the Mohammedan. He still went on begging the lion to let him live, and while they were talking a hare came along.

As soon as the Mohammedan saw the hare he called out to him to come rapidly and begged him to hear the case and make his decision. When the hare had agreed to do this the Mohammedan began to relate all that had passed. Then the hare laughed and said that they were making a fool of him. They asked why, since it was the truth that he had been told. Then the hare said: 'What, do you think I am an idiot? You ask me to waste my time here and make me a fool. I will have nothing to do with you.' And he made ready to go away. But the Mohammedan asked what they had said that displeased him. And he answered: 'You told me that you changed this great big lion into a stone, so small that you could put it into your bag. I do not believe it.'

But the lion then said: 'Hare, I am master of all the bush and I did go into a stone and into this man's bag.' Then the hare laughed and said he would not believe the story. So the lion told the Mohammedan to show the hare, and at once the man took his paper and made writing and changed the lion into a stone, which he put into his bag.

Then the hare said to the man: 'Now, take the stone and throw it away into the large river where it will never be seen again.'

That story shows also how the weak can prevail.

Of other morality tales the following are typical:

There was once a lizard that was the intimate friend of an old and blind buffalo. It would get up on to the horns of its friend each morning and direct the buffalo which way to go for the best grazing ground, and as a reward it would get the grasshoppers and other insects which flew up as the larger animal made its way through the grass.

However, in course of time the lizard grew tired of his big friend and thinking he might make a better one went and called on a hunter. To him the lizard promised that it would lead him to where a fine large buffalo could be found, but the lizard added: 'I have learned, however, that men are ever ungrateful and that if one does one of them a favour the good deed is rewarded with evil.'

The hunter assured the lizard that that was not so and that he would repay the lizard's kindness in any way the latter might choose. So the lizard agreed that if the hunter killed the buffalo it would be quite content with the entrails only, for it could find there a goodly supply of grubs to eat if the entrails were exposed for a short while to the sun.

Next morning the lizard betrayed his old friend and led the buffalo to where the hunter lay in ambush. The hunter killed the animal and left its entrails to the lizard as promised. On the following day the latter repaired to the expected feast and found, sure enough, thousands of nice fat grubs. But while eating them the lizard grew careless and a hawk, swooping down, devoured it.

That story teaches man to be always on guard even against his friends and also that one often falls into the trap set for another.

Again: A certain girl was given by her parents to a young man in marriage. She did not care for the youth, so she refused and said that she would choose a husband for herself. Shortly after there came to the village a fine young man of great strength and beauty. The girl fell in love with him at first sight and told her parents that she had found the man she wished to marry, and as the latter was not unwilling the marriage soon took place.

Now it happened that the young man was not a man at all, but a hyena, for although as a rule women change into hyenas and men into hawks, the hyena can change itself into either man or woman as it may please.

During the first night the two newly married ones were sleeping together the husband said: 'Supposing that when we go to my town we chance to quarrel on the road what would you do?' The wife answered that she would change herself into a tree. The man said that he would be able to catch her even then. She said that if that was the case she would turn into a pool of water. 'Oh! that would not trouble me,' said the hyena-man, 'I should catch you all the same.' 'Why, then I should turn into a stone,' replied his spouse. 'Still I should catch you,' remarked the man.

Just at that moment the girl's mother shouted from her room, for she had heard the conversation: 'Keep quiet, my daughter; is it thus that a woman tells all her secrets to her man?' So the girl said no more.

Next morning, when the day was breaking, the husband told his wife to rise up as he was returning to his home. He bade her make ready to accompany him a short way down the road to see him off. She did as he told her, and as soon as ever the couple were out of sight of the village the husband turned himself into a hyena and tried to catch the girl, who changed herself into a tree, then into a pool of water, then into a stone, but the hyena almost tore the tree down, nearly drank all the water and half swallowed the stone. Then the girl changed herself into that thing which the night before her mother had managed to stop her from betraying. The hyena looked and looked everywhere and at last fearing the villagers would come and kill him, made off.

At once the girl changed into her own proper form and ran back to the village. The story of her adventures was told to all, and that is why to this day women do not choose husbands for themselves and also that is why children have learnt to obey their elders who are wiser than they.

But in the olden time men were very chary of giving to

their sons knowledge. It is to be observed to this day that men who hunt rarely tell of their magics and medicines until the time when they themselves begin to feel too old to go out to the chase. But if one of their sons shows discretion and good sense the parent will teach him many things from his early youth onwards. Thus it is told that once upon a time a hunter went with his small son into the far, far bush and there settled. He made a good camp and each day when he fared forth to search for game he left the boy behind to set out the skins and dry them.

One day the hunter killed a young male lion. He skinned it as usual and gave it to the boy to look after. On the following morning when the hunter had gone into the bush it chanced that the lioness, mother of the slain cub, passed by the hunter's camp and there saw the skin of her son drying. The hunter's boy was there watching the skins. She therefore addressed him and asked the names of the various skins. To each the boy gave the rightful name and mentioned that his father had killed it. At length the lioness came to her own son's skin and asked apparently disinterestedly as to whose skin that might be.

'It is the skin of "mph",' replied the boy.

The lioness was very angry at thus being foiled. However, she could do nothing but went back to her home, determined to return the next day.

Meanwhile the boy's father had come back from the bush and had been told all that had happened. The hunter said nothing, but told his son to have all the skins outside drying in the sun next morning and that if the lioness returned he could tell her everything. Sure enough next morning, when all the skins were laid outside in the sun, the lioness came along and asked the boy what animal each skin belonged to. The boy replied truthfully to each question and at last the lioness came to the skin of her own son.

'Whose skin is that?' she asked.

'That is the skin of a young male lion that my father slew,' replied the boy.

This was the answer the lioness wanted and she made ready to leap upon the boy when the hunter, who had hidden himself in a tree close by, fired his gun and killed her.

That story not only tells us that we should show our knowledge to our children, but it also tells us that when our sons possess magic and medicine they will be of use to us.

But at the same time youth must not neglect to pay respect to his elders, for in the olden times when sons did not teach their fathers, a certain boy who had more sense than most left his home while still quite young and began to trade. In a short while he had made plenty of money, and every time he came back he used to abuse his father for being a fool and not faring forth into the world to make money.

One day the old man got very angry and determined to show his boy that he, too, could succeed in trade. So he called all his slaves together and they came to the number of one hundred and fifty. He then loaded them all up with goods to go and sell. They started from the town and had only gone a few days when the old man met on the road a very old beggar. The latter asked him to give him alms. And the old man gave him all he had, the whole of the hundred and fifty loads.

Then with his slaves he went on to the next village. There they sat down under a large baobab which was in fruit. Now they were very hungry and there was nothing left with which to buy food. So their master told them to knock down some of the fruit. They did this, and when they cracked the shells to their surprise they found nothing but gold inside. They knocked down a hundred and fifty of the fruit and all were full of gold. Then the next fruit had none, but was just full of flour and seeds as all baobab fruit is.

The old man sent a present to the chief of the village and kept the rest of the gold and then returned home. There he

met his son who asked how he had fared. The old man told
him to examine the loads, and when the young man saw the
gold he turned to his father and said:

'Of a truth old men are wiser than we young ones.
I have been many voyages and have travelled far. But I have
no wealth like this. You have been but a short way and have
amassed all this wealth. Now I know that I must be quiet
in the presence of my elders.'

So the young man from that day ceased to abuse his father
and paid him every respect.

But a favourite theme is one which tells how evil comes
to man through his dalliance with women. Of these a
Dagomba story, which is told in the first person, is perhaps
the best. It is related in a toneless monotone as if the speaker
were unaware of any listeners and is merely repeating to himself all the sorrows and troubles which have come to him.
Naturally this is a tale which is not repeated to women nor
told in their hearing.

'I was still a young man and my friend loved me. We
were always together and I used to help him on his farm.
One day he got married, but our friendship did not cease
for all that. I still would go to his farm. And at last he told
me that his wife was expecting a child soon. He promised
that he would give the child to me when it grew up and if it
were a female then I could marry it, and if it were a man then
when it grew up it would help me in my farm.

'This was good and the child was born. It was a woman
child. And I worked for my friend for many years.

'At last the child had grown into a woman and the time
came for me to marry her. I went away to collect some
presents and when I came back I went straight to my friend's
house to see the girl, and I asked her mother where she was.
And the woman replied that the girl had been there only
a short time before. But I did not see the girl. When her
father came back I again asked where the girl was, and he

said that she must have gone to look for firewood. But the girl did not come back. Then I wandered into the village looking everywhere for the girl and asking all the people till they thought I was crazy and drove me away. I sat down and a man came to me. He was the blind man, but could just see a little bit. He asked me what was the matter. I told him that I had lost the girl for whom I had worked for so many years and that I knew some evil thing had happened. He told me then that he had seen a man and a woman and a child pass along towards the sacrificing place early in the morning. I went quickly down the path and when I got to the place where the big tree stands I saw my girl lying down before it. Her throat had been cut, and I knew then that her father and mother had killed her for the Deity.

'I did not know what to do. I sat there by the tree close to the body and wept. I refused to leave the girl and I stayed there for a long time. The body was getting very bad when one night three hyenas came and wanted to eat it. I drove them away.

'Then I saw a very large hyena. He came to me and said: "Why do you drive away the hyenas? The girl is dead and it is better that she should be eaten."

'I told him to go away, that the girl was mine, that I would not leave her till I, too, were dead, and that if she could only return I would give anything.

'He then said: "Oh! that is indeed a small matter. If you want the girl back I will restore her to life. But you must know that if she does come back, then in time to come it is a certain thing that the girl will kill you."

'I said I did not mind that. All that I wanted was for the girl to come back. Then he agreed and gave me a white tail. "This," he said, "is a magic tail. If you wish to raise the dead, all you have to do is to wave it over the body and call them back. They will at once arise and be quite as they were before."

'I thanked him and waved the tail over the girl, calling her to come back.

'At once she arose and greeted me.

'So we went away from that country from her parents. And we wandered far. At last we came to a large village. The people there agreed that we could stay with them and I built my hut on the outskirts of the town.

'One day I heard a noise of weeping and wailing in the town. So I inquired what it was all about and the people told me that one of the young men, a famous hunter, had died. I told them that that was nothing and that I would come along and see the body.

'I went into my hut and took the tail and went to the house where the dead man lay. When I approached the people made way for me to pass and when I saw the young man I took the tail and waved it over him and called his name. At once he arose and was quite well.

'The people marvelled, but I said nothing and went to my hut again. Many times did I do this thing and the people began to show much respect to me. They came often to my house, and among them was a certain young man who made love to my wife.

'One day when I was not at home he asked her to give him the tail. Being a woman she did so, and then followed him away to his house. Now at that time I was in my farm. I heard a great cry coming from the town and then I saw mounted messengers coming to me. They stopped and said that great trouble had come to the village, that the chief's son had been bitten by a snake and had died. They told me that the chief was in great grief, but they had told him I was able to bring back the dead and so they had come to fetch me.

'I left my farm and went with the men back to the chief's house and when I went inside I saw the dead boy and his father grieving. I told the chief to be of good cheer, that his boy would be back again soon.

'So I ran to my hut. But I could not find my tail. I cried to my wife to come. But there was no answer. People came to me and asked what was the matter. I told them and they said they had seen her going away with the young man. I ran to find them, but they were gone from the village. Men came and caught me and took me before the chief, who said: "You have promised to restore my son. Do so. People tell me that you have often done this thing before. Do it that I may see."

'I tried and I tried; but I could not. The boy would not come back.

'Then the chief got very angry and called to his people to take me away and kill me.

'They took me outside the village and there killed me, and left me outside lying there dead.

'When night came the big hyena came to me and he laughed. "I told you trouble would come to you if you called that woman back to life." I said that of a truth he had spoken well and I begged him to restore me to life. He refused and began to eat me.'

In some versions the faithlessness of the woman is omitted and the hearers fully understand that the innate stupidity of women caused this one to throw away her husband's magic power.

Another favourite theme is one which explains that not every man has good luck.

There was once a certain poor man who had three sons. But while they were still babies he died, and so did their mothers. They had nothing at all in all the world, but the big man of their village took pity on them and took them into his house, where they soon began to work for him.

As they grew older they began to make a farm for themselves as well as for the big man who had taken them in. But having no money nor clothes nor anything except their arms to work with, they were unable to obtain wives. This grieved them.

Now as it is customary the youngest of them used to have to fetch the water for them. This he always placed in a large calabash in the field. But a wonderful thing happened here. For the two elder brothers found in the calabash only water, whilst every time the youngest went to drink he found milk. The brothers thought he was not only a liar but also crazy, and did not force him to work so much. And one day when they saw a cow come into their corn they told him to go and drive it away whilst they continued their hoeing. The youngest did so and followed the cow away from the farm. Suddenly the cow changed itself into a fine girl who at once asked the boy to marry her. He agreed to this and brought the girl back to the field and told his brothers. They said that truly it was a wonderful thing from God and accepted the woman as their brother's wife and told her to go home and make them food. The girl did so and thus the youngest became a married man and more important than the two older ones.

So it fell to the lot of the second brother to fetch the water in the farm. One day when he came down to the river side he saw a beautiful girl bathing in the water. She was a stranger to him and, as is usual, he did not go near until she had finished. But the girl called to him and asked him why he was afraid to draw near. He explained that she was a stranger and that he feared to do so. Then she laughed and told him that she had done this on purpose and that she wanted him to marry her. The young man was overjoyed and took the woman back to the farm and showed her to his married brother and the eldest.

Then was the eldest sore distressed. He could not understand how it was that he could get no wife and that his two younger brethren had succeeded. He went home and in the evening went to consult the Bakologo man, who is, as you know, learned in revealing all secret and hidden matters. The Bakologo told him that it was all due to luck, which was given by God to men. Some had good luck and others bad luck.

But this did not satisfy the unfortunate man, and he went out and hanged himself.

It is natural that the subject of evil step-mothers should provide some tales. The Dagomba relate that:

Many years ago there was a certain man who had two wives. To each of these wives was born a son, and the man gave them both the same name, Dramanu. The elder was known as Big Dramanu and the younger as Little Dramanu.

Now it came to pass that the mother of Big Dramanu died while her son was still but a child, but the mother of Little Dramanu did not die. The husband told her that she must look after both children for him, but this she did not like as she had hated the dead woman. Therefore she was always maltreating Big Dramanu, whipping him and giving him but little food. The father was unable to say anything as men have nothing to do with young children.

Always was Big Dramanu crying and hungry. So one day he said to his father: 'Give me some seed yams, so that I can go and make a farm for myself.'

His father agreed to this. But the woman had heard the conversation and called her own son Little Dramanu to come and get some seed yams too. When the man had come back from the storehouse where he kept his seed yams he found the two boys, but unfortunately he had not enough for both. So the woman advised him to give the yams 'Niu-wobo' to the Big Dramanu, and the yams 'Larebako' to Little Dramanu. Now the yam Niuwobo is, as every one knows, a yam that is of no use at all, and the good yam is Larebako. But Big Dramanu was not yet old enough to know this, so he went away with his younger brother to make a farm in the bush.

In due season the yams came up and the boys collected the harvest. Big Dramanu then decided to go and sell his yams and went away to the market-place. But every one laughed at him for being so foolish as to try to sell Niuwobo and made him go outside the market-place. There he began to cry; but a stranger passing by asked him his trouble, and when he heard how the boy had worked for nothing took pity on him and bought the useless yams for three hundred cowries.

Meanwhile Little Dramanu had sold his for a much larger sum, for his yams were good ones. Both boys then went home and reported their adventures at the market-place and showed the money they had got. The woman then advised them to return to the market on the next market day and to buy with their money some fowls. She particularly advised Big Dramanu to invest his in a cock, as then he would have plenty of chickens.

Next market day the two boys went off and they bought fowls, Big Dramanu buying as advised a large cock-bird. But Little Dramanu had been told by his mother to buy only hens.

On their return the boys looked after their fowls, and in course of time Little Dramanu's fowls produced plenty of chickens, whilst Big Dramanu still had only his own cockerel. He therefore asked his parents for advice, and his step-mother told him the best thing to do was to kill the bird and go with the meat to the market and there sell it, and with the money to buy some hens.

Now it is never the custom for any one to try to sell in the market-place the meat of fowls. That is a foolish thing to do. So when poor Big Dramanu came to the place the other children hooted and jeered at him and drove him outside the clearing. Whilst seated there it chanced that a rich young man came up. He was beautifully clothed and was riding a horse magnificently caparisoned. When he saw the naked boy sitting outside the market-place with a calabash of unrecognizable meat, he asked him what it was.

Big Dramanu at once replied: 'Master, it is the meat of my own cockerel.'

The rich young man laughed and said: 'I shall buy it all. That is why I came to this market. I am a sick man and the oracle which I have consulted told me to go to market after market and if I succeeded in buying there the meat of a dead fowl then I should be cured of my sickness. Now I shall pay you my own price. You shall have this horse and all its trappings. For my life is of more worth to me than any horse.' So saying he dismounted and took the calabash of fowl meat and gave Big Dramanu the horse.

Away rode the boy full of joy at his good fortune, and as soon as he came near his father's house he cried out: 'Father, come quick and see what I have got.' The man came out and could hardly believe the story. However, he was overjoyed at the success of his eldest son. But the woman was annoyed, so that night she discussed the horse and said: 'Look here, Big Dramanu, if you want to become a very rich man this is what you must do. To-morrow tie the horse up and build around him a wall without door or other hole. Keep him like that for ten days and give him neither food nor water. Then at the end of that time break the wall and you will find that the horse has had at least ten young ones. All that time the fine trappings will be spoiling and there is only one thing to do with them and that is to take them down to the watering-place and leave them in the water. Thus white ants will not eat them.'

Now Big Dramanu was getting to be more sensible and he doubted the words of the woman, but she so abused him and made so much noise that his father said to him: 'Do as my wife bids you. Is she not older than you and has more sense?'

So next day the boy did as he was told and built a wall all round his horse and left no hole, neither door nor window. And he took the trappings and put them in the water.

At the end of ten days he broke down the wall and found, not the ten promised young horses, but his own dead. When he went to the watering-place he found that the trappings had all rotted and were useless.

Then he began to cry bitterly and said that neither his father nor his father's wife liked him and that he would therefore leave them and go away and see what he could do on his own.

So on the morrow he got up and left his father's house and wandered forth naked, without cloth or money. His sole possession was a flint and tinder.

After wandering a long long way he came to an immense town, the largest town in all the world. And as Big Dramanu walked along the streets he became frightened at his nakedness, for all the children were clothed and only he was naked. Seeing a very large house he ran inside to hide until it was dark. The yard seemed full of people and the boy hurried through courtyard after courtyard till he saw a big room where it was all dark. He ran inside and no man noticed him. Here he stayed till it was night.

But just as he was going to leave the room a man entered and Big Dramanu knew him for the king of the town. The man began to undress in the dark and Big Dramanu began to get very frightened. So he struck a light with his flint and tinder just as the man was going to lie down on his bed. The light revealed a bad snake on the bed, which would most certainly have killed the king if Big Dramanu had not shown the light.

The king shouted for his people and they killed the snake; then the king turned to Big Dramanu and asked him who he was and all about him. When Big Dramanu had told him, the king called one of his wives and said: 'Take this boy, wash him, and give him plenty to eat. He has saved my life and to-morrow I shall know what to do with him.'

And the woman did as she was told and washed Big Dramanu and gave him plenty to eat.

Q

In the morning the king called Big Dramanu and said, 'You have saved my life. Therefore all that I have is yours; I will give you ten women to look after you, ten men to make farms for you, ten sheep, and ten cows. I will give you four horses, and you may go where you please and found a city, and you shall be chief of that city.'

When the king had thus spoken all the people shouted and said he had done well. And Big Dramanu went away with the people the king had given him and many other followers as well. And he founded a great city and he was chief of that place.

In the course of time he wanted to return to his father's place. So he called his people together and they all went to the little village where Big Dramanu was born.

When they came into sight of the place Big Dramanu sent one of his young men forward to announce to his father that Big Dramanu had returned. And while the young man went on, the cavalcade stopped on a little hill looking over the village.

As soon as Big Dramanu's father heard that his son had come back he called to his wife and told her. She, looking up, saw the cavalcade and asked the messenger what it was, and when she heard it belonged to Big Dramanu she did not know what to do. So she ran from the house to meet her son, pretending to be overcome with joy. And as she ran dancing to the meeting, holding in her hand a bowl of water, she saw a bad snake slide into a hole, and an evil thought came into her head.

So she greeted her step-son humbly as a woman should and gave him the bowl of water. He thanked her, and began to ride on to his father's house. But the woman begged him not to be proud, but to walk with her. So Big Dramanu dismounted and walked with his step-mother. When they drew abreast of the hole where the snake had gone, the woman said, 'Oh, look! Put your hand into that hole quick,

Big Dramanu, a fine rat has gone in and I can see his tail. It will make a good dish for you this evening.'

Big Dramanu began to do as he was bid, but his followers came up and told him not to do things like that, for he was a big chief, and one of them would pull out the rat. However, Big Dramanu did not listen, but inserted his arm and pulled it out all covered with gold-dust. Again he put in his arm and again he drew it out all covered with gold-dust. Then the woman began to cry out for her own son, who came running up. 'Look,' she said to him, 'that hole is full of gold-dust. Put in your hand and see what you can pull out.'

Little Dramanu did as his mother bade him and pulled out a handful of dust. 'Again,' she cried, and again he put in his arm. But this time the snake bit him and he cried out, 'Alas, alas! I am a dead man. A snake has bitten me.' And he ran back to his house where he fell dead.

Then said Big Dramanu, 'Verily no man loves me in all mine house. So I shall take myself away and return no more. I and my followers will all go far away and never come back to the dwelling-places of men again.'

So saying, he began to dance, he and all his followers, and as they whirled and whirled faster and faster they began to leave the ground, and whirled themselves right away out of sight into the sky.

And that is how the whirlwinds came, so that to this day whenever the old men see a big whirlwind they say, 'Look, there is Big Dramanu with his men.'

But an Ajati story of the evil step-mother relates that:

There was once a certain man who had two wives. The first one bore him a boy-child and the other had no children. Now it came to pass that the mother of the boy became sick, and when she knew that death was near she sent for the second wife and placed in her charge her son, saying: 'I am going away now and must leave my boy. Take him

and care for him and feed him as if he were your own.'
The second wife agreed, and shortly after the woman died.

But the surviving wife forgot her promise and ill-treated
the motherless boy. She gave him neither food nor clothing,
and the wretched child had to seek what he could find for
himself.

One day the woman called the child to her and said that
he was to accompany her into the bush to get firewood.
The boy obeyed and went with the woman. When they
were a long way from the village the woman went into the
bush for the sticks and the boy sat down in the shade of
a big tree. Presently he noticed a lot of fruit had fallen from
the tree and he began to eat it. He was very hungry and
only when all the fallen fruit had been eaten was his hunger
satisfied. He then fell asleep, and after a while when he
awoke he found he was again hungry. But there was no
fruit on the ground and he was far too small to reach up to
the branches to gather some. So he began to sing, and as he
sang a song in praise of the tree, lo! the branches of the tree
bent down to him and enabled him to climb up. He then
took all the food he could eat and collected some to take
home in the rag which did service for a cloth. Then, still
singing, he climbed down and waited for the woman. She
soon came and they both went home.

Some days later the boy was seated outside the house
eating the fruit he had gathered when the woman saw him
and asked him what he had there. He told her, and the woman
took some and said that it was good. She then told the boy
to go with her to the tree so that they could get some more
of this new and excellent fruit.

They went, and when they drew near the tree the boy
began to sing again, and the tree obediently bent down its
branches, and the woman climbed up. Then the boy ceased
his song and the branches sprang up, taking with them the
woman. The woman called to the boy, but he answered that

Nyame had now given him sense and had shown him how to procure food, and that as she had neglected him so he would now neglect her. He then went home to the village.

Now when he arrived all the people asked him where was the woman, and he replied that she had gone to the bush to get firewood. Evening came and still no woman. So the people assembled under the village tree and again asked the boy, but he replied as before.

On the following morning they again collected, and began to beg the boy to show them where he had left his step-mother. When they had begged him for a long time he at last consented and led them into the bush, where the people saw the woman at the top of the tree. They asked her how she had managed to get there and she told them. Then they all begged the boy to sing. For a long time he refused, but at last as they begged so long he agreed and began to sing his praise of the tree. Immediately the branches bent down and the woman was freed.

Then every one went back to the village and reported to the chief what they had seen. He at once called all the elders and sent for the woman. He told her that had the boy not consented to sing she would not have been rescued, and he ordered her to give an account of how she had treated the motherless child. She confessed she had done wrong, and then the chief said: 'Now let all men know from this that when a man has many wives the children shall be treated as the children of them all. To each woman her husband's son shall be a son, and each child shall call each of his father's wives mother.'

A very good command, but alas! one that Nature itself often refuses to obey.

Chapter Eleven

WHICH DEALS WITH MATTERS OF HISTORY

ETYMOLOGICAL MYTH—TOTEMIC MYTHS—EARLY HUNTERS—
ASHANTI ASCENDENCY—TAR BABY MYTH—LEGENDS OF
FAMINE—HISTORY OF DAGOMBA.

WHEN one starts inquiring about the history of these various tribes of the Togo hinterland one is faced with an almost complete ignorance on the part of the native of any past beyond the first encounters with the Ashanti. The gap is filled with a number of myths and legends which are to all intents impossible to unravel. Except with the Dagomba the favourite story is of some migration and settlement in some spot where an etymological explanation of the name has produced a myth such as that classical one quoted by Sir E. B. Tylor in his *Primitive Culture* which relates how the Romans, coming in sight of where Exeter now stands, exclaimed in delight, 'Ecce terram!' and thus the city had its name.

Of such is the story of Krachi. The myth runs as follows:

In the very olden time Wulbari sent down some men by means of a chain, and they settled in the coppice between Nkomi and British Krachi.[1] At the same time he sent down some women, also by a chain. They were on the other side of the Frao[2] and lived where Krachi itself now stands.

Now it happened that no men were born in Krachi and no women in the coppice. The young men did not seem to like this, and at last they arose one day and said to their elders that they were dissatisfied with their enforced celibacy, adding, 'Ka Achi', which means, 'Let us go to the women'.

---

[1] British Krachi so-called, to distinguish it from Krachi on the opposite bank of the Volta, which was German.
[2] Or Volta.

Therefore they arose, and that is how Krachi came by its name, and how the Krachi tribe originated.

One might read in that a story such as that of the rape of the Sabine women. But the legend of separate towns for women and men is to be found among the Dagomba, who tell that in the beginning of the world Wuni did not want men and women to mix. He, therefore, had arranged for the men to live in one town and the women in another, and to make sure that there would be no intercourse between them he scattered masses of dry leaves all round the towns, so that if some one did venture out at night he would hear the rustling of the leaves and would be able to prevent his reaching the other town.

The women, apparently, did not approve of Wuni's idea at all, and after a while they collected great pots of water, more than ever they could possibly require. This water they poured on the leaves each night and thus were able to get across to the men without Wuni's knowledge.

This was very satisfactory to the men. But one day all the women menstruated and they did not, therefore, arrange for the extra supply of water. Now in the bachelors' town were three very ardent lovers. These grew impatient at the non-arrival of their sweethearts and determined to go across themselves to see what was the matter. No sooner had they left the town than the rustling of the leaves awoke Wuni, who at once challenged them. They explained their errand and then Wuni grew angry indeed. To punish the offenders he said that in future, since they had already broken his wishes, they should suffer—that women would no longer run to men, but that men should ever have to chase and hunt down women. That is why we have such a lot of trouble with them now.

Another very common myth brings one possibly into touch with the beginnings of totemism as understood in these parts. I have elsewhere related how in the Nankanni country the people of Via regard the crocodile with respect, for they relate how one of these reptiles carried their father across a river in the hour of need; how, too, through the kindly services of another crocodile the Navaro people were saved; and how the mole-cricket rescued the founder of the Mayoro. One finds the same type here.

The Konkomba of Palba, in flight from the Dagomba, reached the Oti. There was no means of crossing until a crocodile came out of the water and asked what all their cries were about. When informed he at once offered his back as a raft, and thus the Konkomba were saved. Moreover, when the pursuing Dagomba arrived on the scene they saw their would-be slaves safely across, and without hesitation hurled themselves into the flood. Thus many of them perished.

We are told, too, how the Wurupon were, as a direct result of prayer to their god, carried across the Frao on the backs of river-turtles, and similar myths might be recorded of almost every division in every tribe.

A third story of the origin of settlements is much less of the mythical type, and is probably in the vast majority of cases true. This is the foundation of the village by a single hunter. For it must always be remembered that it is only in quite recent times that the tribes of this part of Africa have learnt the art of farming, and even to this day the wandering nomad spirit is evidenced among such people as the Chumru, Krachi, Nawuri, &c. by their continual migration from one spot to another.

But real history, however, dates only from the time of the ascendency of Ashanti, and already myths and legends have arisen relating to those times. Such, I believe, is the story told by the Ajati, which tells how a long time ago Nwa, the snail, decided to go and make a great kingdom for himself. He therefore sent as far away as Krachi and told the chief there that he was coming and wanted the land. Then he got

up and slowly marched towards Krachi. As he drew near
the first chief's land he began to sing a song of war:

> 'I am coming, I am coming.
> All this land is mine.'

Now when the town people heard this they did not make
ready for war; so Nwa came, and he ate all the land.

Then, when all was finished, he arose and went on to the
next country, singing all the time the same song. But the
people were foolish and did not make ready, so that in course
of time Nwa conquered all the land and was master everywhere.

But in his pride Nwa said that he was not content, and sent
and told God, Wulbari himself, that he was coming and
would make war on him. And God laughed and waited, and
when Nwa came near he smacked his face.

From that day to this Nwa cannot walk straight, and his
face is sideways.

The Ashanti is a great eater of snails; in fact, snails are in
some parts of the country practically the only meat. And it
is not difficult to read in the allusion to Wulbari a reference
to the European, for among all the wilder tribes even to-day
is to be found a half-belief that the white man is divine.

Again: In the old old days, when the Ashanti overran the
whole country, there lived at Zilimon a certain old man who,
as a result of a visit to the great god, Bruku, of Siari in Ajati,
had acquired much magical power. It was said of him that
he could hold fast the arm or hand of any one who might
give him trouble or annoyance. And in the time of famine
it chanced that the people of Zilimon were hard put to it to
get their daily food. The children were forced to beg of their
elders for a little dawa-dawa or locust beans, for that was all
there was except a few roots and leaves. The boys of the
village came one day to the old man's farm and asked him
for some of the beans from his tree. He gave some to them,

and just then an Ashanti soldier came along and tried to take
the food away. The old man protested, and the Ashanti told
him to go away, as it was not his affair. The old man insisted,
and the Ashanti struck him. Again the old man protested
and warned him. However, the Ashanti took no notice but
hit at him again, and the Ashanti's arm hit the wall of the hut.
There it remained stuck fast, and the man could not release
himself. Other Ashanti came and begged, but for a long
while the old man would not release the fellow. At last he
consented to do so on condition that the Ashanti would go
away from Zilimon and promise no more to trouble that
part. This having been agreed to, the arm was released and
the Ashanti went away.

It is said of that same old man that he had another magical
power which enabled him to send forth his calabash to look
for food and to return filled. This, it seems to me, may em-
body yet some older tradition, as throughout the Northern
Territories the calabash is the symbol of productivity and is
among the remoter tribes a magical possession of every
woman when she has reached puberty, and at the same time
is so much her property that it is buried with her or on the
top of her tomb. Farther south among the Dagomba and
Konkomba, as well as among the Ashanti tribe of the Brong,
the calabash is replaced with pottery, and whenever one
goes into the room of a woman one is struck by the great
collection of new pots ranged against the walls. Such pots,
as far as I can learn, are regarded as a sign of wealth and
evidently productivity, for they are handed down as heir-
looms and yet are never used for ordinary domestic matters.

But the former story is interesting as it embodies the idea
of the Tar-baby story, which is so common in West Africa.
Perhaps a short digression to give two of such stories from
Krachi may be allowed.

The one tells the reason why men, who formerly died of
shame, do so no longer. Anansi had three sons, the eldest of

whom was named Ntrekuma. Now it happened that famine
came to the land where the family dwelt, and there was left
but little food in the field of Anansi. He therefore shammed
sick and, calling his children, told them to hurry and consult
a medicine-man. Being naturally obedient they did as they
were told, but their father made haste, and having disguised
himself went in front of them and sat down at the cross-
roads. There he waited for the children, and when they came
near he asked them what was the matter that they were
hurrying so. They told him that their father Anansi was ill
and they were on their way to consult a medicine-man. The
disguised Anansi then said that he was a medicine-man and
if they liked he would find out what was best to do. They
agreed to this, and after consulting his stones and other things
Anansi said that their father was bound to die and that it was
absolutely necessary for them to bury him in the farm. They
were to make the grave a nice deep one with a room for the
body and a good entrance hall and they were to be sure not
to cover it. At the same time they were to set plenty of fish,
salt, meat, and pepper, as well as other foods, each day at the
entrance hall.

The children, hearing this doleful news, hastened back to
the father they were so soon to lose. But unfortunately they
arrived too late and found Anansi already dead on his bed.
There was nothing to be done except carry out the orders
given to them by the old gentleman at the cross-roads. So
they went to the field and dug a nice deep grave with a room
and an entrance hall and brought their father the food they
had been ordered to. They then left him.

Now each night Anansi would get up out of his grave
and take enough yams to keep him well supplied during the
day. At last Ntrekuma began to suspect something was
wrong, and he caused the usual rubber man to be fashioned
and set it up in the farm, and placed in front of it a lot of nice
cooked and mashed yams. That same night Anansi saw the

food and begged the rubber man to be allowed to partake. The rubber man kept on nodding, and Anansi took this to mean 'yes'. He therefore stooped down for the food, and at once one of his arms was caught. He hit out and the other was held. He kicked and his foot was held. He butted and his head stuck fast in the rubber.

Thus he had to remain till morning when his children came. Ntrekuma at once recognized his father, but the latter shouted out:

'Go away, go away. I am not your father. I am like him. Go away. I am full of medicine. Don't come near me, don't touch me. If you do come near me I shall turn into your father.' But the children drew nearer and Anansi kept on shouting, 'I shall turn; I shall; I have.'

Then the children approached their father, and Ntrekuma abused his father for his trickery. And Anansi was ashamed, but because he was a wily man he refused to die, and from that day to the present time many men, though covered with shame, do not go into the bush and kill themselves. Formerly every one did.

The second story runs on similar lines. But in this case Anansi sets the trap. The rubber man catches the farm thief and Ntrekuma and his father cut the unfortunate fellow up into very small pieces and scatter them all over the place. This, seeing that Anansi was a medicine-man in the story, was a foolish thing to have done, as the pieces all became men and kept the thieving propensities of their fore-father. Thus it came about that the world has many thieves in it.

Now it seems curious how in so many of these stories the setting lies in the prevalence of a famine. I venture to suggest that this is either the remembrance of a time when all these tribes lived well out of the forest zone, where shortage of food is frequent, or that it recalls the period before men had learned how to cultivate their fields and had perforce to eke out their livelihood on roots and snails and insects and occasional meat, a manner of living which must often have placed men on the shortest of commons.

The following history of the Dagomba people is a much more elaborate tale than is to be found in most parts.[1]

It is said that their country was once inhabited by giants who are remembered by the name 'Kondors' or 'Tiawomya'. This race of giants is said to have been of so extraordinary a stature that if a hawk swooped down on their chickens and carried one away, they stood up and snatched it back. They were so tall and big that their voices could be heard some twenty miles off when singing to their drums.

Their arm-rings (two are kept to this day as magic wonders; one is at San and one at Dikpeleu in Adele) were so large that the biggest man of modern times could easily pass through them.

But that is myth. There is a story told by the Mohammedans how, after the confusion of tongues, the tribe of Ad, which descended from Ad, the son of Uz, the son of Aram, son of Sem, son of Noah, settled in the province of Hadramaut, where their posterity greatly multiplied. This tribe continued to worship God; but in process of time they fell from the worship of the true God into idolatry. God, seeing this, sent his prophet Heber to preach to them and to reclaim them. But they refusing to acknowledge his mission, God sent a hot and suffocating wind, which blew seven nights and eight days without ceasing, which entered into their bodies and destroyed them all save the very few who had believed in Heber. This tribe is said to have been of a prodigious stature, the largest of them being a hundred cubits or a hundred and fifty feet tall and the shortest sixty cubits or ninety feet. This tribe emigrated and wandered towards the east and the west, settling in uninhabited countries, till they

[1] My coadjutor, Mr. E. F. Tamakloe, is responsible for the collection of the facts in the history of Dagomba from this point to the end of the chapter, myself acting solely as editor.

arrived in this country which is now called 'Dagbon' and their progeny 'Dagbambas'. The first towns built by them were said to be Gunayiri in Karaga District and Yogo in Toma or Safulugu District, and those of them which settled beyond the Oti river were the progenitors of the Kpam-kpamba (Konkomba) races. The story also goes that some of these giants, three men and three women from Yogo and seven men and seven women from Gunayiri, moved on and founded Nanumba and Adele.

The Adites who settled in Dagbon were iron smelters and blacksmiths. As the iron-bearing stones were not to be found in one place in any quantity, these people found it necessary to wander about from place to place, and became scattered over the country which lies between the Kulkpini River (that is the Dakar River; also written Kulpene), the White Volta, and the Nyamalga Rivers. Large kitchen middens, heaps of iron slag, aged baobab and kapok trees, which witness the sites of one-time well-peopled towns, are sufficient proofs that the Dagbamba country was once occupied and inhabited by a numerous and industrious people. It is said that many of them also possessed large herds of cattle, and owing to the dryness of the country they had to dig water-holes in nearly every part of the country.

The religion of the Adites is forgotten, but perhaps the observance of the Festival of fire torches (Muharram) held on the tenth or twelfth October, to commemorate the resting of the Ark of Noah on Mount Ararat, when the people in the Ark came out and made fires, and that of Damba which celebrates the birth and circumcision of Mohammed, indicate its nature.

That is the Mohammedan version of the early days of Dagbon.

The chiefs or the priests amongst these settlers were wont to sit on cow-skins and used the lion and leopard-skins as their authority, which they called 'Ada gbon', meaning

Ada's skin, hence the name of the country came to be corrupted into Dagbon and the inhabitants 'Dagbamba'. The giants gradually disappeared, but their offspring named Gbandimara or Gbandara survive to the present generation.

The posterity of the Adites multiplied greatly. They had no rulers save the priests who exercised a mild control over the people. In some cases, a headman of a compound who had plenty of followers, or was wealthy in cattle, was considered the chief or head man of a town. But the most sacred spot in the country was at Yogo, and its priest was the head of the Dagbamba people. They were in this deplorable condition till Na Nyagse, the great grandson of Kpogonumbo, made war against them, killed all the priests of the Dagbamba, and appointed his sons, brother, and nephews chiefs in their stead.

History tells us the following concerning the origin of these conquerors, whose descendants are the present rulers of the Dagbamba people.

In the wilderness of Malle (not to be confounded with the Western Empire of similar name), a country to the east of Dagbon, there lived in a cave among the hills some four days from the town of Malle, a certain superman whose name was 'Tohajiye' or the 'Red Hunter'.

This man was a great hunter in the wilderness. Once in time of drought, he came out from his mountain and went into Malle where he lodged with a certain old woman named 'Malle Pakurugu' (the old woman of Malle). He asked the old woman for some water to drink. The old woman replied: 'Don't you see all my children and grandchildren lying down half-dead for want of water? But listen to me,' she continued, 'there is a lake in the suburb whence we fetch water in the dry season; but now, for a long time, we have been dispossessed of the lake by a one-horned wild bull, which attacks and kills every one who dares to go there to fetch water.' On hearing this Tohajiye asked where the road to the lake was; upon being shown he took his bow and quiver, and with four calabash pots hanging on his shoulders, he went to the lake to fetch water; no sooner did he dip the calabash pots into the water than the wild bull rushed upon him to kill him. Tohajiye immediately shot an arrow and killed it; he then cut off its tail and, taking some water, he returned to the old woman and informed her that he had killed the troublesome beast. The woman doubted; but upon being shown the tail she was exceedingly glad, and instantly sent off the inmates of her compound, led in person by Tohajiye, to fetch water. The old woman then ordered drums to be made for her children which, being played upon, sang thus:

'Ngun so wayo, onkpi,' meaning that 'One who is grown up foolish, he will die', and every one began to dance and play.

The rejoicing was kept up in the old woman's house for some days until the King of Malle heard of it and asked what it all meant.

The old woman was summoned to the presence of the king, and told him all that had occurred. The king then invited Tohajiye to his compound, and having entertained him for two days sent him back to the old woman with valuable presents. After a few days Tohajiye begged leave of the old woman and returned to his abode in the wilderness.

For some reason which the legend omits, a few hours after the departure of Tohajiye, the old woman sent three of her 'sons' with pumpkin seeds, to follow him secretly back to his house, and told them to plant the seeds there. They did so without being seen by him till the fourth day, when he reached his destination, and they saw him enter the cave (i.e. hole in the ground).

They immediately planted the seeds near the cave and returned home, and in a few weeks the pumpkins had grown, and their branches ran along the bush track towards Malle until they reached the gate of the old woman's house.

Some time after the departure of Tohajiye there arose a war between the people of Malle and the neighbouring tribes, and the Malles, having been several times discomfited, were driven back with great slaughter. The King of Malle then remembered Tohajiye and inquired as to his whereabouts. The old woman was asked to send for him to come to their help. The same three grandsons of the old woman went. They followed the branches of the pumpkin to the cave. There they called and told him of the reason of their coming. He made himself ready and went back with them to the presence of the king. The enemy were even then about to attack Malle; therefore, immediately after his interview with the king, Tohajiye went out unaccompanied against the enemy. His appearance in the field alone caused a great panic among them, and they ran in confusion away from his presence—however, he followed them, and killed plenty of them. The King of Malle was very glad, and proposed to give one of his daughters to the conqueror. He therefore called them together and asked the victor to choose a wife from among them. To the surprise of the king and the spectators around, Tohajiye chose as his wife a lame, crippled girl, and carried her off on his shoulders to his cave in the wilderness.

This woman was called 'Pagawobga, Malle Na bipunga', i.e. 'Lame woman, the daughter of the King of Malle'.

In course of time the girl presented Tohajiye with a boy who was named Kpogonumbo (often called 'Numbo' for brevity). The mother died just after his birth, and a few weeks later his father also died. Kpogonumbo remained alone in his father's cave till he attained manhood. As to the outward appearance of Kpogonumbo, tradition differs, but the general opinion is that Kpogonumbo was of a gigantic stature; blood incessantly trickled from one of his eyes and white matter from the other; flies dwelt in one of his nostrils and bees in the other. Some say he had only one arm and one leg. Kpogonumbo, though bereft of his parents during his infancy, knew that he was a grandson to the King of Malle.

The legend goes on that once more the King of Malle had to defend himself against the neighbouring tribes. He again asked the old woman to send for his son-in-law Tohajiye to come to his succour.

The messengers arrived at the cave and called out to Tohajiye. Kpogonumbo replied that his mother Pagawobga had died when he was but a child; and that his father too was dead, but anything that was required of his father he would do it. He then departed with the messengers and was brought into the presence of the king. During their inter- view the king said that there was strife between himself and the neighbouring tribes; he was very sorry to hear of his bereavement and sympathized with him; he was certain that he (Kpogonumbo) had inherited the intrepidity and valour of his father. Kpogonumbo then undertook to fight for his grandfather. His appearance alone caused panic among the enemy, whom he totally routed. After this Kpogonumbo neither stayed in Malle nor returned to his subterranean home, but went off immediately towards the west.

After many days' travel, Kpogonumbo arrived at Biung[1] in Gruma, and hid himself in the bulrushes and the thickets on the bank of the small stream called Yilinga, from which the Biung people used to drink in the dry season. During this time the high priest Tindan-na[2] of Gruma in Biung had hired young men to make him a farm for the coming year, and placed them in charge of his two brothers, Tindanjiye and Tindanbila. One day the men went to work in the farm, and the sun grew very hot. Knowing the men would have no water to drink, Tindan-na sent his eldest daughter, who

---

[1] Biung is a name commonly found throughout these northern parts; it is invariably that of the oldest village.

[2] Tindan-na = tindana, chief of the earth + na, king, i.e. head of the chief of the earth.

was called Suhusabga or Sisabga, to take water to the men in the field. When she came to the stream the sun was overhead. As she was about to dip the pot into the stream Kpogonumbo appeared from his hiding place and stooped toward her. The woman was so frightened that she could not move. Kpogonumbo then asked her if her father was in the town. Having been told that he was, he bade her go and call him. The Tindan-na and some of the elders in the town, when they had heard the strange story from their daughter, went off to the stream and saw exactly what she had told them. Kpogonumbo performed some miracles (he caused millet to grow, to be reaped, and be brewed into pito at the same moment) in their presence, and went with them into the town. The Tindan-na, having consulted with his elders, gave his daughter to Kpogonumbo to marry.

Kpogonumbo remained in Biung, and a son was born to him. This son he called Namzisielle. During his boyhood Namzisielle used to accompany his young uncles, the sons of the Tindan-na, into the neighbouring bush, where they used to shoot at wild pigeons. His young uncles, who actually hated him, used to give him to eat the roasted feet and the wings of the wild pigeons, saying, 'Were it not on account of our sister, we would not even have given you these, for we do not know from where your father is come.' The boy Namzisielle used, on his return home, to tell all this to his father, who for a long time had wished to make himself chief priest, and he now decided to do so, making this illtreatment of his son his excuse.

Now the time to observe the customs of the big annual sacrifice was at hand, and preparations were being made; pito was brewed and a huge bull slaughtered for the feast. One leg of the animal was sent to Kpogonumbo, who sent it back and asked for its feet and head. The day for the feast came and soon all became intoxicated. During the day, Suhusabga went into her husband's room. Kpogonumbo exclaimed: 'Oi Tindan-na biya!' i.e. 'Alas! daughter of the high priest'.

The woman said:

> 'Mani m-be la,
> Ti nim m-bara bunga,
> N-Kare dore n-wolge piyinga,
> N-duhuru nam
> Mani Tindan-na pakpon.'

meaning:

> 'Here am I.
> We are those that ride donkeys,
> And number the locust-trees
> And rend asunder the flat-topped houses
> And ascend the chieftainship (stool).
> I am the first-born daughter of the
> High priest.'

Kpogonumbo, seeing his wife thus intoxicated, seized the chance of learning the secrets of the sacred things of the priestcraft and where the Tindan-na would be found during the coming night. That evening Kpogonumbo took his wooden spear, mounted his donkey (the custom of mounting a donkey on the day a new king is elected for Yendi stool is observed to this day), and accompanied by his son Namzi-sielle, playing upon a pumpkin drum which his father had made, went into the Tindan-na's residence and called him out.

No sooner had he come out than he was stabbed to death by Kpogonumbo, who cut off his head and threw it into the washing-place of Tindanjiye, the younger brother of the murdered priest. Kpogonumbo then took and arrayed himself in the priestly cap, the three strings of costly aggrey beads, and the priestly gown, which are still preserved, and when kings are elected to the Yendi skin, are worn by them for that occasion only during their lifetime.

At dawn, when the people came to pay their respects to

the Tindan-na, they saw his body lying outside naked and
mutilated, nor did they know who had done this. Great
consternation arose and every one began asking his neighbour, 'Who has done this?' At the same time, they saw the
blood leading from the dead body to the compound of
Tindanjiye. They followed it and found the head in his
washing-place. Kpogonumbo, observing this, came out
immediately from his compound, attired in the high priest's
regalia and shouted: 'I killed him! I killed him!' He then
went into the sacred hut—amid the awed silence of the people
—and seated himself on the skin, and thus assumed the
chieftainship of the country.

During his reign a powerful prince of Gruma, named
Daramani, tried unsuccessfully to fight and dethrone him.
Peace once more restored, Daramani gave his daughter
Soyini or Solyini to Kpogonumbo as his wife, who bore
him Na Gbewa.

The writer has heard no account of Kpogonumbo's death;
but after the death of his sons by Suhusabga—who were
supposed to have succeeded their father as priests—his
youngest son Na Gbewa succeeded to the sacred skin.

Na Gbewa, after having stayed for a very short time in
Gruma, emigrated with a tremendous number of followers
into the Kusanga and the Busanga countries, and made Pussiga his capital town, whence he used to fight the Kussasi and
the Busansi, trying to subdue them. The head chiefs among
his followers were the Chief of Gushiago, the Chiefs of
Gukpiogo, Tugurunam, Gomle, and many others. There
were also priests serving under the king, the head priest.
Na Gbewa had the following issue:

Kachiogo	(Female)	Sitobo	(Male)
Zirili	(Male)	Sibie	,,
Kufogo	,,	Biemmone	,,
Tohago	,,	Bogoyelgo	,,
Ngmantambo	,,		

Na Gbewa was now very old and blind; but as the Kussasi and the Busansi very often raided his settlement near the capital, and were not entirely crushed, he sent his eldest son and Kufogo against them, and they remained a long time away at the war. Now Na Gbewa considered Zirili a wicked man in his manners of life and quite unfit to reign. He therefore proposed to leave the kingdom to Kufogo. Having arranged this with his elders he sent his 'hazo', i.e. one who sits in front, to call Kufogo's mother. And when he came he told him what was in his mind and then confided to the elders who had agreed to help taking the chieftainship from Zirili.

For some reason, which no one knows, the messenger went and called Zirili's mother (it is stated that Zirili's mother was good and Kufogo's mother wicked, and that that was the reason that the front sitter had done this).[1]

Na Gbewa, not knowing the mistake, for he was, as stated, blind, began to tell the woman all he had arranged with the elders. Zirili's mother said never a word; but leaving the presence of her husband the king, she went directly to the camp and informed her son Zirili what his father had said.

During the night Zirili ordered a big hole to be dug and covered with grass reeds. Before dawn he ordered skins and embroidered leather cushions to be placed over the hole. Then he sent for all the elders in the camp.[2]

When they had come Zirili seated himself near the trap and ordered his younger brother Kufogo to sit on the pillows over the hole by his side. Nobody knew that a trap had been set for Kufogo, and no sooner had he sat on the pillows than he dropped into the hole and was there buried alive by Zirili's orders. Great terror reigned in the camp and none dared leave it. Men remained in the camp until

---

[1] Cf. the story of Tano and Bia, p. 49.
[2] Cf. *supra*, p. 43, the story of Nyame and Edubiaku and, p. 129, the story of Antiakoti.

Gushiag Na, i.e. Chief of Gushiago, broke off, and with his party repaired to Pussiga to inform Na Gbewa of what had occurred.

As they drew near the town, the Chief of Gushiago ordered a halt, to consider how Na Gbewa could best be informed of the murder of Kufogo; for according to the customs of those days he could not inform him verbally.[1] At last it occurred to him to fashion a pipe, a drum, and a horn of an elephant tusk. On entering the town he ordered men to play upon these instruments which are preserved to this day, and, whenever a chief of Gushiago visits Yendi, are carried and played as he enters that town.

The pipe says:

> 'Gbewa! Gbewa!
> Zirili ku Fogo!
> Zirili ku Fogo!'

The drum answers:

> 'M-ba ye! M-ba ye!'

The horn then wails:

> 'U-uhu! U-uhu!'

Meaning:

> ' Gbewa! Gbewa!
> Zirili has killed Fogo
> Zirili has killed Fogo
> Oh! Father, Oh! Father
> U-uhu! U-uhu!'

At the time Na Gbewa was sitting outside his compound, and when he understood what the music said he began to throw himself about in such grief that the ground opened and he disappeared from sight.

Zirili was still in his camp when he heard of the death of

[1] Cf. *supra*, p. 38, the story of Nyame and the Gold and Silver children.

his father, and that his elder sister Kachiogo had seized the
skin, saying that she was the eldest. He at once struck camp
and began to move homeward, proposing to enter Pussiga
by night so as to frighten the people; he therefore ordered
a halt, and told all the men who were with him to make
pieces of board (about eighteen inches long and eight inches
broad) and fix one end to a piece of string—each man
to have one—which, when whirled in the air would give
a tremendous humming sound. When night came on, he
moved into the town with his party, and terrorized the town
folk, even the chieftainess ran and hid herself in the cavity
of a large Kapok tree in the town. She was found by her
brother Zirili, who told her to renounce the skin that same
night and, as a reward for complying, when the custom of
'making king' was finished, Kachiogo was appointed the
first woman Chief of Gundogo—a chieftainship for the
eldest daughter of Yendi kings, which is theirs by right to
this day. Gundogo is gunga (Kapok tree), Dogo (hole),
i.e. Chief of the hole in the Kapok tree.

When the elders and their followers came to pay the new
king their respects, he paid particular heed to the attendants
on the person of the late king his father.

One of them, called 'Kpoyo', was asked what his duty
was, and said that he drove 'flies' from the king. Zirili told
him that he was to be Zohena, Chief of the flies, i.e. Zohe
(flies), and Na (Chief). Another one said his duty was to lull
the king to sleep; he was told to be the Chief of the lullers,
i.e. Balona. Another one said his duty was to find cooking-
pots for cooking the king's food, when travelling; he was
told to be called 'Pogo', i.e. cooking-pot. Another one said
he soothed the king's anger; he was ordered to be called
'Malli', i.e. make it (the trouble) good. Another one said
that his duty was not to leave the king alone; he also was
ordered to be called 'Dewalgena', i.e. don't leave the king.
All these appointments were held by eunuchs until recently,

when the last eunuch died, except the post of Dewalgena which was filled by a Mohammedan priest.

During the reign of Na Zirili, there was no trouble with the local inhabitants in the Kussasi country; but when Zirili died there arose a dispute over the succession between his three younger brothers Tohago, Ngmantambo, and Sitobo. The last two joined against the former, and fighting took place. Tohago and his adherents were driven away by his brothers, and the legend informs us that only because Tohago was possessed of some magic was his life saved. For when he saw his brothers' party pressing hard upon his heels, he made magic (with what, is not known) so that a large space between his brothers and himself became covered with trees, and this forest still exists and is known by the name of 'Sunba'. Sitobo and his party had to halt in order to cut a way through the forest before they could continue the pursuit. Tohago then picked up a stone and knocked it on the ground and the space between himself and his brothers became a mountain range, and there he built his town, which he called Nalerigu, which is amongst the Mamprussi—thus Tohago became the first Mamprussi king, and his posterity still rule over that land.

Sitobo and his party still persevered and tried to cross the mountains to find and slay him. When he heard this, he took an egg and struck it to the ground and it became so large a river that their advance was hindered. Thus frustrated from his evil design Sitobo had to find a passage and so came to Gambaga.

The visit of so mighty a foreigner was unknown, and all the inhabitants of Gambaga ran away, excepting an old woman who possessed a large herd of cattle which Sitobo very cunningly got rid of. For no sooner had Sitobo settled in Gambaga than he sent to the old woman for a goat to make a sacrifice. The old woman complied with his orders; and Sitobo continued to demand from her goat after goat and sheep after sheep till all the goats and sheep were finished, and then he began to demand her cows. Whenever he slaughtered anything that was taken from the old woman, he used to send her a leg of the slaughtered animal; therefore, the old woman did not feel so much the ill-treatment until only one cow remained. Sitobo at last sent for the only remaining cow, slaughtered it, but failed to send a leg to the old woman. She then came to him and asked the reason why he did not send her her portion as he had heretofore done. Sitobo said to her that it ill-suited her to ask such a question. The old woman said to him, 'A kunko pun dira,' i.e. 'Did you use to eat (meat) alone before this time?' Thereupon Sitobo ordered her to be killed on the spot.

The legend tells us that, after this old woman of Gambaga had been thus brutally murdered, her ghost was ever by the side of Sitobo—no matter if he was eating, drinking, sleeping, hunting, playing, she was always there, and kept asking him, 'A kunko pun dira.' This state of things so alarmed Sitobo that he left Gambaga for Nabare, a very flourishing town at the time near Walewale. Still the old woman's ghost followed him there, and ever asked him, 'A kunko pun dira.' But here Sitobo made magic and cast the ghost away from himself, and it fell into Safulugu (Savelugu). This ghost was then called 'Yo', and therefore, until this day, the chieftainship of Safulugu is called 'Yo', and a chief to that skin 'Yo-na'.

After some years' stay in Nabare, Na Nyagse, the eldest son of Sitobo, asked of his father some fighting men to wage war against the neighbouring tribes to the east. It was only through the good offices three times given of his uncle Kuga-na Sibie, Sitobo's younger brother, that his father agreed. Na Nyagse set out, therefore, on the war-path, subduing all he met on his way, until he came and settled in Bagale—a Dagbamba village on the Mamprussi-Dagbamba frontier. There Na Nyagse stayed a long time until his father, in order to prevent disputes arising on his death as to the succession to the skin, grew anxious to see and to make him king in the presence of his uncles.

On a certain Friday when all the elders, &c., would come round to pay him their respects, Sitobo proposed to his brothers and followers, that as his son Na Nyagse had remained so long abroad, and he had heard nothing of him, he would go himself in search of him. But his followers told him that he was too old and weak for the enterprise.

Sitobo then ordered a lamb to be taken from its mother and hidden in a room near-by. And the assembled people saw a mother sheep running about calling, calling for her offspring; then Sitobo asked them what was the reason of the sheep's baaing and running about. They said they did not know. He then ordered the lamb to be led out. The mother sheep, on seeing her lamb, ran to it and began to fondle it. By this example he demonstrated to them how necessary it was that parents should love their children. Then all his men agreed that he should go to find where his son Na Nyagse was.

It was in the rainy season that Sitobo, with all his brothers and a great host of followers, travelled to Bagale. On the way he sent a secret messenger to Na Nyagse to acquaint him with the reason of his coming. On hearing this, Na Nyagse bought one red and white striped gown, and a walking-stick to exchange for those of his father. Two days after his arrival in Bagale, Sitobo summoned a meeting of his elders and, in their presence, rose up and ordered a grass-mat to be given him; he then invested his son with the regalia and seated him on the skin; and he seated himself on the grass-mat and began to address the people, explaining his reason for so doing. This, of course, annoyed his (Sitobo's) brothers, and they went away in anger from him. These were Biemmone, Bogoyelgo, and Ngmantambo.

Biemmone went and established himself in Gunayiri. At this time there was a priestess in Binduli (Karaga) who became Biemmone's sweetheart, and from time to time sent him presents of okros and other vegetables. Biemmone was pleased at these presents and went to visit the priestess in her town. Falling in love with her, and at the same time with the intent of seizing the kingdom, he married her and waited patiently until she died, and thus Biemmone became the founder of the big chieftainship of Karaga.

Bogoyelgo and his party went away from Sitobo in Bagale, and established himself in Sunson, amongst the Kpankpamba people (Konkomba). He gradually subdued these savages and became their chief. The second Chief of Sunson removed hence and settled in the far north to control his Kpankpamba subjects the better. There is only one compound remaining on the ruins of the old Sunson which is now called 'Sunson-gbon' between Sekpiego and Zion.

Ngmantan who was also called Ngmantambo went far to the east and, settling amongst the Nanumba, founded the kingdom of the Nanumba in Bimbila, after having killed the priest of that place.

But Kuga-na Sibie, who followed his nephew Na Nyagse to Bagale in the expedition, and acted as a fetish consulter, and burner of sin offering, &c., was appointed Chief of Gbalga, Tannyeli, Nankukpalgo, Nanluo, and many other villages, by Sitobo.

After the installation of Na Nyagse, his father Sitobo remained in Bagale as chief of that place; he died and was buried there. His tomb was encircled by a compound and a house built over it. To this house the souls of the Kings of Yendi return when they leave the king's bodies.

Na Nyagse now took the field against the Dagbamba people; first he went to the west and then to the east, fought with and measured all the Dagbamba priests, and appointed his sons, brothers, and uncles as chiefs in their stead.

He fought with and killed the Tindana of Pigu, and appointed his eldest son Zolkpaba Chief.

He killed the Tindana of Nyinbungu and made his son Mogonyona Chief.

He killed the Tindana of Didoggo and made his son Wombolga Chief.

He killed the Tindana of Sakpli and made his son Frinyanga Chief.

He killed the Tindana of Zosalle and made his son Wunbiele Chief.

He killed that of Diare and made his son Shallon Chief.

He killed that of Gushiye and made his son Kapziem Chief.

He killed the Tindana of Safulugu (Savelugu) and made his brother Biyo Chief.

He killed the Tindana of Dapale and made his son Denzie Chief.

He killed the Tindana of Namogo and made his son Bisunga Chief.

He killed the Tindana of Singa and made his son Layyago Chief.

He killed the Tindana of Dalong and made his son Busubunankape Chief.

He killed the Tindana of Kumbungu and made his son Bimiem Chief.

He killed the Tindana of Zangbalon and made his son Buruzambo Chief.

He killed that of Gbolon and made his son Lokpa Chief.

He killed the Tindana of Vogo and made his son Bambilie Chief.

He killed the Tindana of Timbungu and made his son Lundu Chief.

He killed the Tindana of Lungbungu and made his son Susable Chief.

He killed the Tindana of Tamale and made his son Tulebi Chief.

Though having been made Chief of Tamale, Tulebi did

not reside in Tamale; he appointed a new Tindana whom he named Dakpeme or Tamale-Dakpame, and created a new chieftainship for himself near Safulugu (Savelugu) whence he exercised lordship over Tamale.

Na Nyagse killed the Tindana of Nanton and made his brother Batanga Chief.

Owing to the valour of the Tindana of Tampion, Na Nyagse spared him to live until his death, when Bilyanga, the son of Dimani, was made to succeed him.

He killed the Tindana of Tujo and made his son Ngunawi Chief.

He killed the Tindana of Tugu and made his son Sangmani Chief.

He killed the Tindana of Galwie and made his uncle Zogga Chief.

He killed the Tindana of Zakole and made his son Bembale Chief.

He killed the Tindana of Kukon and made his son Zontulibi Chief.

He killed the Tindana of Ngani (Gnani) and made his son Konsigenili Chief.

He killed the Tindana of Nakpari and made his son Kayiimbagaya Chief.

Na Nyagse, believing that he had now finished his task, went and settled in Yogo, whence he selected a site between Yogo, Dapale, and Diare, and built the capital town of the Dagbamba, and called it Na-ya, i.e. the king's town.

'Tandogo lie mor'le
Ka Tankpa lie Zoya'

meaning:

'The swish[1] hole became a river
And the swish balls (bricks) became mountains.'

It was stated that the swish hole out of which swish was

---

[1] Swish is the word used in West Africa for mud, stamped by men until sufficiently well mixed for building houses, exactly like cob in Devon.

dug for the building became a river and the pieces of swish which fell off from the hands of the carriers became mountains.

This river is shown near Dapale and is a long pool which joins the White Volta in the rains. Owing to the determination of the Gonja to conquer Dagbon, Na Luro abandoned it about a hundred and fifty years after its building, and the site of the ruin which is called Yendi Dabare (Ruins of Yendi) is still visible. Na Nyagse died in Yoggo when invited by his mother to attend her skin-sacrifice, and was succeeded by his son Zulande.

The desire to be masters of other countries had always existed among the princes now ruling the Dagbamba country. Therefore, when Zulande became king, his son Nagalogo, at the head of a large army, waged war against the Tampruma people. He burnt Kulumbuso and Zantani. He went through the whole Tampruma country as far as to Murugu, where he heard of the death of his father the king. Having made ready to return to his father's obsequies, he himself died suddenly at Murugu. These two funeral customs weighed heavily on Galbanga Fatu the first wife of Na Zulande and the mother of Nagalogo, hence the song:

'Murugu yalem ngmaya
Galbanga Fatu n-Kumda
O-yidana Zugu
N-kumda o-bi zugu.'

meaning:

'The salt of Murugu came to nought
Galbanga Fatuma
Bewails her husband
Bewails her son.'

(Galbanga is the title of the first wife of every Yendi king.)
After the completion of the funeral of Na Zulande the

insignia of the kingship were taken to Murugu and placed
on the tomb of Nagalogo, showing thereby that he had
reigned and was to be numbered among the Kings of
Dagbon. The Tampruma country then remained under the
sway of the Dagbamba kings, until Jakpa wrested the place
from them.

Darigudiembda, surnamed 'Shelbema Datolle', the second
son of Zulande, became King of Dagbon. Early in his reign
he took the field against the Wangara people. He stormed
and took Gbona the capital, and married the princess of that
place. Having remained in Gbona (modern Bona) for some
years, he appointed a representative and left for Dagbon; on
his journey back he died[1] at Gbungburi (called by the
Dagbamba 'Binduliya').

A house was said to have been built over his tomb and
thither came the Gbona kings on an annual visit to sacrifice
a black cow to the soul of their great grandfather. (This town
Gbungburi is not far from Bole.)

His brother Bariguwiemda, who was to succeed him, came
to Gbungburi, and after performing the funeral rites visited
Gbona. At this time Darigudiembda's wife, who was in Gbona,
was about to give birth to a child, and Bariguwiemda gave
her a very valuable present, and made all necessary arrange-
ments for the child before it was born. A few days after his
departure messengers were sent to announce to him that his
brother's wife had given birth to a male child. Bariguwiemda
then exclaimed: 'Bun bo nkane?' meaning: 'What is
wanting?' When the messengers returned home they said
the child's name was to be called—as they heard from his
uncle—'Bonkane'. In process of time, Bonkane became
King of Gbona and had three sons; these were Gago,
Kunga, and Banaguri. The present rulers of Gbona are
descended from Gago, the eldest son of Bonkane.

Bariguwiemda was succeeded by Na Zolgo, another and

[1] Cf. L. Tauxier, *Le Noir de Bondoukou*, Paris, 1922, pp. 55–9.

elder son of Darigudiembda, who was succeeded by Zong-mang, son of Zolgo, who was succeeded by his brother Nongmitoni, who was succeeded by his brother Diwani, who was succeeded by Yanzo, who was succeeded by his nephew, Dariziogo. Zongmang's full name was Zongmang kun-she miya, da wata n-nabera, i.e. a broken house cannot be sewn with string, firewood split becomes plenty.

It was during the reign of Na Dariziogo that the Ngbanye (Gonja) people, under the leadership of Sumaila Ndewura Jakpa, came and settled in the Wala country, whence they proceeded to conquer the country lying between the Black and the White Volta, even as far as the Kpamkpamba.

These newcomers are said to have come from Gifi, which is in Mandingo.[1]

Sumaila Ndewura Jakpa was one of the mightiest princes that ever lived in the Mandingo country. On one occasion he interviewed a certain Mallam who told him—from his oracle books—that he, Sumaila Ndewura Jakpa, would never be a king in his own country; his fortune was rather in foreign lands, where he would acquire riches, and would establish a kingdom for himself, his heirs, and successors.

The Mallam's prophecy made a very deep impression on Jakpa, and it was ever in his mind. At last the opportunity came, and he set out with seventy thousand men—men unfit and useless for fighting purposes, women, and children are not counted in this reckoning. The captains of this host were Manwura and Bonwura. A few days after his departure he arrived in a town called Jah, and made friends with a certain Mallam named Fati Worukpe (i.e. Woru-Albino), and told him the reason for his migration, and begged him to enter his service, to pray to God to keep away from him all mishaps and evils that might stay him on his march. In return Jakpa promised him the following articles if he were

---

[1] Cf. Withergill's translation of a Hausa History of Salaga, printed by Government at Accra, 1924.

successful in his adventure: 100 slaves, 100 cattle, 100 pairs of donkeys, 100 pairs of sheep, 100 pairs of goats, 100 pairs of fowls, 100 horses, 100 gowns, and 100 pairs of trousers. Fati Morukpe refused the offer, and Jakpa went on his way. He then arrived in the country of the Biegas, who opposed him.

Fighting took place with much slaughter on either side, but neither triumphed. Jakpa, not knowing what to do, in desperation sent messengers with presents to beg Fati Worukpe to come to him. The latter sent back the messengers saying he could not come without the consent of his elder brother. Thereupon Jakpa sent other messengers, and the Mallam obeyed and came into the camp. On his arrival he upbraided Jakpa for his importuning him, but agreed to pray for him.

The fighting recommenced, and Fati Worukpe, with a firm belief in the holiness of his faith, stretched out his arms with the staff ('Kandiri' which is always carried by the Imams) in one hand, pointed it to the Biegas and exclaimed, 'Run away, ye Kafirs'. The enemies' line suddenly broke and, every one running away to the place whence he came, Jakpa remained master on the field. Here began the greatness of the Ngbanye people.

Jakpa then showed his hospitality by presenting 10 cows, 10 sheep, 10 goats, and fowls to Fati Worukpe who now consented to the former proposal, and an oath was taken on the Koran, whereby it was agreed that:

Mallam Fati Worukpe should go with Jakpa and implore God for his success;

That the articles of reward mentioned before should be paid to Fati Worukpe when Jakpa had established himself as a conqueror and a king over the countries of the far East; and

That if either one of them were to die, or if both of them died together before any empire had been established, the oath and the promises should be honourably fulfilled by the heirs and successors of Fati Worukpe, or vice versa, and that the two races, i.e. that of Fati Worukpe and Jakpa, should live side by side, and regard themselves as brothers.

Things having been thus arranged, Jakpa then resumed his eastward march; and God so favoured Jakpa through the prayers of the Mallam that he met with no opposition, and all the petty kingdoms in the western Sudan fell before him and acknowledged his suzerainty. Sumaila Ndewura Jakpa continued his progress, came and occupied the Wala country, and chose the town Nyanga as the capital of the conquered lands, and named it Gbinipowura-pe. He then appointed his sons as chiefs over different parts of the land.

Jakpa then turned against the Tampruma people on the western bank of the White Volta River. These Tampruma, as has been already told, were the subjects of the Dagbamba kings who had maintained representatives to watch over the salt-making by the natives in Burugu (Daboya). Jakpa fought with and compelled the Dagbambas to leave that country. He then crossed the river to its eastern bank, where Na Dariziogo, the King of the Dagbamba, gave him battle. The fighting was very fierce and the slaughter terrible. The Dagbamba gave way at last, but only when their king was slain on the battle-field. Jakpa then took possession of the Dagbamba towns along the eastern bank of the White Volta and penetrated far inland and took Gbirimani (Birimani), which was afterwards put under the jurisdiction of the Chief of Kpembi (Kombi), and Kasoriyiri under the Chief of Wasope. Having thus taken possession of Tampruma and some parts of the Dagbamba country, Sumaila Ndewura Jakpa removed his son, who was the Chief of Wasope, to Daboya to control the salt-making where formerly the Dagbamba kings had obtained their salt. On the eastern bank of the White Volta there is a salt valley close to the present ferry where the ground is scraped with

hoes and packed into small baskets. These are then placed
in pots and filled to the brim with water. The baskets act
as filters and the resultant liquid is carried into the town.
There it is boiled until only the reddish salt of Daboya is
left. Even now the Chief of Daboya is called not 'Daboya
Chief' but 'Wasope-wura', i.e. Chief of Wasope. (Note
'Wura' the Twi word for chief.) Jakpa then equipped an
expedition for his fifth son, who went and took Kawsaw
from the Dagbamba people.

Having secured chieftainships for five of his sons, Jakpa
then crossed the Black Volta, which is to the south. All towns
and villages submitted to him freely, and while he was still
on the northern side of that river, the Kafaba crossed and
met him with food, water, and honey—a sign of immediate
submission to the powers of Jakpa. He went over and established the kola-trade in Kafaba. From this place Jakpa
travelled as far as Salaga. In those days Salaga was a very
small village of two compounds belonging to the Nanumba
people. The Nanumba were driven away, and the place was
given by Jakpa to the hundreds of aliens who had followed
and fought under him, and transferred the kola-trade from
Kafaba to Salaga, and it became a most flourishing town and
a centre of the slave-trade and for all sorts of products of the
world. The Ngbanye people went a little farther away
from the town Salaga and built the town Kpembi.

His untiring lust for conquest made Jakpa dissatisfied with
the kingdoms and chieftainships he had hitherto won, and
the conquest of the eastern countries became the object of
his ambition. And when he had put things in order and
appointed one of his sons as chief in the newly-made kingdom, he took the field against the Kpamkpamba people. He
raided, on his way, Bo, Tashi, and the Bassari people, who
took refuge in their mountain passes but had to leave great
herds of cattle for the raider to carry off. The Kpamkpamba
were then attacked; the fighting was very furious indeed, but

the tactics of the Ngbanye were superior to those of the savages, who were routed and taken prisoners, with thousands of oxen, sheep, and goats. Jakpa then returned to Salaga by the same route. He planted the captives taken from Kpamkpamba, between Nchumuru, Salaga, and Nanumba, to cultivate the soil, and to supply the Kpembi-wura with food-stuff. They multiplied greatly, and built many towns, such as: Kpandai, Bayim, Baladjai, Kotiko, Nkatchina, Balai, and Katigeli. (It is of interest to note that the people of this last town claim to have come from Tekiman in Ashanti.)

The war-chief became the Chief of Kpandai, which from that time became the residence of all succeeding war-chiefs until 1895, when war broke out between Kabachi and Lempo, and the place was destroyed.

After some years' rest in Kpembi, Jakpa resolved on the conquest of Ashanti; but his men, having been told that the Ashanti were cannibals, and also on account of war-weariness, began to murmur, so that he had to give up the idea. For a time, however, despite the warning given him, he crossed the Volta River in the direction of Yegi to Brumase, where he encountered the Ashanti. A great battle took place in which Jakpa was mortally wounded, and he was carried to Suruminchu or Sumusi where he breathed his last. Before his death, Jakpa gave orders that his body should be entombed in Nyanga. His orders were being obeyed, but when his corpse was on its way through Npaha to Gbipe it became putrid and was interred in the latter town.

The question as to who would succeed Sumaila Ndewura Jakpa arose, and it was decided that the prince or chief who had the largest household and plenty of followers should be his successor. The Chief of Kungu was then elected—hence the town Nyanga was called 'Yagbon', i.e. 'big household', till the present day.

On account of Jakpa's burial in Gbipe, it became a rule that no king of Yagbon should be buried there, and

Mankuma was chosen as a burial-place of the Kings of Yagbon.

The principal chiefs, whose duty it is to decide the enstoolment of kings to the Stool of Yagbon, are Gbipe-wura and Kagbape-wura. Other influential chiefs who are to be consulted are: Mantam-wura, Busuna-wura, Dumangu-wura, Sanyon-wura, and Janton-wura.

When a new king is made, the custom is that he has to give to the Chief of Gbipe one horse, one cow, and 240,000 cowries, and to the Chief of Kagbepe, who is the chief king-maker and also resides in Gbipe, the horse which the new king rides during the ceremony, with the gown, the trousers, the cap, and the turban, as well as 200,000 cowries. The Chief of Kpembi and Wasope-wura (Daboya chief) are excluded from being Kings of Yagbon owing to the extent of the provinces they rule. The Chiefs of Kungu, Kandia, Kaw-saw, and Turugu (Turuwe) are by turns made Kings of Yagbon, and the insignia of the kingship was a fetish 'Aliti' which was lost during the raids of Samori. In the case of Kpembi (in Salaga) the four chiefs quartering themselves in Kpembi are made paramount chiefs in turn. These are: Kalankule-wura, Lempo-wura, Sungbungu-wura, and Kanyase-wura.

The Ngbanye people still held parts of the Dagbamba country near the eastern side of the White Volta, and had even threatened the capital town Yendi. To avoid this incessant fighting Na Luro, who had succeeded Dariziogo, deemed it expedient to abandon the capital and to build a new one in the Kpamkpamba country. Na Luro occupied the Kpamkpamba town Chare, drove the people away to Wang-bun on the Demon road, and Chare became Yendi from that time. Na Luro then managed to drive the Ngbanye away from some of the Dagbamba towns occupied by them, but died when still engaged in the war, and was succeeded by his four sons in turn, viz., Tubugiari, Zagale, Zokuli, and Gungoble.

After the death of Gungoble there appeared four claimants to the vacant stool of Yendi. These were: Timani, Chief of Sunson; Gumachiogo, Chief of Yalzori; Bengahem, Chief of Kpoge; and Zangina, son of Tutugri. Zangina was preferred to the former three chiefs, but to appoint him King of Dagbon would have caused bloodshed. The elders, therefore, secretly sent messengers to the King of the Mamprussi in Nalerigu to inform him of their opinion, begged him to act in their favour, and persuaded the contending claimants to refer their claims to that monarch. But an appeal to a foreign arbitrator required money: therefore, the three rival chiefs, considering Zangina to be too young to fight for the Chiefship of Yendi, began to borrow cowries from Zangina with which to bribe the Mamprussi King. They each borrowed 20,000 cowries from Zangina. But before they could bribe the arbitrator, Zangina had already secretly given 40,000 cowries, a bangle, and a costly gown to him.

A general meeting of the principal men of both Dagbamba and Mamprussi was summoned and a day was fixed for the final decision. When the day came, and the principal men were assembled, the King of Mamprussi addressed them and asked the three rival chiefs to tell him their attributes and titles, commencing from Timani, the Chief of Sunson.

Timani said:

'N-yuli bona Timani, Sunson dana,
Mani Chirigi biogo ni sagam Kurugu,
Tikum-pielgo no zale sa.'

That is:

'My name is Timani, Chief of Sunson,
I am (the) evil punch that spoils the iron,
The dried (white) standing wood
That prevents rain.'

The King of Mamprussi then said to Timani: 'I see that you cannot be made King over the Dagbamba people, because you will cause a scarcity of water, and there will be a famine in the two countries and people will die of hunger and thirst—you are not fit to be King.'

Gumachiogo, the Chief of Yalzori (i.e. Zabzugu), then stepped forward and said:

'N-yuli bona Gumachiogo, Yalzori dana, Mani
Shiogo ni bu-bile zogom kun kpi,
Bargu ban soge dje
Ben-ti zan n-wuhi Kpamba.'

That is:

'My name is Gumachiogo, Chief of Yalzori,
A little goat in the rainy season
Cannot lose its hairs,
Syphilis, when impossible to be hidden,
Must be shown to the elders.'

Then the King of the Mamprussi told him:—'You cannot be King over the Dagbamba, because you have a bold face, and will not give any respect to the elders.'

Bengahem or Ben-nyahem came forward and said:

'N-yuli bona Bengahem, Kpoge dana
Mani Pole-ngmanjie ni yirigi no
Biliere tugsi doya kun ban zolge
Gungumagumde tegse yiliya
Kun ban Kpemma.'

That is:

'My name is Bengahem, Chief of Kpoge,
I am the wild-pigeon (that feeds) by the
Mortar, threatens the fowls' food;
Babies lying together, you cannot know
(Which of them) is the fool;
Fruits of the silk-cotton tree that hang

Down, you will not know (which of them)
Is the first.'

The King of Mamprussi then said:—'My good friend,
it is impossible for you to be a King of Dagbon,
because you will deride the warnings of the elders, and
cannot maintain the peace of the country.'

He (the Mamprussi King) now turned round and called
Zangina, who pretended to have nothing to do with the
matter, to stand up. 'Tell me your name and attributes.'

Zangina said:

'N-yuli bona Zangina
Mani-Singa kun kpe du-noli
Zan tiri goni nan gare
Muni kun nani.'

That is:

'My name is Zangina,
The big pot that cannot be pushed
Through the doorway,
That be leant against the wall,
Then it will pass (through);
Habits (of men) cannot easily be discerned.'

The Mamprussi King then congratulated him and said:
'Bravo! my young lad, thou art a just man and fitted to
be King over the Dagbamba, and to maintain the peace of
the country.'

This was the only occasion on which a King of Dagbon
was made by a Mamprussi King, and it was done at the
wish and request of the Dagbamba elders themselves, nor
have the Kings of the Mamprussi any sovereignty over the
Kings of the Dagbamba.

When there was no war on, the Kings of Yendi were
wont to sit under the shady trees near their compounds,
where they settle palavers, land matters, and differences

between their people. They never go to visit any town or
village in the country. Travelling about, they say, is not
compatible with the customs of the country; because people
outside Yendi, even the important Chiefs of Karaga, Mion,
and Safulugu, would not stay to receive them—they would
all run away into the bush, and leave the town, for they, the
Kings of Yendi, are the 'lions' of Dagbon.

The reign of Na Zangina began as one of the most peace-
ful in the annals of the Dagbamba. His first act was to em-
brace Mohammedanism. His elders and himself were taught
to pray five times a day and make ablutions by Yamusa, the
Imam of Sabare, a town near Nakpari. The Imam Yamusa
and the other Mallams who were in his retinue, had come
from Wangara and settled in this place in the previous
reign. The example of Na Zangina, of being a Mohammedan
and a Pagan at the same time, has been followed by his
successors until the present day.

But suddenly, towards the latter years of Na Zangina's
reign, a very powerful prince of the Ngbanyes named
Mahamman Wari, known by the name of 'Kumpati' to the
present Ngbanye people and the Dagbamba, began a war
against the latter. During his expedition 'Kumpati' built
many fortifications, the swish of which had been mixed with
honey instead of water (an example of these fortifications is
still to be seen in 'Duni', a village of Singa). The Toma, or
Western Dagbamba, fled to Yendi. The king, finding himself
too old and physically unfit to lead his people against the foe,
ordered Andani Sigili, the Chief of Kpoge, who was surnamed 'Bengumanga', the son of Na Zagale, to take the
field against the enemy. Kumpati led his army by by-paths
from Daboya through Singa, to Tamale, sacking every town
en route, and came and encamped in Kurizan. The Dagbamba also encamped in San so as to stop the advance of
the foe against Yendi. The two armies met in the hills near
San, where the battle lasted several days; Kumpati was

unable to break through, and the slaughter was terrific on either side. The Ngbanye were discomfited only when their leader was killed at the hands of the Kumbungu bow-men. Kumpati's body was mutilated and distributed in the following manner as trophies, in remembrance of this terrible war:

His head was given to the Chief of Diari, Bukare Surugu (Kumbungu is the right wing, Diari the left wing, and Tolon the advance guard of the army of the Kings of Yendi); his right arm to the Chief of Tolon, Nahame; his left arm to the Chief of Kumbungu, Sulemani.

His daughter Mariama, who accompanied her father on this what promised to be successful war, became a prisoner, and was married to Andani Sigili, the victor of the battle. This was the last war between the Ngbanye and the Dagbamba, excepting during a civil war between Karaga and Safulugu, when the Yendi skin was vacant after the death of Mahama, King of Dagbon, and both Karaga and Safulugu claimed it.

Na Zangina died in his old age and was succeeded by Andani Sigili, who was succeeded by Na Jimli.

Ordinarily, all the sons of the reigning chief are placed in the care of the most important eunuchs, until they reach the age when they pass through the initiation into manhood. These eunuchs are really the Na's counsellors. They are: Zo-na, the Chief Minister; Balo-na, the Second Minister; Male; Mba Dogo; Kumlana; and Mba Bunga.

When Jimli, the son of Zangina, was a boy under the care of Zo-na, he was infected with yaws and had been neglected by that minister. Jimli ran away to Kpatenga, where he stayed with a Mallam who cured him.

During his early manhood Andani Sigili died. He attended the funeral rites, and while that was still being observed he entered the compound of the deceased king, where the old women of the royal blood were gathered together in a room. They saw him and called out, saying: 'Bunbiogo ngo, kamna,' i.e. 'You ugly man, come here.'

When he went in unto them they invested him with the royal gown and the turban, placed a sceptre in his hand and sandals on his feet and ordered him to walk in the yard, to see if the raiment fitted him as a king. After showing himself off for a little in the yard, Jimli hastened out to the crowds sitting outside the compound, and the drummers instantly began to beat the greetings and the dignities of kings. Thus he became a king, and known by the nickname Na Bumbiogo (Ugly King).

To avenge himself on the eunuchs for their neglect when he was young he gave them all orders, without distinction (at the time there were over two hundred eunuchs in Yendi, the best of whom used to be chosen for vacant positions of Zohe na, &c.), to carry big stones on their heads from the Kulkpeni to Yendi. Many of them preferred death to such undignified treatment.

Na Jimli was succeeded by his younger brother Gar'ba, the second son of Zangina. Unfortunately, he had a rival in the person of Zibirim, a son of Na Zangina's daughter and of Andani Sigili, who secretly sent messengers to Kwsei Tutu, the then King of Ashanti, who reigned from about the year 1697 to 1731, imploring him to send to dethrone and carry away his uncle Na Gar'ba to Kumasi, so that he might be king. Strong forces were then sent to Yendi from the Ashanti monarch with instruction either to deport Gar'ba or fine him 2,000 slaves, but if the Dagbamba were to show any resistance, the country must be taken by force of arms. The Ashanti arrived in Yendi without opposition, and arrested Na Gar'ba in order to take him to Kumasi. But owing to the intercession of the chiefs and the princes, they agreed to take the 2,000 slaves demanded by their king as ransom. As the 2,000 slaves could not readily be paid, the Dagbamba agreed to pay 200 slaves annually to Ashanti left in Yendi for the special purpose of receiving and forwarding them to Kumasi.

Thus Dagbon became a vassal state of the Ashantis, who in about the year 1732—during the reign of Opoku Wari—had extended their power across the Volta River, making the countries of the Dagbamba, Nanumba, Wala, Ngbanye, their tributary states, exacting great numbers of men for their warfare and slave dealing.

Na Gar'ba died and was succeeded by his nephew Zibirim Na-Sa, who was succeeded by Zibirim, son of Gar'ba, who was succeeded by Andani I, son of Gar'ba, who was succeeded by Mahama, son of Zibirim.

When Mahama expired, the vacant stool of Yendi was again in dispute. The two rival chiefs were: Zibirim Kulunku, who was Chief of Karaga, and had been already elected king, and Sumani Zoli, the Chief of Safulugu.

The latter sent and implored the help of the Wasope-wura, Sabunyalung, who was known by the name Tikpiri by the Dagbamba, to fight against his rival. The Wasope-wura determined to lead his army through Kumbungu to Safulugu, where he should arrange matters with that chief. Zakare Yao, the Chief of Kumbungu, refused him passage and gave him battle near Kpiogo, a village of Kumbungu. The Ngbanye were discomfited; a state drum taken from them—still in use by the Chiefs of Kumbungu—was one of the trophies from that blood-stained field. Zibirim Zulunku, the king in whose favour the battle was determined, gave one of his daughters to Zakare Yao, and their issue is Isa, the present Chief of Kumbungu.

He was succeeded by Na Yakuba, whose reign was marked by his conceit, great selfishness and disregard of customary laws, and determination to reign without the advice of his ministers. In the early years of his reign his own sons joined together and fought against him. He was fortunate enough to overcome them; but he had learnt his lesson and reigned afterwards in accordance with the customary law.

When Bukare Gufire, the Chief of Safulugu, was about to

die, though he knew that his nephew Zibirim Idantogma Lagafu, the Chief of Zabzugu, who was the son of his sister Ashatu and a Mallam, had a better claim to the Safulugu skin, yet he bequeathed on oath the Safulugu skin to his brother Mahama Nubila (Bukare Gifire and Mahama Nubila were of the same mother), an act to which he had no right.

Then Bukare Gufire died and Mahama Nubila began to make his funeral rites. At the same time Zibirim Idantogma Lagafu, the Chief of Zabzugu, dispatched his elders with cowries and other presents to Safulugu to perform the rites on his behalf. These representatives were driven out from Safulugu by Nubila and sent back with insults to their master. The Chief of Zabzugu held his peace, but secretly prepared to obtain the skin of Safulugu, held by force of arms, and did but wait the opportunity. The funeral was then finished, and Mahama Nubila proceeded to Yendi to be confirmed in his new office. No sooner was he about to enter into Yendi than Zibirim Idantogma Lagafu met and defied him, and a skirmish took place in the vicinity of Yendi in which the Chief of Zabzugu fell. Mahama Nubila was then confirmed in the Chieftainship of Safulugu by Na Yakuba. Safulugu's example was at once followed by Karaga. For, when Mahama, the Chief of Karaga, expired, his brother on the mother side, Adama, seized the skin and wished to be confirmed in that chieftainship; but his aspirations were not entertained by Na Yakuba, who instantly appointed Yahaya Sunson in preference to him. Yahaya was dispatched to Safulugu so that his brother Mahama Nubila, the chief of that place, might assist him to get the skin.

Na Yakuba's own sons, who were chiefs of some important towns, found fault with their father and sided with Adama. These were: Abdulai, Chief of Tampiong; Mahama, Chief of Nakpari; Andani, Chief of Pishigu; Bukare Shiog-ba, Chief of Nyong; Adama, Chief of Pigu; Sulemanu, Chief of Saganerigu.

The escort from Safulugu were routed before they could reach the neighbourhood of Karaga.

The chiefs who were on the side of Na Yakuba were: Mahama Nubila, Chief of Safulugu; Isa, Chief of Mion; Yahaya Sunson, Chief of Sunson; Kabonna Kpema, the War Chief.

The king mustered his forces in Gamanji, a small village about fifteen minutes distant from Yendi. Adama of Karaga at first took the offensive but was repulsed, and the king then advanced. Adama and his party were gradually driven away and pursued. He fell, and Abdulai took the leadership. The battle continued, but as Abdulai was unable to withstand the triumphant army of his father, he retreated and took his last stand at Vetin, a village about half an hour's distance from Tamale. The night before the battle, Abdulai convened all the Mallams in his camp, and told them to consult oracles to find out what would be the result of the morrow's engagement. They told him that the battle would be fatal to him, and that he would fall, and the result would be that all those princes who took up arms against their father would be exiled, and their sons would have no place in the kingdom. For this reason, it was found necessary to transfer by magic death from him to his younger brother, Sulemanu, the Chief of Saganerigu. Sulemanu agreed to the sacrifice, but requested all the princes in arms against their father the king, and the principal Mallams, to swear on oath, to be recorded in writing, and on the Koran, that when his children (sons) grew up they should be greeted as Princes of Dagbamba, and eligible to the Yendi skin. As there was no time to lose the whole camp agreed, and the oath was sealed hurriedly. At dawn the fighting was resumed with vigour, and it was not till noon when Abdulai's army began to retreat towards Banvem. They were pursued by the king's forces, and the battle came to an end. Sulemanu fell in Dohene, a small village under Banvem. Sulemanu's body was interred at the front of his compound in Saganerigu.

After this battle the Dagbamba, who were in favour of the insurgent princes, migrated to Salaga, Yegi, Kintampo, Ejura, and Kratchi. Mahama Nubila, the Chief of Safulugu, abandoned his chieftainship, and died miserably in Kumbungu, his mother's town.

Na Yakuba was succeeded by his eldest son Abdulai, the leader of the insurgent party. During the previous reigns very little was done to meet the payment of the slave-tribute. Raiding parties only had been sent out, and sometimes they were very unlucky. These raiding parties reached even as far as Tumu itself, and it is recorded that there two men were killed. The Ashanti representative in Yendi began to threaten the king that the non-fulfilment of the promise would result in the destruction of their capital, and that all the royal family and the principal men of the country would be carried away into Kumasi as slaves, and they would never again see their country. To make war against the Grunshi[1] and Basari[2] now became the sole object of the Dagbamba, and preparations were made, the king went with his army to Basari, while the Chiefs of Karaga and Kumbungu went to Grunshi.

The king was successful and brought into Yendi some hundreds of Basari captives, while Karaga and Kumbungu were less successful. To complete the enormous payment in slaves the chiefs began to catch their own people on big market days, in the bush and on the principal trade routes; and thus, gradually, the two thousand slaves were paid off.

Na Andani II, the most tyrannical of all the kings of Dagbon, succeeded. In the early years of his reign arose a frivolous palaver which resulted in open fighting between the king, the Kumbungus, and the Karagas. The palaver was as follows:

On one occasion, a certain Salufu, one of the headmen in Kasoriyiri, was afflicted with a whitlow, and a man from

---

[1] Tribes living to the north along the eleventh parallel of latitude.
[2] Tribes living in the mountains to the east of Yendi.

Kumbungu was engaged to cure him. The cure was successful but Salufu sent the man away empty-handed. He went
and kept company with one Yakobu, a vagabond prince, for
some time, and then complained of his treatment to his
companion, and gave the latter his grievance, bidding him
collect £25 from Salufu. Yakobu was pleased with the
offer, but as he could not openly demand the sum mentioned,
he proposed to infest the Kumbungu-Kasoriyiri main road.
(Princes who had no chieftainships lived on robbery, and
are called 'Nabiyonga', vagabond princes.) So it happened
that on a certain weekly market day of Kasoriyiri, he hid
himself in the bush, and, having seen women from the
villages going to Kasoriyiri to attend the market, he attacked
them and caught the wife of one Adu, of Chisiogo, an important follower of the Chief of Kasoriyiri. The matter was
reported to the Chief of Kasoriyiri, who sent and requested
Yakobu to free the woman from her slavery, on the plea that
a native of Kumbungu could never be sold for an offence
of a Kasoriyiri man. The messengers were sent back with
words of defiance to Kasoriyiri. By this time the Chief of
Kasoriyiri had gathered his forces on the left bank of the
lake which lies between him and the Kumbungus, and some
of his people even commenced to cross it, for it was but
knee-deep. The Kumbungus asked them: 'Shall we fight?'
The answer was 'Yes'. The Kasoriyiris first attacked, but
they found that they were too weak to fight the Kumbungus,
so their chief, Aduna, fled to seek the protection of the
Paramount Chief of Safulugu who, thinking it an easy task
to defeat the Kumbungus, took the field against them.
The fighting took place on the Safulugu-Kumbungu road,
where the Safulugus were repulsed and were driven back
into their homes. Kumbungu was now accused, before
King Andani, of taking up arms against his superiors, and
that he had actually intended to fight the king in Yendi.
Na Andani, on hearing this, did not inquire into what was

T

the cause of the fighting, but instantly summoned the War Chief (Kabon-na Kpema) and his captains and distributed gunpowder. On account of his mother being a native of Kumbungu, Alasan, the Paramount Chief of Karaga, joined with the Kumbungus against the king. The two armies met about an hour's distance from Kumbungu, in the direction of Zugu and Tarkpa. The fighting was very fierce and lasted the whole day. The Kumbungus did not tremble, even in the presence of the Lion of Dagbon who led his army in person against them, and they did not give way until their dauntless leader, Chief Abdulai, was killed. For a further punishment the king dispossessed the Kumbungus of the important town of Zugu, and allowed his army to remain in the vicinity of Kumbungu, robbing and carrying away the people and goods of the Chief of Karaga.

The king led his army through Tampiong; Karaga also mustered his forces and awaited the appearance of the king in the neighbourhood of Karaga. The fighting took place quite close to Karaga and was at first disastrous to the king. But, gradually, after much difficulty, the king got the upper hand, and Alasan was killed. His body was buried just at the entrance into Karaga, and a deleb-palm stands on the tomb.

King Andani continued to trouble his people in this despotic manner, and it was in his time that Dagbon became so depopulated a country.

During the reigns of Andani's predecessors a lonely baobab tree was selected far in the bush, under which any person and any wife of the king's who had sexual intercourse were led and killed by an executioner (Cherilana), whose special duty it was to execute such ill-doers. This spot and the baobab were named 'Na-Data' or 'The King's Rival'.

The Kings of Dagbon usually keep over a hundred wives. These women are closely guarded, yet they are allowed to attend the weekly markets in Yendi, where they easily find a way to find lovers to whose arms they climb over the walls of the royal compound in the stillness of the night.

The depopulation of Dagbon is said to be due to the following:

When Na Andani was busily engaged in having his wives and their sweethearts executed under the Na-Data, a certain Mallam—in that quarter of Yendi called 'Balogo'—was suspected of having had intercourse with one of the king's wives. He was brought to trial before the king, but the guilty woman could not be discovered. The king, however, ordered the Mallam to be killed in his quarters. When his head was cut off, instead of blood, milk was seen to drop. From this time the Dagbamba country began to decrease in population till to-day.

The blindness of King Andani, which has been inherited by all his sons, is traced to one of the fairest and most beloved of his wives, who was accused of having been made pregnant by a lover. She was brought before the assembly, but she swore that the pregnancy was from the king. In spite of all her defence, she was condemned and led to Na-Data together with her sweetheart, there to be executed. The executioner first killed the man, and then the woman, who was, as customary, first cruelly mutilated. The executioner returned to the presence of the king, dancing with the right arm of the woman between his teeth, as was the custom. A week after her execution her ghost appeared in the presence of the executioner and demanded her arm, saying:

'Cherilana, timma m-bogo
M-bi kumda
Ka n-kuli ka o-ti moge.'

meaning:

Executioner, give me my arm,
My child is weeping
That I may return to let it suck.'

T 2

The executioner went mad with fear and remained so until his death, and no one has since been appointed. The woman's ghost is said to have driven her fingers into the eyes of Na Andani so that he became blind in both eyes. The blindness of the father has been transmitted to the sons, and when they grow old they must be and are blind.

During the Kumbungu and Safulugu civil war, Binger had passed through the country,[1] and a little earlier Lonsdale had reached Yendi. The white men had entered the country, and the fall of the Dagbamba empire was at hand. The traditionists relate this misfortune which took place on Adibo-date, i.e. 'The day of Adibo', that memorable day on which the Dagbamba defied the soldiers' carbines with cries of 'Anasare Malfa Cherebo kane', i.e. 'White man's gun has no flint stone', and despised the white man because 'Sereminga yi-la kuom na, o-nye la zaham', i.e. 'The white man is come from the water, he is a fish'. These were the words of encouragement from the war-chief to the captains under him. About one year or so after the settlement of the Germans in Krachi, they organized an expedition under Baron von Massow, Dr. Gruner, and a Lieutenant Hermann; this expedition was intended to proceed to Sansanne-Mangu. En route it was to pass through Bimbila and Yendi. The Nanumbas collected large forces in both Wulenshi and Bimbila to stop the advance of the expedition.

The fighting took place in a small village near Wulenshi, and the Nanumbas were driven towards Bimbila. On the next day the expedition arrived at Bimbila, where the fighting was again resumed by the natives. They were mown down with a heavy slaughter, and the rest fled with their blind king to Chamba. Next day the expedition proceeded on its journey toward Yendi. On hearing that the white men (the fish) were advancing towards Yendi, Na Andani summoned the war-chief and all brave men to go and bring these fishes

[1] 1886.

in ropes into his presence. Some few hundreds of men equipped themselves with Dane guns, bows and arrows, and spears; and the rest of them all took ropes. Especially men from Sunson and its surrounding villages brought no other weapons than ropes in their hands, and sacks with them so as to meet and catch the white men, and to put them in their bags for the king. Spies had been sent out to Langadja, who returned and said that white men were coming with their short guns without flint stones. The war-chief arrayed his men according to their fashion, and he himself with his chief captains seated themselves on the war-chairs and fettered their feet. Servants who would load their guns stood behind them. It was in Adibo where the fighting took place. The Dagbamba were terribly slaughtered; heaps of dead bodies were to be found in all directions, with horses that fell under their riders. The war-chief with all his captains died on the battle-field. A few of the men who escaped in the heat of the fighting ran and informed the king, saying:—'Na, tobo sagamya, kabonna kpeme kpalemya,' i.e. 'Oh, King, the battle is spoiled, the war-chief is dead.' The king was then led on horseback to a safe place.

Before the Germans entered Yendi darkness fell, and with it a very heavy rain, and it is noticed that since that time no rain has ever fallen so heavily as on that day. The Germans burned the whole of Yendi the same night, and left for Sansanne-Mangu. On the return of the king from his retirement, he prophesied that 'while he lives, no white man shall ever set his foot in Dagbon'. This prophecy was and is believed by the Dagbamba that, had Andani lived, no white man would have come to Dagbon to settle, and they still maintain that there is a time when the white men now in Dagbon will leave their country. King Andani then gave cattle and plenty of cowries to the Mohammedan community in all parts of his kingdom to make him charms which would prevent the white men coming any more into his country.

These amulets were said to be hung on the branches of the kapok and the baobab trees in Yendi, and some were buried on Yendi-Bassari roads, Yendi-Demon road, Yendi-Sansanne-Mangu road, Yendi-Salaga road, Karaga-Gambaga road, Safulugu-Diari road, Tamale-Daboya road, and Kumbungu-Yagaba road. Na Andani died three years after the battle of Adibo.

After the funeral custom Idi, the eldest son of Andani, who was then Chief of Tugu, but was blind, wanted to be Chief of Safulugu; he therefore prevailed on the Elders to make Kukra Adjei, the insane Chief of Safulugu, king. During this time, Alasan, the Chief of Karaga, was the rightful heir to the Yendi stool. The Elders reluctantly did what was asked of them. Karaga did not agree and the country was in a state of war. At the same time, Bukare, the son of the deceased King Andani, was helping the Zabarmas, who were finally driven into Yendi by Captain (later Sir) Donald Stewart, and defied the authority of the British in Gambaga; therefore an expedition was organized against them under Major Morris, accompanied by Moshi levies, who had been recently driven by the French from Wagadugu. The insurgents were pursued into Karaga, which was sacked by the Moshis who carried away with them young men and women and plenty of cattle. The news was brought to Alasan of Karaga, who then withdrew himself from the fighting for the Yendi stool and went to interview the English who were encamped in Gunayiri. Idi, who was now thinking of himself as paramount Chief of Safulugu, went with his Safulugus into San, where he kept up orgies and feasting for some time.

Dr. Rigler, the German Resident in Sansanne-Mangu, was informed of the disturbances in Yendi relative to the election of a king to the Stool. Although the Dagbamba country was a neutral zone at the time, Dr. Rigler came down with his cavalry and foot-soldiers, and fell upon the Safulugus in San, and Idi was killed. On his return from San he interviewed the Elders upon the question of electing a king. They all unanimously told him that Alasan of Karaga was the rightful heir. Alasan, therefore, was sent for to be made king. During the reign of Alasan there was nothing important in native affairs, but in the early part of his reign the Germans settled in Yendi in 1900.

He was still reigning when the Great War broke out, but died in January 1917. His son Abudulai succeeded him and reigns to this day.

INDEX

For Product Safety Concerns and Information please contact our EU
representative GPSR@taylorandfrancis.com
Taylor & Francis Verlag GmbH, Kaufingerstraße 24, 80331 München, Germany

www.ingramcontent.com/pod-product-compliance
Lightning Source LLC
Chambersburg PA
CBHW050703280326
41926CB00088B/2435